WITHDRAWN

AMERICAN POLITICAL MOVIES

GARLAND FILMOGRAPHIES
(VOL. 1)

GARLAND REFERENCE LIBRARY
OF THE HUMANITIES
(VOL. 970)

GARLAND FILMOGRAPHIES

AMERICAN POLITICAL MOVIES
An Annotated Filmography
of Feature Films

James Combs

GARLAND PUBLISHING, INC. • NEW YORK & LONDON
1990

Library of Congress Cataloging-in-Publication Data

Combs, James E.
  American political movies: an annotated filmography of feature
films / James Combs.
    p. cm. — (Garland filmographies; vol. 1) (Garland
reference library of the humanities; vol. 970)
    ISBN 0–8240–7847–0 (alk. paper)
    1. Politics in motion pictures—United States—Catalogs.
I. Title. II. Series. III. Series: Garland reference library of
the humanities; vol. 970.
  PN1995.9.P6C66 1990
  016.79143'658—dc20   89–78521
  [347.3073509]   CIP

Printed on acid-free, 250-year-life paper
Manufactured in the United States of America

Dedication

In memory of
two cherished relatives

Earl B. Combs
and
William A. (Billy) Hobson

Acknowledgments

I would like to acknowledge the able assistance and encouragement of several individuals who aided in the completion of this book. My editors, Jared Lobdell and Marie Ellen Larcada, were instrumental in signing up and guiding the work through to publication, and they deserve thanks for a job well done.

I would also like to thank Carol Lewis and Gayla Crosmer, whose work in the preparation of the manuscript was professional and invaluable.

Special thanks are due to Maxine Fleckner Ducey, archivist of the Film and Photo Archive at the Wisconsin Center for Film and Theater Research, and her able staff, all of whom have made research into the movies both professional and painless. The author appreciates their help in many trips over the years.

Last but not least, warm thanks are due Sara Trowbridge Combs, who now shares both my movie and my personal life.

Table of Contents

Introduction

Historians of the motion picture are fond of telling stories of the reactions of the earliest audiences to the new medium as it emerged at the turn of the twentieth century. We are still amused by the uncomprehending awe with which they greeted this spectacular experience. People ran from the theater in terror from trains approaching on the screen. Others ducked and screamed when a gun was fired at the audience. But most appear to have simply been transfixed, sitting and gazing in silent wonder at this visual marvel that brought worlds of sights, and very quickly stories, beyond their everyday existence. Some observers of these brave new "moving pictures" were exultant. "The universal language has been found!" exclaimed a spectator at an early Lumière film. The Russian writer Maxim Gorki wrote after seeing his first motion picture in 1896, "Last night, I visited the kingdom of shadows." The dramatic and turbulent tale of how the toy that evolved from the magician's magic lantern into a multibillion dollar worldwide industry has often been told. The questions about what the movies have meant, and continue to mean, for the conduct of our lives still haunts us. Now that the movies have a history, the question nags: after all the experience so many millions of people all over the world have had with the movies, has it made any significant difference in their lives? The converse is equally intriguing: if we study the movies, can we infer anything of significance about movie audiences? Let us be even more inquisitive: can we infer anything from the movies about the climate of opinion at a particular time, the *ethos* of an historical period, and more directly here, the political temper of an age and place?

Such questions have burdened film scholars for a very long time now. But the reader may quite rightly object that such questions, while not illegitimate, may be unanswerable and even unimportant. It may be ultimately impossible to conclusively demonstrate how the movies have affected thought and action, since any such impact might well have been long-term, diffuse, and even unconscious. Making inferences from the movies to society, and from society to the movies, involves intellectual leaps of faith that only the most daring have attempted to jump. Too, it may also be objected that the subject itself is a frivolity. In this view, movies are bubble gum, popular entertainments without either significance or consequence, something used by audiences seeking diversion and then discarded. The movies are not worth studying because of their inherent marginality and levity. They are therefore marginal to the cultural process, and lack the high seriousness that a student of culture should expect.

Those of us who love movies leap to their defense, usually winding up arguing in favor of the significance of something called "the cinema," asserting the aesthetic significance of a few (often subtitled) films. But what I want to do here is to assert a bolder argument. In the twentieth century, the movies have been a central aspect of the American popular experience. They have expanded and enriched the popular imagination while deriving much of what they depicted from that imagination. The relationship between us and the movies is truly transactional, an interplay of influence between moviemakers and movie audiences (as well as the larger population and power structure) that takes subtle twists and turns in the relationship as time goes by. The imagination of moviemakers extends popular experience, and the experience of moviewatching extends the popular imagination. Although we shall never know for sure, it seems reasonable to conclude that the movie experiences have made a difference in the shaping of our national imagination, or in other words, that we would not be who we are, nor do what we do, without the movies. We may state this also in the negative, as a thought experiment. Suppose there had been no movies made in America this century: would we be the same? I think not. The movies are such a powerful and compelling form of popular communication that even those not directly part of the mass movie experience have been subtly affected by them. Many of those who voted for Ronald Reagan likely did not fully appreciate the intermingling of fantasy and reality, the blending of movie experience with political experience that gave Reagan his particular attraction and familiarity. Like so many other things that we do, we vote on the basis of our imagination, and the movies have long become an integral dimension of the popular mind that Reagan understood and represented so well.

Hollywood has been derisively called "the Dream Factory." In one way, the criticism is quite accurate, but in another it is quite telling. It is quite correct to say that Hollywood is the purveyor of collective dreams, often sensational fantasies of thrills, chills, and spills associated with popular adventure and mystery, and romantic fantasies of sensual or marital happiness achieved in exotic or idyllic circumstances. The movies did not create the practice of devising entertainments that appealed to popular tastes and interests, but they did give it new power and force. They were selling dreams, giving legitimization to the vicarious experience involved in moviewatching. But they were also guiding thought, evoking emotion, and suggesting action. If those cues were romantic fantasy, they could lead to frustration, since they were beyond attainment. Love and sex could not reach the erotic heights of love stories; our own natural cowardice and weakness could not match the bravado of adventurous heroes and heroines; and our lack of wit and daring prevented us from seeking and solving extraordinary mysteries. If movie metareality led for some to frustration or even aggression, for many others it filled a void by imagining an "as if" universe in which things do work out in ways different from the immediate and palpable conduct of our own mundane lives. For many, the movies offer a vicarious answer to the question, wouldn't it be wonderful (or awful) if the world were like that? Movie dramas are something that we are not: life that is more romantic, adventurous, mysterious, or frightening than our lives. We may wish it so, and even seek to make it so. But the basic attraction of the movies is their dreamlike quality.

The idea of "movies as dream" is a useful one for our purposes here. Like dreams, the movies have the power to transport us to worlds beyond our existence with rules and characteristics of their own. They are full of wish-fulfillment and wish-denial, powerfulness and powerlessness, triumph and torment. Dreams, both day and night, are ways that let us deal with the fantastic threats and promises of our lives. The movies no less became a socially approved way of dealing with reality through the medium of a metareality. In that sense the movies are no different from theater. But they built upon theatrical and narrative traditions by extending their dream-experience to many millions, and by their grasp of popular dreaming, depicted a remarkable interplay of the extraordinary and ordinary that permitted mass audiences to learn from them. The movies tell us what stuff our dreams are made of.

If this idea is correct, the movies are not some marginal triviality, but rather a repository of cultural dreams transformed into dramatic and visually rich stories. We are dealing with the interplay between a people seeking culturally valid entertainment and an industry that is sensitive to the cultural shape such dreams should be made of. If it is important to understand the continuities and changes in the popular mind, then it is worthwhile to examine the artifacts of popular communication designed to appeal to, and in some sense represent, aspects of the popular imagination. The movies, like all important art, are thereby vicarious representations of the experience of Americans engaged in popular imagining, and by extension popular learning. At any given time, our relationship to the movies is essentially metaphorical. Like dreams, movies stand in metaphorical relation to reality. They are not reality, but are something *like* reality, only more so. They are symbolic realities that unfold in tacit and implied analogical communication with ourselves. Movies are not literal but are familiar to us; they do not present reality, they represent reality. Metaphorical representations are not copies.

Movies are not series of photographs. They are rather more a familiar mystery that unreels before us as a dream we both understand and do not understand. Like any metaphor, the movies use our familiarity with narrative and visual conventions to introduce us to a mysterious world that represents but does not replicate our experience. We are irresistibly drawn to the movies because they give us a glimpse of our own temporal and cultural existence, a moving picture of something recognizable but also spectacular. The paradox is that the movies are also strange precisely because they are spectacular. We see ourselves in the movies, and the movies in ourselves; but we also see someone else not really ourselves, someone larger-than-life in the movies. We see both life and metalife combined in the form of cultural dream. If it is the case that we live out our metaphors, when we watch the movies we live in our metaphors.

Moviewatching, then, is a symbolic activity wherein the watchers form a bond of communion with what they see on the screen. The act of watching is not mindless diversion, but rather absorption in a play-activity that involves learning. Indeed, moviemaking and moviewatching, although separated in many ways, are reunited in the mutual process of learning: both are sensitive to what the other is communicating. The movie transaction involves the interplay of communicants in the metaphorical action of the photoplay, attempting to "re-cognize" what is significant in a given cultural and temporal setting. The relationship is not "reflective" in the simplistic "mirror and lamp" theory. Rather it is ritualistic play, ludenic involvement with a prescribed form of metaphorical communication that has ceremonial conventions in both setting and representation. We go to the movies as a ritual interlude, obeying the norms of silent deference to the proceedings and acquiescing in the familiar mysteries of filmed drama. The movies invite us to suspend disbelief and make a leap of faith into the mythic metaworld recreated on the screen. By accepting the canons of the movie faith, we have participated in ritual celebration of the cultural and temporal myths that unfold in the dramatic structure of movie narratives.

Myth may take many forms, from the personal myths an individual has about himself or herself to the overarching and deeply imbedded myths of an entire historical culture. Such shared myths are the imaginative tales that are the stuff of cultural dreaming. People get many idiosyncratic messages out of the movies, much of which is likely impossible to trace. But we can study the movies with a view of understanding popular myth, those ideas and images, both longstanding and immediate, that large numbers of people share and enjoy seeing translated into story. Popular myth is of course rooted in, although not limited to, traditional forms of myth, such as folktales and legends. It also includes more recent and "created" forms of myth that are products of popular commerce. As a form of popular communication, the movies absorb and use both, and audiences like and expect adaptation also. The Western, for example, is rooted in the myth of the frontier, but has been utilized in subsequent eras for metaphorical statements of various kinds, and indeed many ostensibly non-Western film genres (space epics, return-to-Vietnam, private detective and rogue cop films) share its assumptions and formula. Popular mythmaking is not a morbid celebration of archaic tales, but rather is a dynamic usage of story as metaphors for living.

The movies as metaphors for living suggest uses for mythic tales other than pure diversion. Like all storytelling, the movies both delight and instruct. The unique and unprecedented power of the movies stems from the ability to do both for large popular audiences in memorable and even enduring ways. The movies educate our imagination in compelling ways of vicarious learning. We do not fully understand how popular learning works because it is so diffuse, uneven, long-term, and even unconscious. But the subtlety of popular learning does not decrease its importance. The movies were not the first great popular medium to invite widespread play-learning, since popular print had preceded them, not to mention visual media such as the photograph, and moving representations such as stage productions. Yet it is fair to say that the movies constituted a breakthrough, and probably did more to legitimate play-learning than anything that had preceded them. Since then, the movies have been complemented by other related and even derivative media, especially radio and television. But the movies established the popular habit of learning about the world through their metaphorical representation of it.

If our argument is correct, then we may say that the movies do constitute a major form of *popular evidence*. But evidence of what, and how do we use it? What we assert here is a movie pragmatic, the idea that people, both in active and derivative audiences of the movies, make practical use of movie experience. Play, after all, from childhood on is a pragmatic undertaking, with learning acquired in play and applied elsewhere. The symbolic play of movies is a learning experience through the use of imaginative narratives that identify and explore relationships that one might encounter, at least in one's conception of the world. The "reel world" is imaginary, but it is also comprehensible in evoking imagination of a real world that has some relationship, however concrete or imaginary, with our movie experience. We may therefore be able to make use of the movies as popular evidence of the imaginary life of a culture living and coping with the unfolding dynamics of time. Movies are a form of popular mediation, metaphorical communication that people utilize in their understandings and undertaking in the always changing temporal reality of their collective lives.

In this way, we may posit a discoverable relationship between movies and politics. Politics is an ongoing activity that people, both popular artists catering to audiences and the audiences drawn to that popular art, are trying to understand. Since politics involves power, people are trying to understand the nature of power: Who tells other people what to do? Who ought to? Whose values are to prevail? How is power conducted in this particular political culture? How is power conducted at this particular time? What is happening in politics now? Politics is not on people's minds when they go to the movies, but it is in the backs of their minds. If moviegoing is an occasion for implicit learning, then we cannot exclude the possibility of political learning, or more accurately, learning that in some way, however subtle, affects our attitudes and actions about politics. Even the most apolitical souls among us are not immune from popular learning through the movies about the nature and exercise of power. Indeed, even the non-moviegoer may acquire derivative knowledge from other people's movie experience that affects political thinking. Such a process is difficult if not impossible to trace, but its subtlety and subjectivity make it all the more intriguing as a source of political knowledge. But if we cannot fully study the mercurial process of popular use of movies as political learning, we can fully study the cultural and temporal artifacts of the process, the movies themselves.

Most movies are made without any conscious political intention, and even those that do include political themes and messages are often vague in their political perspective. Even "political movies"--movies explicity about politics--do not constitute a "genre" in the same sense the Western or the horror film does. But movies are a major popular art form that occurs in a political culture with a particular history and values, some of which is celebrated in story as myth. So we should expect that some movies will include "American themes," stories that treat politically relevant themes deemed important in the conduct and distribution of power. Stories that extol heroic individual achievement rather than collective action, depict males rather than females as legitimate social authority, expect conflict to be resolved in violent rather than peaceful ways, or simply appeal to patriotic and democratic emotions are *political thematics* from which we may learn. Too, deeply rooted cultural themes reappear in stories that tell anew an old folktale that retains temporal salience. We have recurrently been drawn to the "captivity narrative," stories involving the capture and rescue of Americans by an alien force that threatens their life or identity. This ancient tale dates to Puritan times, but is as current as tales of MIAs (missing in action soldiers) held in Indochina or hordes of children spirited away by cults or fiends. Such a powerful story has obvious political salience during hostage crises, and inspires both political and movie fantasies about heroic rescues to save our fellow citizens and punish the evil captors.

This is not to say, of course, that everyone gets something out of the movies that affects their political perspective, or that people get the same political message out of the movies. Movies may use cultural myths (the conquest of the West) and folklore (the virtue of individual acquisition) as the basis for stories, but they will tell it in different ways and audiences will learn from it different things. It is silly to say that the movies perpetuate an elite-imposed "ideology," even though there are cultural and political constraints on what goes into movies. Movies are not propaganda in the obvious sense, and are about as subversive of "ideological hegemony" as they are supportive. In any case, such learning is audience-centered. In a very real sense, moviemakers have to be very sensitive to what audiences want, or at least what they think they want, and how those wants change over time. Audiences are not fools. Hollywood could only perpetuate an "ideology" if there is audience consensus on values, and in the American twentieth century these values have been of such generality that they are essentially myth and folklore, ideas and images of popular value rather than elite imposition. It is true that there is a complex interplay between Hollywood and audiences, but movie fare is not without popular mediation. Indeed, it is precisely because moviemakers are audience-sensitive that we do indeed see things in movies that are useful popular evidence because they have been mediated--in the sense of being catered to--by popular audiences. Movies are in that way "audience-driven": both their form and content, their continuities and changes, their "residues" and novelties are mediated in the interplay of influence of the movie process.

We may therefore usefully speak of movies as a mediated political reality. They are a popular medium of communication that exists in rough aesthetic concomitance with the political culture. They utilize the heritage of popular myth and folklore to create visually compelling narratives that include depictions of the exercise of power. They help people mediate politics by offering popular learning about reality, and political reality in particular. But as Machiavelli teaches us, political reality is not a static thing but rather a dynamic process. Political learning goes on precisely because people are always trying to figure out what's happening. What we call "reality" is an interpretation of states of affairs as they exist at a particular time. Even in the context of an ongoing political culture with continuous habits and institutions of power, political change necessitates new and different definitions of the political situation. The instability wrought by the occurrence of political events and processes tests the stability of our vision of political reality. Popular art such as the movies is a source of communication-learning about the world, and by inference the politics that characterizes a distinctive political period. If all politics is local, it is also located in time. Our ideas and images of the political world exist in time also, and the movies made at that time become an indirect and subtle source of our vision of power. When we see movies from a past political period--the Depression, the Fifties--we are seeing stories and themes that are important politico-cultural artifacts of that time. Movies are part of the communication process wherein a political-culture-in-time is defining what's happening politically in the context of temporal immediacy.

We may say, then, that movies are political communication, even when those movies are not overtly about politics. Ostensibly non-political feature films are "about" politics in the sense that we may interpret them politically as part of a political-culture-in-time. They are popular evidence of how we conceived power at a particular time. If political reality is "conventional," then the perspective on those conventions as seen by the movies helped people then, and people now, understand the dynamic conventions that characterized an age. Indeed, movies, and for that matter all popular art, participate in the unfolding process of temporal self-definition as the *ethos* of a time is identified and dramatized. For the "temper" of a political time is made up in the interstices of events as they happen, or the prospect of events that might happen. If we can locate a movie in political time, it can serve as an imaginative map into the foreign country that is the past, wherein they do things differently. In seeking to establish some degree of explanatory or indicative power for the movies, we assert the tacit relationship forms of popular communication have with the political immediacy of a time. As with the study of all art, we seek nothing more than to see in that art representations of the sensibilities of an age as it were being revealed to itself. In a sense, every past time is a mystery to us, and even to itself. Popular art such as the movies helps us to demystify the political character of that time by interpreting representations of the period. A movie may be an oblique and ambiguous map, and certainly is no "snapshot" or "reflection" of a political time, but neither is it a meteor that happened to fall to earth then. We may use it like any map, as a clue to understanding the terrain and getting where we want to go without mistaking it for the topography itself.

Movies survive from our past as imaginative narratives of something that is both absent and present, mysterious and understandable, immediate and timeless. When we see a movie from the early 1930s, for example, we have the odd experience of encountering a world that is at once alien and familiar. The political immediacy of the unresolved Depression is interwoven into many movies of the time, in both overt and covert ways. But even if we did not live through that time, we can use the movies to understand the political fears and hopes that obtained in that present. We can use movies to help us understand how that present saw the political culture that it had inherited, and how the present would (or would not) resolve its own vagaries and vicissitudes now for the benefit of the future. Finally, we can use movies in our present in order to understand our present in relation to the past. Not only do movies give us a glimpse of the political past, but they also make us aware of the similarities and differences between that culture-in-time and ours, between their political dynamics and what's happening now. Now we see the reality of the Depression through an historical glass, darkly; but the movies at least give us a vision of that past denied us before, and let us compare it to our own reality. In that way, the political interpretation of the movies broadens and deepens our political horizons. Although many objections may be raised concerning this mode of inquiry, we may proceed with the tentative curiosity of the pathfinder, confident that our arduous journey is not a fool's errand. "Only connect," suggested the writer E.M. Forster. It is to the difficult task of only connecting the movies and politics that we now turn.

American Political Movies

Chapter One

Politics in the Early Movies of Hollywood

The student of the cultural and political history of the era encompassing the beginning of the twentieth century down to the aftermath of World War I can find a number of films of assistance in understanding the political *ethos* of the era. There is always a kind of "law of diminishing returns" in watching the films of any particular era. After watching a good many films, one realizes that certain genres, themes, and styles dominate and repeat. But certain films stand out as representative of the politics of the age, and as that age advances, blends, and is transformed into another, certain films are of interest as indicative of the kinds of changes underway. The 1910s, like any decade, did not arrive or leave "on time," nor did it occur in a vacuum devoid of a past and future. But it did constitute an identifiable political period whose politics found its way, as it always does, into popular art, including the explosive and exciting new art form emerging during that time, motion pictures.

It was during this time that the nickelodeon evolved into a major industry centered in Hollywood. People were lured to the spectacle projected onto the screen in increasing numbers. If we are correct about the learning dialectic between moviegoers and moviemakers, and that what we see on the screen tells us something of the political process at that time, then our task here is to select those films which still offer us the most useful popular evidence. As early film became more sophisticated in both subject and technique, and as the film industry developed in wealth and distribution power, films succeeded more and more in offering identifiable narratives of contemporary American life that appealed to increasingly large audiences. By the end of World War I, the movies had become a major cultural force in the United States, and "Hollywood" had become a symbol of the power of this new and awesome form of mass communication to attract and fascinate us, and even perhaps to shape our consciousness of ourselves in ways that no previous medium had been able to do. The new medium of the movies was not just an image of a single sign audiences could see (such as a photograph or painting), nor a diagrammatic arrangement of signs that audiences could scan (such as a map). Rather now audiences were seeing a kinetoscopic photoplay, a dynamic spectacle of signs in action that both represented and superceded life through the persistently unfolding imagery that projected a "metaworld," both hypothetical and topical, "metareal" and real, dramatically distant and identifiably close, an interplay of Other and Self without peer. In ways we do not fully understand, the genesis of the movies corresponded with the "new consciousness" of the period (most evident in philosophy, psychology, and literature) that explored dreams, the meaning of time and duration, relativity and simultaneity, the "stream of consciousness"--all told, a reality that was complex, dynamic, and visual. The movies were all those things, capturing and shaping the modern imagination.

In the United States, the birth of the movies corresponded with several important social processes that were to have impact on the politics, and concomitantly the popular aesthetic context, of the era. These included the closing of the frontier; the completion of the establishment of much of the industrial base of the economy and the great fortunes derived from industrialization; the growth of urban populations through migration both from the native countryside and foreign immigration; the increasing organization of society in both public and private bureaucracies; and the potential for explosive social conflicts because of the new "mix" of peoples and institutions. Like so many societies undergoing rapid change, there was considerable nostalgia for a pastoral and prelapsarian Eden of mythic memory and celebration. The considerable political upheavals of the period--Populism in the 1890s, succeeded by the more successful Progressive movement of the 1910s--had a nostalgic strain that gave them almost a reactionary myth: we had lost or were fast losing ourselves and our values in the alienating whirlwind of the present. Both William Jennings Bryan and Woodrow Wilson were men who venerated the past as a model for the future, in the spirit of our curious political habit of trying to run a large national and capitalist empire on the popular imagination of pastoral and small-town life. We entered a century of increasing organizational gigantism armed with our own sense of individual rectitude and premodern heritage, we thought in our innocence, would sustain us through the colossal changes under way without losing our identity.

The new medium of the movies responded to the "brave new world" of the emerging urban and industrial order, so the immediate imagery and narratives that emerge even in the earliest and most crude of films are of interest to students of politics. Let us mention two early short films in passing as quick examples, before we discuss in greater detail later and more complex films. In the famous *The Great Train Robbery* (1903), the Western frontier motif and setting is introduced, beginning the long tradition of the Western movie genre. The movies may have done more than any other popular medium to perpetuate the power of that past mythic time, forever underscoring our faith in the vitality and uses of violent action, our distrust of cities and the quasi-European "East," our need for "frontiers," and with figures such as Theodore Roosevelt and Ronald Reagan, our incorporation of juvenile fantasies of direct heroic action in the manner of the fictional Western hero into the Presidency. But our political cleavages were not all mythographic. In our populist yearnings, we also imagined the tension over social justice involving the privileged and the ordinary citizen. In *Kleptomaniac* (1906, directed also by Edwin S. Porter), a rich woman and poor woman are each tried for the same crime, but the poor woman is jailed while the rich one is freed. Here the conflict is rooted in the persistent inequality in our history that led to the recurrent sense of injustice so explosive in the Progressive Era.

Many of the famous Chaplin films from this period offer a glimpse of the new urban order at the bottom, peopled by slumdwellers and immigrants. Chaplin's sense of injustice, of the rich against the poor, the necessity of becoming "streetsmart" in order to survive, and the brutality and stupidity of authority recur again and again. The popularity of his early films--*The Tramp, The Immigrant, Easy Street, The Adventurer,* for instance--captured some of the resentment of ordinary people, who could cheer the poetic justice of Charlie's "little fellow" against the agents of arbitrary authority (policemen, immigration officials, bankers), yet sympathize with Chaplin's pessimism about the possibility of social reform.   The Chaplin character had pretensions to respectability and wealth that are ultimately unsatisfied, so he had to set off shuffling down the road again (or suffer through an absurd and contrived "happy ending" that mocks social optimism). The Chaplin films of 1915-1917 captured something of the contempt for authority and wealth the "lower orders" of the new cities felt, the irony of America as a "land of opportunity" when they lived in slums, yet the desire to achieve some of the wealth and position from which they are excluded. In an odd way, Chaplin's little fellow and his friends had in common with Horatio Alger's fictional heroes their pluck, but not their upward-mobile luck.

The populist bias of Progressive Era movies did not only appeal to those audiences caught in the new urban maze, but also included those with nostalgic yearnings for the simplicities attributed to rural culture, the familial devotion of common folk, and indeed the moral certainties of the common life. With the lingering feeling that the urban environment lacks all that, and having to live in the wake of social upheaval, audiences could relate to parables that extolled the tenacity and triumph of loving families in the face of threat and injustice. This attitude helped make the films of D.W. Griffith popular and indeed indispensable for understanding the politics of the era. Griffith himself was a southern Romantic who used women as symbols of domestic gentility to contrast to a world of violence and injustice. He corresponded with Woodrow Wilson, and sympathized with the brand of Progressivism that would somehow "restore" the past in the future, as symbolized by the family and the virtue thought to reside in its sanctity. Audiences responded to his kinetoscopic dramatization of that fundamental popular institution, felt to be so threatened by social change, and his contempt or fear of those forces or groups that threatened the family, including social reformers, plutocratic wealth, war, urban crime, sexual promiscuity, and the threat of alien races.

A *Corner in Wheat* (1909) begins with pastoral imagery familiar to audiences of that day, farmers sowing wheat, exemplifying a natural unity between man and nature. But quickly we are in the city, and the market in wheat is cornered by the "Wheat King." We are seeing an image of a dreaded "trust," the sort of market monopoly that agitated the populists and which the progressives hoped to control or break up. The price of flour doubles, many cannot pay, and farmers cannot sell their wheat, while the Wheat King revels at a lavish party. Bragging of his wealth while touring one of his grain elevators, he falls down a shaft and dies, suffocated by the wheat. Audiences could intuitively sense the justice of the fall of a plutocrat who had disturbed the economics of the popular order. This film expressed a villain worthy of Populist tracts against the conspiracies of the plutocracy, and the Progressive faith that those who have violated the canons of the imagined past economy--competition, fair prices, the sanctity of the yeoman farmer--were subject to divine, and even anti-trust wrath.

Griffith's famous *Birth of A Nation* (1915) is of interest to us here on two counts: first, because of the immediate political furor that arose over the movie, and second, because of the reactionary populism inherent in his interpretation of "progressive" history that would shape the reform program of Wilson, literally "re-forming" the State around a conception of the major political crisis of the recent past as it gave "birth" to a new society. In this view (shared in more sophisticated form by Wilson himself), the industrial North defeated the plantation South, but unleashed an uncivilized force in the freed slaves and their carpetbagger masters bent on revenge and greed. In order to restore a civilized and virtuous community, they were stopped by the vigilante action of the Ku Klux Klan, restoring the peace and virtue of community and family. The two families, one Northern and the other Southern, who reconcile and intermarry at the end stand as metaphors for the reunion of the nation founded on the natural sentiments of home and family, defeating the evils of cold-hearted industrialism (exemplified by the Radical Republican Senator Stoneman) and alien forces (exemplified by miscegenation: villains are either mulattoes or black). The film was an immediate sensation, and inspired protests by black and liberal groups incensed by the blatant racism of the story. With *Birth*, observers began to sense that the movies' power to make a political statement and shape political consciousness was greater than anyone anticipated. *Birth* gave imaginative shape to not only a Progressive interpretation of the past, but also as a parable of the politics of the present. Not only did it justify the "Jim Crow" laws of the time, it also warned of the dangers of a manipulative industrial elite using power to destroy traditional bourgeois life so dear to the hearts of mythologists such as Griffith. Wilson was a spokesman for that tradition who sought, like the powerless but respectable white men of *Birth*, to restore a sane and understandable political order that reflected the values, and power, of the large middle class that saw itself as the backbone of the country. *Birth* was not only, as Wilson was supposed to have remarked, "History written in lightning"; it was also Progressive politics written in lightning, offering a parable of the righteous power of Wilson's middle-class voting base standing for the virtue of the family-based middle against the plutocracy on the one hand and a degenerate proletariat on the other, and the possibility of a conspiratorial coalition of the two. Progressive order would now be restored, as it was in the movie, not only by concerted political action by the "good people" of the community, but by moral regeneration symbolized by the triumph of familial rectitude and the vision of pristine peace and order governed by the principles of Christ (this, recall, after bloody racial war and vigilante murder). But in the political visions of Griffith and Wilson, violence, like reform legislation, could be used both ruthlessly and morally for the Progressive cause. *Birth* represents something of the nostalgic and "reactionary" element in Progressivism, uniting on screen both the cinematic and political imagination of a restored and regenerate moral order.

Both Wilson and Griffith were essentially imbued with the romantic sentimentality at the core of popular Victorianism, so dealing with the onslaught of modern urban and industrial change was difficult but compelling for them. Much of Griffith's work deals with the tensions wrought by modernity, always coming to a resolution in which traditional morality is upheld even in the roughest of circumstances. Griffith's subsequent work represents some of the periodic political tensions that emerged with the fear, shared by rural folk and urban reformers, that modernity would bring chaotic consequences. Many of his films, from the early *Musketeers of Pig Alley* (1912) to "The Mother and the Law" section of his masterpiece *Intolerance* (1916) and subsequent films such as

Way Down East (1920), deal with the "postlapsarian" world of modernity and how the moral order of "prelapsarian" tradition can be saved from ruin. What is fascinating to the political observer of the times is that both Wilson and Griffith were eclipsed by events, Wilson by World War I and the impulse toward modern life that the war speeded up, and Griffith as an anachronism in the Twenties making movies about the very pastoral life and morality that the Progressive Era and the war had done so much to destroy. *Intolerance* is of interest not only because it is one of the greatest of all films, but also because of its immediate political eclipse and subsequent political influence.   Griffith's theme is injustice through the ages, in which innocent ordinary folk are subjected to the abuses of the powerful and haughty. His populist roots show in his depiction of the social tension between wealthy industrialists and their "society" wives against the innocent pursuits and urban travails of the new working class.   But his Wilsonian ties also are clear, in that both ancient and modern rulers can be just if they are on the side of popular morality, including familial autonomy from a meddlesome, elite-sponsored welfare state and protection from the predatory powers of both industrial magnates and vice lords.   Griffith, like Wilson, still retained a kind of sentimental idealism that suggested a political coalition between benevolent authority and the virtuous individual could produce social harmony without disturbing the actual concentration of power in industrial and social elites.   Still, one reason given for the box office failure of *Intolerance* was that the new urban middle classes just discovering moviegoing didn't like the theme of industrial strife which placed culpability clearing on the shoulders of greedy and hypocritical industrialists.   Too, *Intolerance* not only included some of the more explosive Progressive criticisms of the arrogance of power, it also proceeded on pacifist sentiment and concluded with a moving Utopian vision of a world without war.   When Griffith began making the film in 1915, much of the public agreed with this sentiment, and Wilson ran for re-election in 1916 with the claim of moral superiority over the warring nations of Europe, declaring that we were "too proud to fight." But by the time the film was released late in 1916, the public mood and political realities had changed to a bellicose and interventionist stance, and Griffith's views seemed curiously if quickly dated.

The Great War raging in Europe was much on the minds of Americans, and the new medium of the movies became a popular forum for us to entertain fantasies about what war was like and what our attitude should be about this war.   Some took a "preparedness" stance that advocated intervention, others a pacifist stance that emphasized the horrors of war.   The most famous of the former is J. Stuart Blackton's *Battle Cry of Peace*

(1915). It depicted an invasion of New York by an army from an unnamed country sporting spiked helmets and handle-bar mustaches who ravaged the city and its population, raping women, looting stores, and altogether living up to the nefarious reputation the Germans were acquiring in Allied propaganda. (The film was based on a novel by Hudson Maxim, the brother of the inventor of the machine gun, entitled *Defenseless America*; was praised by Theodore Roosevelt and condemned by Henry Ford; and is one of the first examples of War Department cooperation with the makers of a film they found agreeable, since General Leonard Wood put 2,500 Marines at the director's disposal as extras.) Similarly, *The Nation's Peril* (1915) involved a foreign spy attempting to steal the plans for an aerial torpedo through the pacifist sweetheart of an inventor but when she discovers the schemes she kills the spy. The movie climaxes with another foreign invasion and capture of an American city, but this time the U. S. Navy bombards them into submission, and the nation is saved. On the pacifist side, Thomas Ince's *Civilization* (1916) promoted the still powerful idea that modern warfare was a horror to be avoided by imagining a war between two fictional countries, one of which is clearly Germany. A German submarine commander, envisioning the consequences of sinking a civilian ocean liner, refuses an order to torpedo the ship, and indeed sinks his own submarine and crew rather than defile the innocent (this was the era, recall, of unrestricted submarine warfare by Germany). By sacrificing his life to a "Higher Power," Christ takes on the commander's bodily form and preaches peace to the warriors, escorting a military leader that resembles Kaiser Wilhelm across a battlefield, where troops in spiked helmets herd wretched women and children, and a dead soldier is mourned by his dog ("See thou thy handiwork," Christ enjoins the Kaiser). Ince claimed that Wilson praised the film, and others claimed that the film helped Wilson win the 1916 election, but today it reminds us how much American and Progressive Era pacifism has been rooted in a political interpretation of Christian love that takes precedence over assertions of national interest or even national peril. Since then, pro-war movies have depicted the adventure and glory of war, and the existence of foreign threat to our "way of life"; and anti-war movies have abandoned the "moral" argument against war in favor of depictions of war as a savage reversion to barbarism and an existential nightmare. *Civilization's* religiosity is clearly of another era.

With American entry into the war, moviemakers took up the Allied cause and the national commitment with the same enthusiastic innocence that made us believe that this was "the war to end all wars." It is at this point that the narrative and visual power of the movies was united with political power in the production of officially sanctioned propaganda. The emerging studies of the new institution of Hollywood sought political respectability and sanction, so they threw themselves into making the patriotic fare designed to provide motivation to fight, suppress doubts, and promote the sacrifices and attitudes that would underwrite the war effort. In particular, the propaganda films made pacifists either cowards or naive fools, and associated the willingness to fight and die as the test of a "manly" patriotism that not only won battles but also women's hearts and men's admiration. The crucible of war not only would purge us of selfish or weak impulses, it also served a democratizing and moralizing purpose by bringing men together in egalitarian military camaraderie and offered an opportunity for moral regeneration of slackers, effete lounge lizards, and the sons of the idle rich. In other words, these films offered a vision of war that served domestic Progressive purposes of "moral democracy" making not only the world, but also America, safe for Wilson's grand vision. But this moral crusade also meant the depiction of the enemy in the darkest of imagery, yielding to the Allied folklore of German culpability and atrocities. The Kaiser was a familiar target, becoming in films such as *The Kaiser, Beast of Berlin* (1918) and *The Kaiser's Finish* (1918) either a bloodthirsty monster who enjoyed slaughter and torture, or a beer-soaked buffoon presiding over a bloated and pampered royal family. In the same vein, German officers were usually depicted as cruel and monocled Prussians, and German soldiers as louts interested in rape and pillage. Even big stars got into the act, with Charlie Chaplin's *Shoulder Arms* (1918) showing a lustful German officer menacing an arrested French peasant girl, and Charlie capturing a befuddled Kaiser when he visits the front. Mary Pickford's *The Little American* (1917) has the captured Mary threatened by menacing Huns as she attempts to steal German war plans. Perhaps the most ambitious of these war films, Griffith's *Hearts of the World* (1918) is still representative enough. Shot at the behest of the British government and with Wilson's blessing, even though he began work on it before American entry, Griffith's story (some of it actually shot at the front) includes murderous German troops, a rape-minded German officer with designs on Lillian Gish, the mistreatment of French civilians, a French girl flogged by a boorish German sergeant, and rescue from the Hun by brave French troops. (Griffith may have overdone it: when the movie was viewed at the White House, apparently neither President nor Mrs. Wilson cared much for it.) The overall impact of these propaganda films was such that it solidified a tradition of military-movie cooperation that would only begin to break down in the 1960s.

By 1919, some of the realities of war and peace were beginning to sink in, along with the political exhaustion of the

Progressive movement symbolized by Wilson's incapacitating stroke. The war had given impetus to a number of political forces, such as the persecution of foreigners in the Palmer raids, the rise of radical and labor groups, the rebirth of nativism, and political reaction against two decades of reform. We were on the verge of true modernity, a modernity that was not going to be leavened by the moral restraints and promise of redemption inherent in Wilsonianism. With Wilson's removal from the political scene, it was clear that the nation was moving into a new political--or perhaps apolitical--era. The movies were now established as a major cultural force, ever sensitive to changes in popular mood and the political dynamics of a new age, a habit of representation they will continue down to the present.

Chapter Two

The 1920s: Movies in the Politics of Normalcy

The student of the interplay of politics and popular art is keenly aware of the fluidity of political reality in the dynamic, and perplexing, unfolding of events and processes. But the intriguing, and revealing, thing about studying the movies is that this potent form of popular expression offers us indices of political change. Although art historians have always agonized over the relationship between change and expression, there is enough concomitance between politics and popular aesthetics to warrant serious examination of the relationship. In the political period of the 1920s, this relationship is profoundly evident but not directly so, making our problem of cautious but useful interpretation difficult but worthwhile. For the political world of 1924 was really different than 1914, and as the political past of Progressive reform was undermined in the *ethos* of the Twenties, one could observe very clear change in the political assumptions and agenda of the age. Indeed, President Harding's watchword for the time-- "normalcy"--captured a popular desire for respite, signaling an end to the reform impulse. But what is astonishing about the Twenties is that it was able to characterize the previous period of domestic reform and foreign involvement as something of an aberration, and thus legitimated the present as a "return" to normal American practice. Yet even with that assumption, the Twenties were anything but normal, unleasing some of the most striking changes in American life in this century, and breaking with the past in ways of which we still are feeling the impact. In many ways, it is correct to date American "modernity" from a time presided over by archaic figures such as Warren Harding, Calvin Coolidge, and Andrew Mellon. The Republican beneficent plutocracy, wedded to the rhetoric of tradition and even nostalgia, nevertheless acquiesced in the effects of the new consumer economy, the rise of advertising and public relations, the speculative and merger fever that led to the Crash of 1929, and the technological innovations (such as the radio and the automobile) that were to write significant changes in social mores and folkways. Too, there was a very real sense, for all of the unimaginative passivity of its presidents, that the Twenties was a vibrant if often frivolous time, with revolutions in art, music, and literature, the massive explosion of popular culture, and in truth a good bit of the "wonderful nonsense" we associate with the Jazz Age. Hollywood enjoyed during this time its silent "Golden Age," and many of its stars--Valentino, Clara Bow, Louise Brooks, John Gilbert and Greta Garbo--became famous as representations of the new sophistication, and indeed sensuality, associated with the changes in moral and social climate.

The Twenties make our interpretive task even more difficult, since that period is what we might call "metapolitical," an era tired of the political turmoil of the time just preceding it, determined to ignore politics, and certainly not interested in directly political subjects in the movies. To be sure, there were a few films among the many hundreds made that used a political setting as a dramatic context, but politics usually was a convenient background without much significance. These films were obscure, and unnecessary for our purpose of selecting a few representative films that one can usefully and conveniently examine. Guided by our principles of parsimony and serendipity, let us look at a few movies that give us popular evidence of the unfolding political climate of the Twenties.

For a beginning, one of the striking things about the advent of the Twenties was the speed with which the political atmosphere changed. For example, the moral tone of political and social life was transformed from the essentially Puritan "moralistic" imperatives to a more relaxed and oddly permissive environment of the Harding Administration, whose wink-and-nod attitude toward wealth, acquisition, and conspicuous consumption would lead to the Teapot Dome scandal. In a more general sense, the new attitude gave enormous impetus to conspicuous consumption spread among the expanding middle class emboldened by new prosperity and leisure. The revival of the old myth of "the rugged individual" in the role of new businessman, and the complementary role of consumer of leisure, made privatism take precedence over reformist political goals. In this sudden new milieu, the movies began to treat the change toward the avowedly nonpolitical, even anti-political, life that admitted no mass political role nor necessity of political reform. Hollywood's celebration of leisure, its play with the joy of sex and the display of the body, its images of sensual European sophistication, and its dance around the possibility of sexual freedom focused attention away from the moral and "social" questions that agitated the Protestant reformers of the prior age towards essentially privatistic or individual questions that denied the relevance of a political perspective. The change is made quite evident by comparing earlier and later movies. In Griffith's *Way Down East* (1920) the tensions were on traditional Progressive lines: country against wicked city, ordinary virtue violated by sophisticated chicanery, the moral Protestant family pitted against idle and arrogant wealth, the struggle to preserve the moral center of a way of life against the onslaught of modern problems, a struggle so severe in its strictures that it condemns a "fallen" woman to social exclusion and almost death. But at the same time, directors less wedded to a vision of the past quickly becoming obsolete were capturing on film a very different new attitude. Stroheim, in his *Blind Husbands* (1919) and *Foolish Wives* (1922) and Cecil B. DeMille, in such films as *Why Change your Wife?* (1920) and *Forbidden Fruit* (1921), proceeded from very different assumptions: the problem was not how to prevent, but how to adjust to and enjoy modernity. The unspoken politics of these films was how to create the economic condition for a new pattern of private life that included a "fun morality," self-display, and the family as a unit of leisure consumption. Traditional Republican notions of *"laissez-faire"* now filtered down into the new economy, which included travel, the emulation of European elegance and even a bit of decadence, and how to incorporate the new morality into marriage (with allusion to the possible joys and uses of infidelity). These new experiences virtually always strengthened marital bliss, to be sure, but now in the new consumer economy marriage was more a sensual than a moral agency, just as work was not only a means of creating social wealth but also as the way to finance the pursuit and trappings of leisure. By the time of the late Twenties, the images of the "flapper" and "flaming youth" who party in the mansions and yachts of the very rich seemed to be the legitimate recipient of the new prosperity: money was not to be saved, but spent, and life was not to be devoted to work but play. In their tuxedoed-and-champagned best, see *Our Dancing Daughters* (1928), *Our Modern Maidens* (1929), and *This Modern Age* (1931).

Yet there is a more serious question implicitly lurking here than even the purpose of the work ethic: the persistence of inequality. Progressivism, like previous reform movements, had not been able to significantly change the highly unequal distribution of wealth and power. A good bit of the country did not really share in the booming economy of the Twenties. But the political *ethos* of the time did not favor either admitting or depicting the hopelessness of the have-nots, but quite the contrary wished to propagate the myth of the essential harmony of fluid social classes and the widespread possibility of urban organizational mobility by ordinary but ambitious people. In fact, there was more social tension and less mobility than the political structure was willing to admit, but both the Harding-Coolidge normalcy and popular institutions such as Hollywood extolled this new version of American exceptionalism. The private power of individual pluck rather than concerted political action was applied in the large and remote world of urban organization and rural plantation settings. In the case of women, the pluck of both a traditional (but poor) and "liberated" (but poor) girl can overcome poverty. In *Sparrows* (1926), Mary Pickford leads a wretched rural existence that is overcome through private rebellion against

oppression by lowlifes and eventually a courageous act that ends
with a marriage to a plantation-owning and handsome millionaire.
In *It* (1927), Clara Bow is a shopgirl working in the urban
monumentality of a large department store, whose wealthy owner
is only committed to work; eventually she teaches him the
importance of fun and then possibility of fulfillment with her, and
in the end they, and social classes, are united. The 1920s was a
political culture of achievement that saw potential class conflict as
something overcome by sexual allure or character, suggested that
upward mobility and affluence did not imply "conservative"
austerity or self-denial, and that lingering democratic concerns
about equality could be quelled by private unions of capital and
labor, symbolized by shopgirls and tenants marrying up, and
college boys and clerks marrying heiresses. In *Safety Last* (1923),
Harold Lloyd plays an ambitious youth clerking in a department
store who tries to impress both the acquisitive girl of his dreams
and his boss, eventually literally climbing up the face of the store
building as a stunt, exemplifying the peril but also the rewards of
the achievement ethic. Even in more exotic parables, such as
Fairbanks' *Thief of Bagdad* (1924), the confident and wily thief
wins through mental and physical agility a highborn princess and
riches beyond dreams, proving the movie's motto that "happiness
must be earned," a political aphorism worthy of Coolidge. For the
Twenties, the last could come first without the egalitarian
nuisance of the first having to come last.

The era's optimism about the essential beneficence of
political capitalism was occasionally challenged by negative images
of crooked capitalists who are duly punished for their violation of
a restraining ethical and business contract (as in *The Winning of
Barbara Worth*, 1926), or simply obsession with money and
philistinism (as in *Beggar on Horseback*, 1925). The
entrepreneurial optimism of the age usually took form in the
movies as a happy ending defined by individual achievement
(winning a mate, a game, or a promotion). But as the romantic
struggles of the stars suggested, they were up against monumental
powers in the new gigantism of organization. Comics like Lloyd
and Buster Keaton could make fun of every person's technological
ineptitude and organizational degradation, but it was rare to
witness treatment of the sense of *anomie* the new economic order
was creating. The most serious depiction of the meaning of the
new organizational regimentation into what the German
sociologist Max Weber was calling "the iron cage," and its
implication for democratic society was in King Vidor's *The Crowd*
(1928). In this film, the individual ambition and earnest idealism
of self-help of a young man are destroyed by the quotidian reality
of urban organizational work. As in so much of American
mythology, the city becomes the symbol of the dream of success

and the nightmare of failure. As the protagonist views the skyline of Manhattan, he is told, "You've got to be good in that town if you want to beat the crowd." Relegated to the grind of routine office work, we are given alternative images of the hero either immersed in the conformity of mass society or starkly isolated in metropolitan hallways and streets. The tool of work and familial problems robs him of ambition to the point of becoming suicidal, but his wife and child give him the fortitude to go on, sobered by the fact that the romantic myth of capitalist achievement is a rare if celebrated event. At the end, they are trying to come to grips with the fact that the organizational hierarchy of modern corporate order is for most people impenetrable and unsurmountable. Now aware of their own social and political marginality, they sit in a theater trying, as so many millions of others, to forget their ordinariness through entertainment. As they laugh (at themselves or unfunny clowns?), the camera pulls back to reveal them as only two of many sitting in the theater, forgettable and unremarkable faces in the crowd, the democratic mass in which the individual becomes a lost cipher in a gigantic world from which there is no exit. *The Crowd* takes issue with the fundamental political myth of the age, a myth that would be shattered for so many the very next year, 1929.

There is an odd sense in which the Twenties thought things foreign both a threat and a promise. For all of the audience interest in foreign aristocratic elegance, the recent bitter experience of World War I and the rise of alien doctrines such as communism in the new Soviet Union inspired moviemakers to provide negative treatment of both. In the latter case, a number of films attacked the new Soviet Union as barbaric or just silly, as in *Bullin' The Bullsheviki* (1919). But the most sustained cautionary tale about the dangers of the Russian Revolution is Griffith's parable, *Orphans of the Storm* (1922). Set in the French Revolution, the Revolutionaries are shown to be self-serving, vengeful, cruel, lust-crazed and murderous. The movie was shown at the Harding White House, and Griffith compared the "tyranny of small but aggressive parties" (presumably the Jacobins) who parallels a "similar condition (that) exists in Russia today." The capitalist American fear of communism was not only economic, it was also moral, contrasting the "mobocracy" of the French Revolution as antithetical to the moderate bourgeois democracy of the United States. Russian Bolshevism, like Jacobinism before it, was characterized as an aberrant and twisted grab for power without true popular roots or legitimate purpose, a theme that would persist in political movies down to the present, justifying hostility to Soviet power and interests.

There was also in the Twenties a strong impulse toward "isolationism," an old American political strain made all the more compelling by the very real disillusionment and nagging sense of betrayal and failure over World War I. But the American war experience was still on people's minds, and war is after all an exciting setting for a movie. What emerged was a cycle of World War I films that celebrated the sacrifice and camaraderie of the American soldier, suggested that the adventure of combat and romance with English nurses and French peasant girls was thrilling, but that altogether war was futile and wasteful of brave young men. This interest in the "lessons" of the war became obvious with the success of *The Big Parade* (1925), continuing through such subsequent films as *What Price Glory?* (1926), *Wings* (1927), and *Lilac Time* (1928), and into the sound era with *All Quiet on the Western Front* (1930), *Hell's Angels* (1930), and *A Farewell to Arms* (1932). Gone were the grand moralizing and political vision of the Wilson era in favor of a focus on the existential grit of warfare, with due respect being paid to an equally brave but doomed enemy, as in the moment in *Wings* when victor and vanquished in a dogfight salute each other, or the scene in *The Big Parade* where the American hero gives a cigarette to a dying young German soldier. Films like *The Big Parade* suggest a public mood skeptical about foreign intervention although not clearly "antiwar" or denigrative of the military, as would be some of the Vietnam films much later. People seem to have been willing to be reminded of the horror of trench warfare (as in *The Big Parade's* horrifying attack of machine gun positions) or the maiming of even heroes (as when *Parade's* protagonist returns to France on a wooden leg). The war films of the Twenties spoke to a widely held popular attitude that World War I was a courageous and noble effort on behalf of foreign powers fighting ancient feuds that we regrettably became embroiled in, and that while the people we met were worth remembering, we should avoid such high-costing interventions in the future. One suspects an attitude toward the foreign governments involved in the war not unlike that directed at the Russian Bolsheviks, that somehow "the people," as symbolized by the suffering soldiers of all countries, were separate from "the powers," and it was the powers that got us involved in that unholy mess. These war films functioned to convince Americans all over again that the United States works best as a perfectible isolate, and that foreign ideologies and involvements should be avoided. The war was not so much being refought as rethought, and in the movie retelling in films such as *The Big Parade*, it seems as if the people had decided that Wilson, quite ironically, was correct when he said it was a war without victors.

By the end of the decade, the political assumptions of the Republican ascendancy were becoming unraveled, and the contradictions inherent in their approach to politics were made painfully apparent by the Great Crash. The movies captured many of these contradictions--the tensions over morality in a consumption economy, the uneven distribution of prosperity and opportunity, the barely suppressed fear of failure, the impulse toward isolationism and "Americanism." The Twenties was an "axial" period in American political history, since many of the trends and processes we associate with national modernity were given great impetus by a conservative elite presiding over the dismantling of tradition. In the 1920s, the movies became the great popular spectacle wherein the mass of moviegoers could witness the world they were creating unfold before them in make-believe metaworlds on the screen, and learn something of what we were becoming as a political culture. As modern Americans, we were buffeted by the tempest of political and cultural change, change which was difficult to take and comprehend. The movies were a form of play-learning, helping people to figure out what was going on by watching the "photoplays" that had become a national habit. By watching the "symbolic realities" of the movies of the Twenties, we may still gain insight into the popular mind, and the political process, of the time.

Chapter Three

The 1930s: Movies in the Depression

In Woody Allen's film *The Purple Rose of Cairo* (1984), the heroine is a harassed and abused wife and diner waitress in a shabby Depression era town. Life at home and at work is almost unbearable, so her only joy in life is going to the movies. In a marvelous fantasy, a character comes off the screen to woo her, and indeed takes her into the elegant movie story. Eventually, she is betrayed by the real actor from the movie, and is returned to the confines of her shabby existence. At the end, without hope of escaping her plight, she sits alone in the movie theater watching *Top Hat*. As Fred Astaire and Ginger Rogers dance, and he sings "Cheek to Cheek" to her, the heroine gazes on the grace and elegance of the screen fantasy in bittersweet adoration, reminded of the agonizing chasm between the perfection of screen life and the hopelessness of her own.

Such a touching scene would remind us of the argument that the major political function of movies during the Depression was escape. If one's existence was a grim fate dictated by the collapse of economic forces beyond one's control, then escape into the easily available movie world of adventure, mystery, romance, and fright offered momentary respite from that fate. It is easy to see in the musicals, costume dramas, romantic comedies, and so forth of the period something steadfastly antipolitical, where the movie theater becomes a sanctuary of play away from the economic blight outside. But if our orientation here is correct, the movies of the Thirties were a good bit more political than one might at first think. The era obviously was "politicized" by the sudden and catastrophic decline of economic prosperity, and indeed the quick and bitter rejection of the political mythology of the previous time. It is interesting to note how much the movies blamed the ills of the Thirties on the folly of the Twenties (gangster films from *Public Enemy* to *The Roaring Twenties* traced the power of the underworld to Prohibition and the public flaunting of the law). So even if most Depression Era films avoided direct confrontation with the political situation of the day, they still "participated" in politics through the inclusion of themes, sometimes explicit and at other times implicit, that told people what kind of fix they were in and what they could, or could not, do to make things right. It was not hard to convince people that something was wrong. The movies were part of the popular search for explanations that placed the blame and provided hope, so in that sense they were much more part of the political process than simply a vehicle of denial.

The political problem posed by the Depression was not only how to recover material prosperity, but also how to recover political mastery. There was a very real sense in the early years of the Depression that things were out of control, and that not only economic but also political paralysis had set in. President Hoover's rhetorical assurances that everything was "fundamentally sound" became more and more ironic as events eclipsed the social philosophy of rugged individualism and heightened the perception not only of injustice but also incompetence. The movies responded by becoming more "socially conscious," treating the problems posed by the Depression in often oblique and inverted ways, but certainly light years away from the flapper fantasies of only yesterday. In the early Depression, the mood of many movies was bleak almost to the point of despair, and solutions offered were often desperate. As the Thirties progressed, and the New Deal worked its impact, Hollywood offered more hopeful and light-hearted resolutions to our plight, restoring a sense, if not completely the reality, of political competence and benevolence.

As the Depression deepened during the period of 1930 to 1933, movies turned to themes of social disarray stemming, it was often implied, by a lack of political power to thwart the temptation of anti-social action or solutions that derived from politically unsanctioned sources. Movies began to show the dark "underworld" of crime-ridden cities, depicted the apparent impotence of political authorities such as police and mayors, played with the efficacy of vigilante or extralegal action, and even inverted the success ethic that had been so extolled as a core social virtue in the Twenties. In *City Streets* (1931), law and order, as represented by the police, is virtually irrelevant to the resolution of conflict, and real urban power resides with the lords of the underworld. (Indeed, some fifty urban crime films were released in 1931 alone.) The most famous of the "cycle" of such movies were *Little Caesar* (1930), *The Public Enemy* (1931), and *Scarface* (1932). The gangster-hero was an ironic "success tragedy," a play on the role models of possessive individualism of the previous period that had produced social chaos and poverty. He displayed the kind of virtues--enterprise, ambition, cunning, daring--that was central to the Horatio Alger myth, and endorsed by Coolidge and Hoover. But now the drama of business enterprise seemed savage, and the gangster a kind of proletarian robber baron bent on social destruction. A figure such as Tony Camonte of *Scarface* represented the ambivalence about capitalism that pervaded the early Thirties, as someone obsessed by raw ambition untempered by moral restraint or social responsibility. "Scarface" is driven to acquire, to exercise at any cost the kind of economic power that overwhelms all other values. "Do it first, do it yourself, and keep on doin' it," asserts Camonte, as he accumulates wealth, women, clothes, and all the material signs of power. But the gangster is doomed by the very nihilism of the "survival of the fittest" ethic of monopoly capitalism. As he grabs for more power ("Scarface" is entranced by a neon sign that reads "The World is Yours"), the logic of social Darwinism becomes self-destructive, and his own popular *hubris* destroys him, punishing him for his own greed and success, much as the speculators on Wall Street were destroyed for theirs in 1929. The analogy between business and crime was not lost on audiences in the early Thirties, who were willing to entertain the notion that the unfettered marketplace was by its very nature criminal. A Tony Camonte loosed on society was individualism run riot, both cause and effect of an urban hell where unbridled power stems from the authority of a gun barrel and extends to the exercise of pathological power, symbolized by Camonte's incestuous control of his sister. The subtitle of *Scarface* was "The Shame of a Nation," but the question was left open as to what was shameful: the shameful social conditions that produced the gangsters and gangs, or shameful individuals that produced shameful social conditions? The New Deal was to subscribe to a kind of pragmatic environmentalism: if "society" improved social conditions, included everyone in expanded opportunity, provided housing and hygiene, then as poverty and exclusion disappeared, so would anti-social behavior. However, the depiction of the power of the gangster was so shocking that Hollywood was soon to restore authority and competence to the police, and former "criminals" such as Edward G. Robinson (in *Bullets or Ballots*, 1936) and James Cagney (in *G-Men*, 1935) were engaged in fighting and winning against the mobs and rackets.

The movie imagination of social disarray eventually resolved by a restored political authority was not confined just to gangsters. One of the enduring themes of the movies of the Thirties was the impact of the Depression on children. In William Wellman's *Wild Boys of the Road* (1933), adolescents are forced out of their homes and onto the roads and rails because their out-of-work parents can no longer support them. The kids of the movie learn how to cope in a tough and unforgiving world. They resort to violent revenge, theft, homesteading in a garbage dump, and learn from hobos about the evils of authorities such as railroad officials (one of whom rapes a teenage girl). At one point, they even start an alternative society, a "sewer city" outside of Cleveland founded on ideals of cooperation and equality, but it is destroyed by the authorities, turning firehoses on the kids. When their inevitable brush with the law comes, they are brought before a benevolent judge who is a clone of Roosevelt, treats them with kindness, offers them help and reassurance, and radiates a federal authority that stands with rather than against the downtrodden and helpless. Kids are recurrently shown throughout the period as the ultimate victims of social ills. In *Dead End* (1937), poor teenage boys live in a hopeless tenement neighborhood juxtaposed with a ritzy apartment building. Their choice of role models are an idealistic architect interested in urban planning and a successful gangster, but their environmentally determined destiny seemed to be the reformatory. Hope did derive from authorities who believe in the benevolence of social planning. In *Boy's Town* (1936), Father Flanagan clearly believes there are no unreformable wild boys destined to dead ends by creating a utopian society of children from the slums as a model for a reformed social future comprised of benign and sociable Andy Hardys.

Although political reform might save the next generation, many of the generations trapped by the logic of Depression were viewed as sacrificial victims of circumstance. The gangster might be a popular tragic figure, but it was his own will to power that destroyed him. Thirties movies also had a strain of everyman betrayed, pathetic figures caught in webs of social injustice from which they cannot extricate themselves. These were the closest Hollywood came to showing us a prototypical "forgotten man" who society has let down, rather than like the gangster, who lets down society. In *Heroes for Sale* (1933), the first of our popular victims is wronged and persecuted: a World War I hero (in the direct wake of the Bonus Marchers) denied his medal with war injuries that make him into a drug addict who embezzles for his habit. Later, at work in a laundry, he is a model worker and leads in innovation and investment, but new owners betray the workers, he is accused of being an agitator, and his wife is killed. Wrongly sent to jail, when released he is persecuted as a "Red" and joins the army of the jobless and homeless sleeping under bridges, still holding out a faint hope for the triumph of "common horse sense" and Roosevelt's agenda. He is humiliated, forgotten, and ruined, but he treads on stoically in the rain, refusing to assign social blame or affirm a radical ideology. Similarly, the hero of the famous *I Am a Fugitive from a Chain Gang* (1932) is a decorated veteran in search of work caught in a holdup and sentenced to hard labor; he escapes, becomes a respectable success, but is betrayed by his alcoholic wife, and is returned to the nightmare of the chain gang; he escapes again, to be permanently on the run against the injustice of justice, another hero destroyed by the brutality and rigidity of an institutional system. The institutional authorities who sentence innocent men to such a fate are cruel and smug ignoramuses who serve an evil system of power. The malignancy of that system itself compels their victims into antisocial rebellion, living on the margins by stealing. Even after the institutionalization of the New Deal, this theme was to persist in such powerful films as *You Only Live Once* (1937). This Fritz Lang film depicts a luckless young man with a "record" who is determined to "go straight" with marriage and a job. But at every turn, he is thwarted by mistaken identity, social hostility, and again, a rigid and venal legal system. Eventually he and his pregnant wife are hunted like animals, forced to live a life of crime on the run, and are finally shot while escaping into Canada as we, the audience, peer through the rifle sight. The politically explosive undertone of these movies was one of profound distrust of authority, disbelief in the fairness of the law, and a feeling that government was an unfeeling and malignant master.

If these films did express dark political feelings, perhaps this helps explain the sense of political urgency that some early Depression movies expressed, to the extent of both fearing and hoping for the appearance of a strong leader who is at least charismatic and at most a dictatorial savior. In *The Phantom President* (1932), portraits of past great presidents such as Washington and Lincoln came to life to sing "The Country Needs a Man." In *Washington Merry-Go-Round* (1932), a brave congressman learns of the nefarious plans of a powerful political boss, who reveals that "I have plans. Italy has her Mussolini, Russia her Stalin. Such a man will come along in America." But the most remarkable such vision from this early period of despair is surely *Gabriel Over the White House* (1933). *Gabriel* was financed by William Randolph Hearst, whose editorials fantasized about the necessity of a strong leader able to take decisive, and supralegal, action. In the movie, a traditional president is transformed after an accident by no less than the angel Gabriel into a virtual dictator who vows to end unemployment, crime, and the defiance of other countries. He declares martial law, disbands Congress, forms a national police force and public works corps, and rallies support over the radio. After gangsters try to assassinate the president, his police force is dispersed to try all such criminals before military courts and summarily shoot them. He blackmails other nations into a disarmament agreement, then blows up the American fleet. With all major problems now solved, the president is killed by the angel Gabriel, but what happens to the Constitution is unknown. Such political fantasies tended to fade with the success of Roosevelt (and, perhaps, of Hitler), but it was a clear sign that people were having grave doubts as to whether democratic institutions were equal to the task at hand.

Many of the films we have discussed conveyed a deep and uncomfortable sense of political impotence and inertia felt at both the bottom and top of the political order. The usual outlets for cultural heroism had been thwarted and denied, and both individual and political power seemed thoroughly emasculated.

Further, as the fear of chaos spread, the necessity of social coordination and cooperation became more urgent. The thrust of the New Deal was to promote the political will to overcome pessimism and "fear itself." In subtle ways, this was given imaginative form by the early Warner Brothers musicals, such as *42nd Street, Footlight Parade,* and *Gold Diggers of 1933,* all released in 1933. These musicals were not only cheery and optimistic, they were also affirmations of the possibility of reward for enterprise, the coordination of group effort where everyone pulls together and plays a part, and the recovery of heroic potency symbolized by young and beautiful female fecundity. These films revolve around putting on a show in an atmosphere of economic scarcity, which they overcome; class gaps are overcome by sexual attractions wherein the wealthy become tolerant and generous and poor working girls marry up, revitalizing an economic elite that needs a common touch; a strong but benevolent leader manages social cooperation in the coordinated effort of the show; and collective effort, as seen in the famous Busby Berkeley dance sequences, can be both functional and beautiful. The Depression is very much on their minds, as a gold digger sings of her "forgotten man" with images of unemployed veterans, and as *Footlight Parade* ends with the dancers forming an American flag, portrait of Roosevelt, and NRA eagle. The dangers of irreconcilable political conflict were overcome in musicland by a renewed sense of potency and momentum.

Yet the movies did not leave the discredited economic elite who were blamed for the Depression completely free of censure. Hollywood was not interested in making Marxist statements, but they knew that negative images of the wealthy and their haunts were popular. The tendency was then to portray the wealthy not so much as venal but as silly, wasting their self-indulgent lives on frivolity and living as "the idle rich" in palaces and pleasuredomes remote from the mainstream of American life. For Hollywood, this was the thrust of the Astaire-Rogers musicals such as *Top Hat* and the genre we term "screwball comedy." From *It Happened One Night* (1934) to *Philadelphia Story* (1940), screwball comedies made fun of the rich, contrasting their social irrelevance with the folk wisdom of ordinary people, such as reporters, farmers, and butlers. Such movies did not urge that we should displace the rich, but they also didn't suggest that we admire or envy them, since they are useless, spoiled, and irresponsible. The rich are almost always degraded, but are capable of learning when confronted with the realities outside their domains, and often form private unions with "streetwise" people who restore their utility and respect for the democratic folk. Typical of these is *My Man Godfrey* (1936). A rich madcap heiress at a tuxedo-and-gown party goes on a scavenger hunt to find a "forgotten man" in a city dump "Hooverville." Taken to the party, the derelict proceeds to berate the smug revelers and wants to return to "a society of really important people" at the dump. Hired as a butler, he runs the household, obtains the affection and respect of the family, and saves them from bankruptcy. He affirms the dignity of labor, and invests wisely in a restaurant that will employ his former friends: the "difference between a derelict and a man is a job," he says. Such an enterprise is a benevolent capitalism oriented toward "production for use" rather than hoarding money to live an idle life. The butler turns out to be an aristocrat who had fallen on hard times, and in the end he is to wed the adoring and chastened heiress, uniting the classes in a new deal in social relations based on a sense of social justice, with all restored to using their energies in "more constructive ways." The screwball comedies gave us a look inside the corridors of wealth, wherein we were more amused than appalled. We could conclude that the useless rich were out of touch but reformable, if they regained contact with their social superiors, the wise and worthy democratic many.

As the decade matured, many of the movie resolutions of the political crisis changed and even stagnated--the gangster genre lost its social bite, and the musical its gritty urban edge. But people were still looking for cinematic resolutions that could help them explain and cope with the emergent situation. What Roosevelt was able to use to build public support for the New Deal was reference to "the old deal," the unifying attitude of social solidarity and cultural consensus that was thought to sustain the democratic folk throughout the crisis. The values and programs of the New Deal were alleged to have their roots firmly in American folk traditions of neighborliness and mutual aid, benevolent capitalism and pragmatic innovation, Jefferson's yeomen and Jackson's craftsmen. Even though the economic problems wrought by the Depression remained unsolved, the political crisis was ended by the regime's association with cultural tradition, making it patriotic to favor its program and leader. In this regard it is useful to compare two films with differing assumptions about community and competition. The first is King Vidor's *Our Daily Bread* (1934), in which the director tries to find a better life for his strained couple in *The Crowd* by putting them in a rural communal farm run by a community of the dispossessed. Vidor tries to place the communal operation in nonideological and culturally sound tradition, with the leader of the group simply deemed a charismatic "strong boss" not bound by ideological "fancy words." But the problem was that the movie depicts the successful operation of a non-competitive and non-individualistic communitarian society, folksy as it is. Even though the social organization of the community is only roughly egalitarian, resembles rural traditions of neighborly help, and makes decisions in the manner of a town meeting, it likely failed with audiences and some reviewers because it represented a way of life that was unfamiliar and vaguely alien. By contrast, Frank Capra's *Mr. Deeds Goes to Town* (1936) deals in rural revitalization, but with a key difference. A folkish small-town innocent inherents twenty million dollars. After considerable humiliation and betrayal by urbane snobs and cynics, he decides to give the money away, is committed as insane and tried, where he defends himself and his plan, slugs a shyster, and wins the girl. Unlike the leader of *Our Daily Bread*, Longfellow Deeds (Gary Cooper) is established as completely within the American grain, someone who is romantic and commonsensical, and a benign capitalist uninterested in social experimentation (he owns a small tallow factory). So rather than trying to establish a rural commune, his plan is to purchase and equip 2,000 ten-acre farms, give them to needy farmers for a period of "homesteading," at which time it becomes theirs. This would create individual, competitive farms for which the owners are responsible, a much more palatable kind of rural reform. *Deeds* was a big success, suggesting that if there was an emerging social consensus on the legitimacy and effectiveness of political institutions and programs, certain alternatives were excluded and others deemed wise.

Perhaps this thesis of the emerging social and political consensus of the late 1930s goes a long way in explaining the popularity of the subsequent Frank Capra films of the period. Capra's heroes are moral leaders drawn from the common culture who speak truth to power, suffering servants who represent popular verities to institutional authorities and hidden powers. Their strength comes from the ideals they know and embody, and their weakness from their powerlessness that leads to their degradation in public. Despite their apparent failure and even fraudulence, they succeed in spite of themselves because they revitalize faith in the political contract between the sovereign people and power. This popular theme is developed in Capra's *Mr. Smith Goes to Washington* (1939) and *Meet John Doe* (1941). In *Smith*, a young and naive patriot is cynically named to fill out a senate term by a state machine. He inadvertently discovers the depth of the corruption of the much admired senior senator from his state and the political boss behind him. They set out to destroy him and the senate itself seems their unwitting tool. Smith filibusters, and speaks the popular truths of romantic democracy to a political body that had forgotten them and a political machine that would subvert them. In the end, he collapses in apparent failure, but the senior senator confesses. In *Meet John Doe*, a derelict is hired by a newspaper magnate with political ambitions to claim that he is the author of a letter to a paper announcing his imminent suicide because the world is so bad. When he discovers that the magnate is sponsoring the "John Doe Clubs" as a springboard for the presidency, and a quasi-fascist program backed by bosses and his own Nazi-resembling police force, Doe attempts to speak to a convention of the clubs, but is thwarted and humiliated by the magnate. In the end, he is saved from suicide, at least a segment of the John Doe movement survives, and we learn that the people can't be licked. It may seem curious that in both films, the powerful, as far as we know, remain powerful, and the virtuous remain powerless. But as Capra understood, a sense of cultural power is something that transcends mere political power, almost to the extent of resignation: Senators and bosses and machines may come and go, but the people, and the revitalized faith in popular democracy that sustains them, go on forever.

This same sentiment was echoed in another of the culminating movies of the Thirties, *The Grapes of Wrath* (1940). Although villainy for the plight of the dispossessed "Okie" farmers is murky ("Who do we shoot?" asks one frustrated by foreclosure), very real villains appear in the form of farm operators and goons who exploit the hapless Joad family trekking West in search of work. Despite all the hostility, and their indignation at the injustices they witness, their unity as a group holds them together in a barren universe. Their faith is rewarded when they enter the benevolent confines of the Farm Security Administration, which acts as their protector and sponsor. Not only does the government seem to be on their side, it seems to share their values and hopes. The shared consensus between government and people made them undefeatable, despite the economic and political powers that beset them. This was perhaps the dramatic outcome on screen of the New Deal, a reform alliance that had restored the popular valuational base of government without altering very much the distribution of wealth and power. In the end, the son is on the run for murder, the family is still poor and desperate for work, but a sense of cultural solidarity and even superiority has been restored to the democratic folk. The matriarch of the Joad family ends with the sentiment that the common folk are the true embodiment of *vox populi*, and that the rich and their progeny are an unstable and immoral force doomed by their own violation of populist moral law. So like Capra's heroes, even though this elite retains the materials of power, it does not possess the symbols of power.

These, then, are some of the representative political movies of the 1930s. We should remind ourselves again that movies function for audiences as symbolic resolutions, dramatic narratives that let us interpret the ebb and flow, and even the sudden convulsions, of political processes. The Thirties was a "politicized" age in that what government can and should do was once again an unsettled question, and popular media such as the

movies could hardly ignore politically significant themes. Some
have even suggested that the movies of the Thirties helped avert a
real political crisis by offering up substitute film resolutions to
urgent problems. This is impossible to know, but we can be sure
that one of the major ways people learned what was happening in
their world that was shattered and then put back together was in
the many movie houses where they would watch an imaginative
universe unfold before them.

Chapter Four

The 1940s: Politics in the Movies of the War Years

The movies of the 1930s tended to have a domestic orientation, since the concerns of moviegoers centered around how to cope with economic deprivation, and what that could do to our political system here at home. But as the Thirties waned, that domestic crisis achieved some popular resolution, and was being superceded by a foreign orientation, with the rise of the ambitious and aggressive new imperial powers of Germany and Japan. During the mid-Thirties, the movies responded cautiously to "the gathering storm." For one thing, studio moguls knew from the success of antiwar movies in the past that there was a recrudescence of isolationist sentiment among the populace that might make movie advocacy of foreign involvement both financially and politically risky. There was a well-organized isolationist movement adamant against American intervention in any future European war. There was also a visible anti-British sentiment that opposed helping them, and a more subtle but nevertheless real if unspoken opinion in some circles that was not so much pro-German as anti-Semitic. But as Hitler's power became more and more alarming, and his threats against European Jews and indeed liberal democracy in general became more than just rhetoric, then Hollywood began to commit itself more and more to a position that coincided with the Roosevelt Administration, moving cautiously towards a pro-Allied, anti-Nazi and eventually anti-Japanese stance. The political cooperation between Washington and Hollywood developed even before the American entry into hostilities, and pre-war movies began to include propaganda content.

At first, the success of the fascist movement around the world invited hostile treatment by independent producers. Walter Wanger produced a pro-Republican movie about the Spanish Civil War (although the country is never named) entitled *Blockade* (1936) that cast the Spanish Republicans as the popular democratic force and Franco's forces as alien and murderous. It included fantasies about fascist air attacks and invasion of the U.S. Later, Charlie Chaplin brought out *The Great Dictator* (1940), an attempt to spoof the pretensions of Hitler and Mussolini while reminding audiences of their ambitions, as in the scene where the Hitleresque dictator of Tomania, Adenoid Hynkel, playfully kicks a helium-filled world globe in the air, as if it were his possession. The film ends, like *Blockade*, with an impassioned anti-fascist speech delivered to the audience by Chaplin himself. But the studios were more cautious and their pre-war messages usually more covert. Costume dramas and other genres began to include themes and images that not only validated liberal (and specifically New Deal) democracy but also impressed upon audiences the alien and authoritarian dangers that threatened popular rule. Warner Brothers in particular began to interweave politically charged themes in movies that communicated a new stance toward the rapidly unfolding events in Europe and Asia. *The Adventures of Robin Hood* (1938), for example, makes the black-clad Normans into the kind of cunning and ruthless exploiters and murderers that it was becoming popular to believe that the Nazis were. By the time of *The Sea Hawk* (1940), movies were clearly abandoning the anti-war and anti-interventionist stances that had persisted throughout the Thirties (cf., *The Dawn Patrol*, 1938, and *The Private Lives of Elizabeth and Essex*, 1939) in favor of stories that emphasized the dangers of isolationism and appeasement. In *The Sea Hawk*, Elizabeth I first appeases Spain until Captain Thorpe (Errol Flynn) convinces her of "fifth columnist" treachery at court and Spanish designs for world conquest, finally resisting invasion and defeat by the Armada. Similarly, "cautionary tales" in other settings warned of the rise of fanatical mass movements led by charismatic leaders bent on revolutionary action or conquest. *Santa Fe Trail* (1940) depicted a monomaniacal John Brown bent on social destruction, and *Gunga Din* (1939) showed the Thugge movement in India as devoted to world conquest. Movies began to appear that legitimated military mobilization and mock heroics of army training, such as Abbott and Costello's *Buck Privates* (1941), ending with a militant and marching troop number led by the Andrews Sisters.

Another subtle political trend in the movies of the pre-war period was the return to the "lessons of the past" in American history. Notable figures from the past were conjured up to remind us of their commitment to popular leadership and commitment to patriotic ideals. The populist hero of the Thirties, Abraham Lincoln, was represented in Ford's *Young Mr. Lincoln* (1939) as courageous and idealistic, the kind of young American needed today to lead the fight against injustice and bullying. Daniel Webster reappears in *The Devil and Daniel Webster* (1941) to defend America against Satan and his minions who would destroy the country. In *Drums Along the Mohawk* (1939), ordinary pioneer families living in the troubled times of the American Revolution are put to the test of sacrifice and bravery, and are equal to the test because of their loyalty to family and above all country. Like so many of the "historical" movies that flooded the market during this time, *Drums* reasserted national values and achievements at the end of a decade of hard domestic struggle now about to be followed by difficult international struggle, and provided an inspiring historical reference with political uses in the present.

Too, the movies' attitude toward World War I undergoes a change, either reassuring us of the essential heroism of American fighting men in that war (*The Fighting 69th*, 1940) or the extent to which that heroism is justified by American values and mission (*Sergeant York*, 1941). *York*, as the top-grossing film of 1941, was accompanied by a promotional tour by the real Alvin York. It was viewed by President Roosevelt, who told the visiting York (and Gary Cooper, the York of the movie) that "the picture comes at a good time"; but it was also condemned by isolationists as pro-interventionist propaganda. *Sergeant York* centers on York's "conscientious objection" to warfare, since killing is "agin the book," the Bible of his deeply felt religious conversion. His commanding officer, impressed with both his moral fiber and shooting ability, argues that he has an obligation to the Constitution also, since "all men must defend the rights of each man, and each man must defend the rights of all men." When York retreats to the Tennessee hills to ponder the question, a holy wind opens the "book" to the passage on rendering unto Caesar, and York is convinced of his patriotic duty to the extent of winning the Medal of Honor in France for killing twenty Germans and capturing almost singlehandedly 132 others. Returning home, he is lionized as a hero, but in the true spirit of a mountain Cincinnatus, returns to farm and family. *Sergeant York* did not so much glorify combat as it did virtuous warfare led by the American salt of the earth against a Teutonic evil that must be defeated again. *York* was "noble propaganda," presaging the almost existential attitude Americans would take into the war, that it was something "we had to do" with the ruthlessness of the righteous, a sense of right combined with efficiency which would enable our resolve that "God's on our side." This is certainly a very different view than that of *The Big Parade*.

In the mounting atmosphere of preparation for the seemingly inevitable entry of the United States into the conflict, and the often simplistic appeals to patriotic fervor and military heroism, there did emerge two mature and sophisticated treatments of political power that offer us a useful contrast deeply rooted in American popular thinking about politics. In American popular thought, there has been a strain that regards political icons such as Washington and Lincoln as figures who were above politics and of the people, and that political redeemers, such as *Mr. Smith*, are attuned to the ideals of the political culture and not the Machiavellian machinations of politics nor the lust for power that obsesses the political megalomaniac. In the former case, the movies have portrayed politics as a corrupting force, the stuff of machines, deals, payoffs, strategems and betrayals, a not very elevating but certainly very native, and in some ways accepted, part of our national life. On the other hand, the movies have

tended to view the overly ambitious seeker of power as alien and
pathological, someone whose will to power propels him or her so
against the American grain that he or she becomes doomed by
demonic excess. From *Corner in Wheat* on we have liked to see the
mighty fall and the arrogant get their comeuppance. We expect
the machine politico to take a minor fall, since he or she is, after
all, an almost venerable character type, and the would-be dictator,
too, take a drastic fall, one in which he really suffers for his
excessive reach for power. In this regard, two films from the
immediate pre-war period are instructive. The first, Preston
Sturges' *The Great McGinty* (1940) depicts the rise and fall of a
corrupt machine politician as a comic story. A bartender recounts,
via flashback, the story of his political career, beginning as a bum
who falls in with a sharp political organization by voting thirty-
seven times for the machine candidate for two dollars a vote. The
ward heeler explains the political logic of this, arguing that for
various reasons, some voters just don't make it to the polls, but
that is no good reason for their candidate to be cheated out of
their vote: "All we're doing is getting out the vote." As the young
politico's career and political education advances, he learns the
wrongheadedness of reformers (a "Civic Purity League" is formed
to fight the machine) by the same political philosopher: "They're
always talkin' about graft, but they forget if it wasn't for graft,
you'd get a very low type of people in politics--men without
ambition--jellyfish." The bum McGinty advances from alderman to
mayor to governor by using means of persuasion from lies to fists.
But the twinges of political conscience on which the culture relies
affects him, and he tries to do the right thing, resulting of course
in his downfall. More petty than the gangster, the machine pol
such as McGinty lives to reminisce on another ironic American
success story turned sour by the essential corruptions of ordinary
politics, yet one we do not regard so much with horror as
amusement. By contrast, we judge more harshly someone like
Charles Foster Kane of Orson Welles' masterpiece, *Citizen Kane*
(1941). Kane, unlike McGinty, has truly fervid and soaring
ambitions, is characterized by a truly monumental ego and need
for power and love, and wishes for nothing less than that the
world be organized on his terms. In him, we see something
profoundly "un-American," someone capable of identifying his own
interests with the public interest and thus reaching for power that
was nothing less than absolute. Kane (partially based on the
newspaper "Magnate" William Randolph Hearst) is a commanding
but forbidding figure, imperious and extravagant, living in the
pretentious manner of an oriental potentate in his many
mansions. Kane flirts with a kind of American populist fascism
but is defeated by scandal. As he ages, he openly states his
manipulative powers ("People will think . . . ," his wife begins, ". . .
What I tell them to think," he finishes), and abandons his early
"principles" in favor of power associations (he poses with Hitler).

His defeat in politics is engineered by a McGinty character, Boss Jim W. Gettes, who is "a cheap crooked politician" no doubt, yet he humbles the mighty Kane and destroys his vaunting ambition to rule. Kane eventually retreats to his own domain wherein he can play "absolute monarch" over his own world, a world that finally includes no one, and he dies wistfully reminiscing about a lost and treasured object of his childhood. A political adventurer like McGinty is merely comic and even part of our native cultural charm, but a Kane is a more threatening if more tragic figure whose reach for power could have been a much greater threat to American political values than the "honest graft" of a McGinty. McGinty becomes "great" because he finally wanted to do the right thing; Kane is reduced to being a mere "citizen" because he finally was willing to do the wrong thing. In the former case, power became oddly ennobling; in the latter case, power was sought as an adornment of the ego, and became a destructive intoxicant that made its seeker predictably ignoble. At a time when the world was being engulfed in a war that stemmed from the power of a collective national ego represented by one demonic man, a McGinty certainly was preferable to a Kane.

By 1939, the parabolic references to fascism and war began to wane in favor of more explicit treatment of the Nazi enemy. Under immense pressure and even Nazi threats, Warners' brought out *Confessions of a Nazi Spy* (1939), which depicted the evil machinations at the top of the Nazi hierarchy and the "fifth column" tentacles of Nazism here in America. In one scene, Goebbels himself orders the dissemination of Nazi propaganda in major American cities, and in another, a whispering campaign against Roosevelt is organized. We see German-American children at a Bund summer camp in Wisconsin singing Nazi songs and goosestepping; and newsreel footage of Bund rallies where intruders are beaten up. *Confessions* was not a critical nor popular success, but it did legitimate Hollywood "taking sides" in the political debate about American involvement. As the Nazis overran Europe, other studios joined the anti-Nazi chorus. *The Mortal Storm* (1940), for instance, was released by MGM the week that Hitler toured defeated Paris. Whereas *Confessions* had editorialized about Nazi threats to American security, *The Mortal Storm* focused on the destructive powers of political fanaticism in Europe. Here that great symbol of European culture, the German university professor, is renounced by his stepsons for his democratic views and is sent to a concentration camp where he dies. His daughter is appalled by her fiance's Nazi beliefs and runs away. Pursued and shot at by stormtroopers on skis, she dies across the Swiss border. The two motifs of foreign invasion or subversion here at home and the horrors of Nazi rule in Europe would dominate the anti-Nazi films made throughout the war years. Sometimes the results would be ludicrous: in *All Through the Night* (1942), the American underworld is recruited to fight Nazi spies on the argument that a Nazi takeover here would be bad for their rackets, truly a move to make all segments of American society part of the war effort. Similarly, the lurid vision of Nazi Germany in such sensationalist fare as *Hitler's Children* (1943) was so preposterous as to undermine serious propaganda efforts.

As the Nazi Occupation and Blitz unfolded, pro-British and pro-Resistance sentiment in the movies became legitimate. The political motive for showing Americans the gallantry of our soon-to-be allies was certainly to demonstrate their courage in the face of a ferocious and ruthless enemy, and to remind us that the same fortitude would soon be expected of us. The most famous, and probably the most politically influential, was *Mrs. Miniver* (1942), a movie that portrayed the British as civilized but courageous in the face of the German onslaught. Mrs. Miniver presides bravely over a gentle middle-class world, although all classes and professions are in essential harmony and resolve. All the men are courageous, but so too are the women, as Mrs. Miniver disarms a downed German pilot. The widespread suffering caused by German attacks is endured by maintaining a patina of normality. The film concludes with a sermon to a microcosm of the British nation gathered in a destroyed church that makes an appeal to democratic solidarity, clearly including our American cousins in the "war of the people." There is even a suggestion of the social benefits of war, as an old lady remarks, "War's brought us to our senses in more ways than one." The film was an enormous hit, was praised by the Secretary of the Navy as "worth a flotilla of destroyers," Roosevelt himself told director William Wyler that it made increased aid to the British politically easier, and indeed ordered propaganda leaflets of the vicar's sermon in the film dropped over cities in Occupied Europe.

Many other films would depict Americans helping out, usually decisively, various resistance groups inside Nazi-held Europe, who were almost uniformly stalwart and heroic against overwhelming odds and brutal reprisals. There was, however, one ally that constituted a problem: the Russians. If the movies are a guide to the popular mind, they suggest that we have been hostile to the Soviet Union from its very inception. Movies of the 1920s and 1930s typically portrayed the Bolsheviks as brutal and tyrannical, or sometimes as comic bunglers or bureaucrats. The hilarious Lubitsch film *Ninotchka* (1939) depicts a serious and drab female communist official in Paris on a mission who is lured and won by an American playboy who introduces her to the pleasures of decadent capitalism and Parisian romance. But the Soviet-

American alliance necessitated that positive films should be made about Russia, just as negative films were being made about the Nazis (the funniest satire was Lubitsch again, in *To Be or Not To Be*, 1942). The Soviets had an "image" problem with Americans, who were suspicious of their government, official ideology, and recent actions, such as the Non-Aggression pact with Hitler, the division of Eastern Europe with him, and the invasion of Finland. The propaganda content of the "pro-Soviet" movies was to make both the Soviet government and the Russian people acceptable as allies. In such films as *North Star* (1943) and *Song of Russia* (1944), the Russian people are portrayed as peaceable and happy peasants far removed from the grim new cities of Stalinist industrialization. Thus they could not be associated with an industrial proletariat of Marxist theory, but rather with the American myth of pastoral simplicity and democratic good sense. By contrast, the Nazi invaders were portrayed in the harshest terms, with emphasis on their penchant for outrageous atrocities. In *North Star*, for example, the men of the village who had fled a Nazi medical unit that had occupied their village counterattack when they learn that the unit is killing the village's children by using too much of their blood for transfusions given to wounded German soldiers. But the most remarkable of the "pro-Soviet" films is certainly *Mission to Moscow* (1943), based loosely on the reminiscences of former ambassador Joseph Davies. Made with the support of the White House, *Mission* follows Davies' diplomatic travels. But the political purpose was to demonstrate Nazi villainy and Soviet trustworthiness and resolve. While Nazi Germany is a grim and regimented society bent on world conquest, Soviet Russia is a friendly and peaceable place not unlike America. Not only do the men--Litvinov, Molotov--get along well with Davies, Mrs. Litvinov and her daughter become friends with Mrs. Davies and daughter, giving a tea party in which Mrs. Litvinov explains her job as Commissar of Cosmetics, concluding with the sentiment that "women are much the same the world over." Davies witnesses the famous purge trials and declares a confession to be valid. The purge trials, the pact with Hitler, and the invasion of Finland are explained away. Finally, Davies meets with Stalin himself, who is pictured as the avuncular and wise "Uncle Joe" of official propaganda rather than the master of the Gulag. Such a sympathetic treatment of the Soviet Union invited a great deal of hostile reaction to its distortions, both when it was released and after the war with the new perception of Soviet enmity.

With the American entry into the war, the central political communication from the movies was commitment. This theme of the necessity of firm political commitment is so pervasive that one is tempted to think there was considerable anxiety in the corridors of power about the depth of our national resolve. Whatever the case, in all of the "war-related" genres of the period--the combat film, the "home front" movie, the gallant allies film--the drama centers on heroic forms of commitment that serve the common effort of defeating the enemy. It was common to depict the Nazis and Japanese as fanatically dedicated to their purposes to reinforce the idea that we had to be more committed than they. The best-known wartime commitment drama was *Casablanca* (1943), in which Rick's "Cafe American" becomes the stage for the formation of the Grand Alliance, a haven for the Resistance, and a place for the display of Nazi cruelty and ambition. Everyone is committed except the disillusioned American, who could have been a World War I veteran, an unemployed Bonus Marcher, and was an anti-fascist activist, but now is described as an "isolationist" who wisely sticks his neck out for nobody. But such an attitude represents the bitter fruits of parochial non-commitment: cynicism, selfishness, refusal to face the realities of a world at war. His cafe is populated by a virtual united nations, but without American leadership, a political state of affairs that makes the outcome of the conflict in doubt. America is still The Promised Land to which Bulgarian newlyweds and Czech patriots must go to continue the fight or escape the horrors of occupation. The story is set in December 1941, when we were politically "asleep all over America," but now through Rick we are going through the agony of re-commitment. American power is seduced by Europe, who trusts us to make the right decision, involving sexual renunciation, intervening against the Nazis, and accepting world responsibility on the side of Right. "Welcome back to the fight," the voice of European intellect tells him, "this time I know our side will win." The sentiment revived in Rick is for active and resolute patriotism, signified by his union with France, an ancient but now reactivated political alliance in defense of the values of the democratic revolutions against the Nazi peril. Like the nation, Rick reluctantly came to realize that he could not "escape from himself," reconciling himself to his responsibility to the civilization from which he sprang. *Casablanca's* theme of commitment was to be much imitated, but not equalled.

The commitment theme appears in a wide variety of dramatic contexts, from the highly serious to the ludicrous. In the former instance, the movie version of *Watch on the Rhine* (1942) approaches the fight as a matter of ideological commitment of a vaguely left-wing but also nationalistic identification. A German aristocrat in America before the war announces that his profession is "anti-fascist," and much of the film is taken up with him explaining the issues involved. But again the plot centers on his ability to rouse the Americans to understand the gravity of the threat and join in the cause. Like *Casablanca*, Americans are suddenly confronted with the face of the enemy with the presence of a Nazi sympathizer who learns of the anti-fascist's plan to return to Germany with resistance funds and threatens to inform the German Embassy, stirring the Americans out of their political lethargy. The many war films typically depicted democratic heroism at great personal sacrifice for both fighting men and the multiple nationalities (French, Chinese, Filipinos) who were our allies. From *Wake Island* (1942) to *Objective Burma* (1945), the tendency in war films was to contrast not only our fighting skills, but also our cultural superiority and indeed commitment to humane values that undergirded our efforts. This involved the use of outrageous racial and ethnic stereotypes (sly and cunning "Japs," oversophisticated but barbaric Prussians,) warfare that excluded the possibility of American cowardice or ineptitude, and rhetorical appeals for patriotic support. Indeed, there were some films *(This is the Army*, 1943 and *Yankee Doodle Dandy*, 1943) that mixed patriotism and militarism together in an emotional medley of national commitment. Too, the "home front" movies usually centered on the commitments necessitated by the war for women, both working and maintaining a "manless" home. Exemplary here is *Since You Went Away* (1944), in which a mother and two daughters maintain "the unconquerable fortress--the American home." The film served the purpose of providing heroic role models for the girls left behind. The mother acquires the ability to decide things, make ends meet, help her daughters deal with separation from their boyfriends, and even takes a job in a defense plant. Her war experience teaches her female responsibility and democratic empathy, but tests her the most when her husband is reported missing in action. However, neither Hollywood nor Washington liked downbeat endings that might suggest great casualties (a movie called *The Fighting Sullivans*, about five real-life brothers who all died on a ship at sea, was so upsetting to the public that it was quickly withdrawn), so on Christmas Eve the cable comes that "he's coming home." The fortress has held and the family is reunited. Those who have kept the faith are rewarded with survival. By war's end, practically everybody on film had taken part in the war effort--Tarzan, the Three Stooges, Donald Duck and Bugs Bunny. There were even wartime Westerns, including one (*Wild Horse Rustlers*, 1943) in which Nazis in Western clothes show up in the West to rustle Army-bound horses, only to be foiled by cowboy heroics.

During the imminent ending and immediate aftermath of the war, the movies began to respond to newly emerging political concerns: the nature of the coming peace, the return to civilian life, and the rewards of victory. It was a time of political fatigue, with people tired of the sacrifice and deprivation, but also of hope, that the political tremors of the previous decade might finally settle. There were hopes that the lofty Rooseveltian and

Churchillian rhetoric could now be translated into international cooperation. It was a moment that the international-minded wished to seize. To that end, Darryl Zanuck produced *Wilson* (1944), reviving the memory of that president's failure to secure the peace after World War I because of isolationist opposition at home. The movie attempts to "humanize" Wilson as a college professor who reads detective novels, with a beautiful wife and three teen-age daughters, all the while pondering the structure of international peace. He is thwarted in his dream, warning of another world war in a generation, by petty and duplicitious politicians here at home such as Senator Henry Cabot Lodge (whose opposition was rigidified by a snub on Wilson's part). Zanuck's movie was an obvious attempt to rally support for Roosevelt's post-war plans for a United Nations founded on Wilsonian principles updated in "The Four Freedoms" and "collective security" to be enforced by the Great Powers in a Security Council. Wilson was portrayed as wise and prophetic, urging on audiences the idea that we now had a "second chance" to secure the peace, and that Roosevelt (up for re-election) was the heir to the Wilsonian internationalism that we must implement. The movie was condemned by FDR's opponents, but it probably failed at the box office because of its own sense of self-importance, the rather obvious code of special pleading just beneath the surface, and the fact that moviegoers are often put off by high-toned political fare (it was defeated for the "Best Picture" Oscar by *Going My Way*).

What people were becoming much more interested in was the homecoming, and realistically what that was going to mean for our lives. (It is interesting to note that the movement toward "social realism" in the movies corresponds with the veteran-inspired antipathy against romanticism: the last war films, such as *A Walk in the Sun* (1946) and *The Story of G. I. Joe* (1945), are grim naturalistic dramas of tired and cynical soldiers fighting a seemingly endless war for survival rather than glory or political principles.) Another film, *Pride of the Marines* (1945) makes the transition from war to peace: it focuses on a soldier who survives, but is blinded in truly nightmarish battle scenes. Returned to a rehabilitation center, he and other wounded veterans are bitter about their fate and anxious about their future. But in the end we are offered hope that he will both see and adjust to civilian life. The most celebrated "coming home" movie of the period is *The Best Years of Our Lives* (1946), a compendium of the political concerns and agenda of the time. It is true, as critics of the film have charged, that it avoids taking an obvious political stance and opts for personal solutions; yet it does depict returning veterans from different social classes who are all quickly disillusioned with the civilian world. They feel excluded from power over their lives and see no realization of the ideals for which they presumably fought. The film suggests a political agenda that spreads the spirit of democratic cooperation experienced during the war to domestic institutions, with banks giving loans to seasoned veterans, jobs to war heroes, and wives to men maimed in combat. In all cases, the returning veterans overcome their sense of emasculation as aliens in a civilian world suspicious of them, unite with the right women, and then hopefully enjoy the fruits of victory by building the post-war world of peace and prosperity. *Best Years* has many romantic touches and resolutions, but it doesn't hedge on the very real fact that it would take veterans "years to get anywhere" and that they would be "pushed around."

It was also the case in the immediate post-war years that there was considerable expectation that Roosevelt's liberal domestic agenda could now be completed. The war was fought with several tacit ideals delayed but now to be realized--the end of racial inequality, the eclipse of the kind of prejudice that had motivated the Nazis, the realization of labor power, the completion of an agenda of health care, housing, and so on. This of course didn't happen, and the conflicts that persisted gave inspiration to the wave of "social problem" films of the period. Some of them, indeed, even involved veterans: *Crossfire* (1947) concerns a soldier who murders a Jew out of pathological hatred reminiscent of fascism, and *Gentleman's Agreement* (1947) reveals the ways in which Jews, and by implication other minorities, are excluded from social institutions. Movies also began to presage the black revolution that would come. In *Home of the Brave* (1949), a black soldier suffers discrimination at the hands of an embittered white sergeant, revealing an implicit racism in an army that prided itself on its recently successful defense of democratic ideals against a racist ideology.

As the war receded, a new mood of pessimism began to creep into the public consciousness. Simply presenting a social problem in a movie didn't solve it, nor stating the ideals of the war didn't mean they became practice. What began to emerge was a feeling that power was somehow implacable and irredeemable, regardless of the ideals that are the stuff of political rhetoric. This was evident in the darker view of politics that began to emerge at this time. Even Frank Capra, chastened by his war experiences, returned to view American life in much darker tones: his much-beloved *It's a Wonderful Life* (1946) is a hauntingly pessimistic view of American life, characterized by malicious elites, class divisions, and unheroic entrapment by family and friends.   He explicitly dealt with politics in *State of the Union* (1948), the story of a rich and opinionated man with a sense of capitalist *noblesse oblige* who is drawn into the political arena. His candor about the supremacy of the public interest makes him popular, but the lure of power makes him compromise with traditional political methods and powers, including having his estranged wife make a speech about him she doesn't believe. Although in the end his principles prevail, he is excluded from power and power and principle remain estranged. In *All the King's Men* (1949), Robert Penn Warren's demagogue (loosely based on Louisiana's Huey Long) makes democracy itself suspect, as a populist leader who cites ideals takes on fascist overtones with himself as a kind of would-be American *Fuhrer*, suggesting that the democratic mass is irrational, fickle, and willing to follow a facile and exciting leader who offers them bread and circuses. In *Born Yesterday* (1950), a brutal and crude junk magnate in Washington buying influence is not seen as just a time-honored politico in the tradition of McGinty, but rather is elevated to the status of fascist, suggesting that capitalist, as well as democratic, power has now become suspect.

In this atmosphere, it is no wonder that the movies began to explore the darkest corners of the public mood, in the film movement now termed *film noir*. Dark in both lighting and mood, these films seemed to reveal a post-war malaise that could only appear in art: a world of betrayal and suspicion, of dark motives and evil acts, of the inescapability of one's fate and inevitability of doom. Beginning with films such as *Double Indemnity* (1944) through *Out of the Past* (1947) and finally petering out with films such as *The Big Heat* (1953), the movement in subtle ways did relate to the political mood of disillusionment with public ideals betrayed and liberal hopes unfulfilled, making the individual feel that power was something completely out of one's hands, that hidden and impersonal forces govern life, and that both personal and political trust are unwarranted and destructive. *Film Noir* was probably the closest that Hollywood ever came to popular tragedy, emerging in a post-war political world whose bleakness and dashed hopes gave credence to a dark and foreboding movie landscape that suggested both moral and political exhaustion. *Film noir* was almost never about political subjects, but it was very much about a political mood of sudden powerlessness to affect a world that seemed hostile and corrupted beyond political, or individual, redemption.

By the late 1940s, political conditions in the country and the world were altering drastically and quickly. All of the pious hopes of 1945 seemed far removed in time, as new and harsh realities impinged. The movies were responding to mercurial changes in public opinion and audience interests, vacillating between the light optimism of musicals and comedies and the heavy pessimism of the social problem films and *Film Noir*. They knew that audiences wanted certain symbolic resolutions on the screen, but the political atmosphere mitigated against certainty. With the solidification of the Cold War, the Forties began to evolve into the Fifties, and we begin to see the emergence of new political foes and causes, a new reality that is more appropriately treated as part of the 1950s.

Chapter Five

The 1950s: The Creation of the Post-War World

The political drama that unfolded in the late 1940s stemmed from a lack of triumphant resolution to the war. Unlike World War I, World War II had been a clear victory, and Americans thought that not only did they have a great deal to be proud of, they also had gained much from the war. The war was supposed to have ushered in an American-dominated world, a world in which American values and benevolent empire were to triumph as our gift to other nations, friend or foe. We would Americanize the defeated Japan and Germany, revive Western Europe through the Marshall Plan (thus opening up the new Europe to American values and goods), and enforce a *Pax Americana* through far-flung alliances (the frontiers of the "American Century"). We viewed the model of American capitalist democracy as beneficent and appropriate everywhere.

When the realities of peace sunk in after World War I, the response was one of disillusionment expressed in the existential tone of "Lost Generation" art (such as Hemingway's stories) and the vaguely "anti-war" films of the Twenties. After World War II, as we noted, there were half-hearted attempts in the movies to represent the liberal values and agenda that were to be the promise of the war through the "social problem" films, keeping alive the hope that problems addressed in art would inspire solutions through political action. Too, we saw that post-war *film noir* was a kind of existential response to the moral and political exhaustion engendered by the war and the uncertain peace, expressing doubt and official optimism. But also like World War I, there was a political reaction that we might term a drama of recrimination, a search for enemies, scapegoats, and those to blame for the perceived failure of the war and peace. After the first war, the movies were not expected to become part of this in any major way, although they did produce some anti-Bolshevik films. But after the second war, Hollywood was not only put under political pressure to adhere to certain political orthodoxies (vaguely pro-capitalist and anti-communist), but also to prove itself patriotic and worthy of trust by banishing from its midst those whose loyalties were questionable and making films which attacked the new enemy. As it became clear that the great new power in Europe, the Soviet Union, did not accept the terms of an American-dominated post-war world, the fury of our political rage over this defiance became focused on dramas of political purification at home and political confrontation abroad. A nation that had before been portrayed in the movies as a remote and strange Ruritanian "ice kingdom" of Mongolian cruelty and Slavic soul became suddenly a gigantic political and ideological threat to us. Soviet villainy and culpability for the disorders in the world became almost an article of faith, and our search for someone to blame was over. For Hollywood, this meant the House Un-American Activities Committee (HUAC) hearings that forced movie figures to "name names" or face contempt of congress charges, pressured film studios to fire and "blacklist" those that thought all this persecution was ridiculous or at least unconstitutional, and suggested a thematic code that would avoid criticism of the "free-enterprise system" or, horror of horrors, "deify the common man." Ardent searches were undertaken to discover hidden "communist" content in movies that left-wing writers and directors had worked on with predictably preposterous results, such as a "suspicious number" of happy Russian children in MGM's *Song of Russia*.

As a sort of penance for past sins of being "soft on communism," post-war Hollywood was encouraged to make "anti-communist" movies that would dramatize to movie audiences the nefarious designs of communism and the extent to which communist agents were attempting to infiltrate and subvert American life and institutions. Hollywood grudgingly complied, with practically every studio from MGM to Monogram dutifully making films that were politically correct in their attitude to the Cold War. What is astonishing in retrospect is the felt necessity for such films, since the political reactionaries who insisted on them seemed to feel that blatant propaganda in the harshest black-and-white terms was the surest way to alert the public as to the dangers of Soviet expansion. Their estimation of the gullibility of the American populace and the fragility of American institutions was only matched by the iniquity of communist agents they forced Hollywood to portray on film. However, the moviegoing public was smarter than they thought: despite the felt urgency for these films on the political right, they all lost money, and the hysteria began to abate. With the election of the generally trusted Eisenhower and certainly with the fall of Joe McCarthy in 1954, they disappeared as a genre, more out of studio embarrassment than perceived success in arousing public concern with the Red menace.

The anti-communist movies did display American confusion as to exactly what this new enemy was and what it was that he and she wanted. One of them involved espionage by the Soviet government that leads "good Russians" who see the virtues of Western life to defect (*The Iron Curtain*, 1948); another involved international intrigue over a defecting ballerina, whose death teaches an agnostic British officer the evils of communism and renewed faith in God (*The Red Danube*, 1949). But most of them incorporated standard generic formulas, simply transforming the struggle with communism into a matter of catching spies, gangsters, and assorted accomplices such as fallen women and overeducated intellectuals. They would use the semi-documentary style of the FBI-police thriller, following the heroics of the government on the trail of subversives (*I Was a Communist for the FBI*, 1951; *Big Jim McLain*, 1952, with John Wayne himself as a HUAC agent and also with guest appearances by HUAC committeemen), who are simply assumed to be part of a political movement and government whose motives are not explored. When communist intellectuals were portrayed, they tended to be stereotypes of effeminate and myopic professors hungry for power. Communist gangsters are another matter; they tend to resemble the seedy and thick-necked brutes of the gangster films, with the only difference being that rather than wanting to take over the West Side, they want to take over the Western world. But Red bosses and eggheads in the movies live well in fancy apartments, with the pleasures of power (champagne, cigars, and beautiful mistresses). They will stop at nothing--murder, bribery, prostitution, torture--to achieve their aims, although usually those aims are so murky as to make audiences wonder what communists are after that is so different than previous political gangsterisms (the Nazis and Japanese had often been portrayed as political gangs who had seized power for their own profit and pleasure). The Commie gang films (*I Married a Communist*, 1949, *The Red Menace*, 1949), gave us a new politicized underworld that was as alien as the Thirties Italian gangsters and with a foreign sponsor (rather than the Mafia, it was the Soviet Union) and Machiavellian rules (like the Mob, you can never quit; you have no private life; betrayal or failure or even questioning the rule of the Party bosses means death; one is expected to obey orders without question, the men to kill, the women to use their bodies to extract information or lure new members into the Party). In all cases, they are foiled, but innocent and naive Americans who have fallen into their bad political company pay a heavy price.

The most remarkable of these films remains *My Son John* (1953), because it suggested that beneath the surface rhetoric of anti-communism both in the country and in the movies was in fact simply an anti-intellectualism and anti-cosmopolitanism that wished to cling to patriotic simplicities and xenophobic parochialism. John is the son of a superpatriot and altogether repellent father who hits his son with a Bible when he makes some critical remark about the United States, and a devout Catholic mother who urges him to abandon intellect (and a professor he admires) and rather mindlessly "think with your heart, not your head," like his father, who is a bigot and drunkard. John is displaying all of the symptoms associated at the time with communist intellectuals: he reads critical books; he didn't play football but rather studied seriously in college, which makes him not only a liberal intellectual who can be duped by communism but probably a homosexual to boot; and he works in the Washington bureaucracy, which gives him access to state secrets. Not only the FBI but also his mother have him under surveillance, and she patriotically turns in her own son to the FBI, who confront him with his political sin ("'The lower you sink, the higher you rise in the Party, don't you, John?") which he runs away from. Beset by both parental and governmental disapproval, he agrees to become a patriot and informant, but it is too late for one so mired in alien betrayal, and he is killed by the Party on the steps of the Lincoln Memorial. The wages of political sin are death, but he is not even in death beyond repentance and example, since he had made a tape, replayed for an assembly of students at his Alma Mater almost like a speech from the gallows, that recounts his descent into a political fate worse than death. But the implication remains that fooling around with political thought, erudite friends, foreign women, and urbane lifestyles can make one lose proper conformity to the canons of "Americanism." Like the other anti-communist entertainments, *My Son John* offered no exploration of the appeals of communism, nor why a political culture (in the movies version) that justifies government surveillance of "those with something to hide," familial demand for ideological conformity and repetition of a political catechism, expectation that family members inform on each other to police agencies, and defensive fearfulness of alien political affiliations is much of a superior alternative. In any case, *My Son John* captures much of the anti-communist zeal of the political time of "the great fear."

The political turmoil in Hollywood itself during this period was divisive and bitter, "politicizing" the film community as never before. The careers of some political nonconformists were ruined (see Woody Allen's 1976 film, *The Front*, which uses many of the surviving victims of the infamous "blacklist"), but the careers of others who were politically correct (such as Ronald Reagan) were enhanced. Even given the constraints of the studio system, there were films that did comment on the political conflicts in Hollywood and the nation, although in metaphorical form. Two are notable: *High Noon* (1952) and *On the Waterfront* (1954). In *High Noon*, a small Western town with a successful sheriff retiring to marry a Quaker is suddenly faced with the return of an evil force, the Miller gang, that had once dominated and corrupted the town. The courageous sheriff stays to resist, but the town abandons him, either in cowardice or allegiance to Miller, and he has to face them alone. He succeeds, and as the townspeople materialize after the shooting is over, the sheriff contemptuously removes his badge, the symbol of legal authority, flings it into the dust, and leaves with his bride.   The director (Fred Zinnemann) and screenwriter (Carl Foreman) were well-known Hollywood liberals, and the film was condemned by movieland conservatives such as Howard Hawks and John Wayne, who in response made an "answer" to *High Noon* in *Rio Bravo* (1959), wherein a few gifted professionals resist evil without seeking very much help from a passive community.   But *High Noon* certainly condemns the unwillingness of a democratic community to resist external evil that would impose its will.   That evil could be interpreted not only as Washington imposing a political orthodoxy on and seeking scapegoats in Hollywood, but also any kind of external threat, including communism.   Perhaps the political point of *High Noon* was not so much ideological as historical: in the Fifties, observers of American society were beginning to see the post-war world as one of complacency and timidity, with an unwillingness to take a moral or political stand against anything, and a preference for material acquisition and predictable bourgeois life that mitigated against heroic autonomy or support for doing the right thing. *High Noon* was not so much about political leadership as it was about followership, or rather the lack thereof.

On the Waterfront (1954) was directed by Elia Kazan, an ex-communist who cooperated with HUAC and was much criticized for doing so.   Many have interpreted *Waterfront* as a political parable justifying informing to the authorities about subversive evil in a community, thus purging it of an alien force.   The story involves the progress of an ex-boxer and now minor operative for a corrupt longshoreman's union boss from fool to hero.   His moral egoism is undermined by the preachments of an activist priest and a loving girl, and after both his social consciousness and his ire over his brother's murder are aroused, he testifies before a crime commission.   After confronting the boss, he is badly beaten, but rises to lead the now defiant union rank-and-file back into the approved moral and political mainstream.   But *Waterfront* could not have succeeded if it were merely a justification of testimony that named names.   Like *High Noon*, it sees the American community under threat, and relies on heroic individualism in spite of the cowardly or cowered community it serves.   The union members are no more capable of concerted action to resist or purge evil than the Western townspeople, despite the urgent reality of the threat and their collective interest in resistance.   We are again observing the curious perception of the post-war world as incapable of action, or even of admission, in the context of community consensus, that something was terribly wrong.   The theme of community consensus requiring everyone to live a lie was to persist in other films of the Fifties (see *Bad Day at Black Rock*, 1955).

The anti-communist theme was perhaps a too direct treatment of a perceived new political threat. But as we have seen, political themes can persist in movies in covert metaphorical fashion, whether the "politics" of a movie's "subtext" is understood by filmmakers or not. The political fear that accompanied the rise of Soviet and communist power remained salient as the events of the Cold War seemed to prove the alarmists correct--the Berlin Blockade, the "fall" of China, the Korean War, and spectacular domestic spy cases such as the Rosenbergs and Alger Hiss. The political struggle of the Cold War was still very much on people's minds, especially since after 1949 it involved the possibility of nuclear war. So people feared either annihilation at the hands of our new enemy, or conspiratorial subversion and invasion leading to totalitarian dehumanization. Rather than deal with this fear directly, the movies learned how to "displace" a looming political fantasy into a setting and genre that let people play with the fear without direct threat. This was the science-fiction formula, displacing the threat into a fictional and futuristic fantasy of invasion from space. The "sci-fi" genre was flexible enough to include a great many politically charged themes specific to the time. For instance, the threat of war or conquest was exacerbated by the advent of the atomic bomb. Science-fiction films became a convenient way to address the questions raised by the Bomb in a fantastic way. In *The Day the Earth Stood Still* (1951) a visitor from outer space lands his flying saucer in Washington on an urgent diplomatic mission: either the nations of the earth disarm and live in peace, or the federation of planets he represents will destroy us as a threat. Although it is still in doubt whether we will when he leaves, his rhetorical appeal for the end of the atomic threat is a strong one. Atomic power also created monstrous consequences, as nature wrought its revenge for fooling around with Frankensteinian forces. In *Them!* (1954) giant ants, mutants created by atomic testing in the desert, threaten civilization, and also Los Angeles. Eventually they are destroyed after the usual Fifties conflict between soldier and scientist, but not before there is much apocalyptic talk abut the end of the world, the end of man as the dominant species on earth, and the uncertain new world of the Atomic Age. The political undercurrent here was that science and technology were now feared to have become agents of doom rather than the handmaidens of progress. As the western United States was recurrently attacked by giant radioactive grasshoppers, rabbits, lizards, squids, mollusks, leeches, and so on, it was clear that the volatile and mysterious new force of the atom had become part of the popular nightmares of the Fifties.

The invasion fantasy displaced from the Soviet Union to outer space inspired a large "cluster" of popular films of varying quality. Some of them were simply bent on the annihilation of earth (always the United States, which we equated as the center of the earth). In *The Thing* (1951), the alien is a vegetable-creature who crashes his flying saucer into the ice at a remote Arctic air base; when he thaws, he appears not a superintelligent being at all, but rather a raging monster unreached by the appeal to communication and reason by the scientist, therefore necessitating his destruction by the soldier. This was followed by a string of invasion films with the aliens usually anonymous and uncommunicative, bent on nothing but destruction (cf., *The War of the Worlds*, 1953; *Earth vs. the Flying Saucers*, 1956; *This Island Earth*, 1955). But a bit more subtle was the theme in some invasion films that suggested the concern about our potential conquerors establishing alien controls over us was widespread enough to warrant recurrent movie treatment. The political fear expressed in these films was more than just physical conquest and control; rather more, it was a fear of Orwellian psychological controls to the extent that the individual was either converted or controlled by an alien force against his or her will. This was the era of "brainwashing," of the image of New Soviet Man as a totalitarian robot devoid of emotion, autonomy, and freedom. Further, in the height of the McCarthy era there was the paranoid fear that the enemy could secretly subvert us without us knowing it by gaining control of our minds, making us over into something "un-American" and alien ourselves. By becoming Other than American, we would then be "dehumanized" into a new and different state of political being that was not ourselves. At base, this sensibility was a fear of political possession, that somehow a free people could lose their freedom through subversive processes conducted by shadowy forces that could "possess" us without us really knowing it.

The first impressive depiction of this in the movies was *Invaders from Mars* (1953). Unlike the other invasion films emerging at the time, these invaders do not want to conquer us through direct military means, but more indirectly through possession; they implant devices connected to the brain that makes us "different"--emotionless, obedient, ruthless, what we might expect out of communist soldiers and spies. Significant members of the community are brought under the spell of a superior intelligence (a bodyless head enclosed in a glass dome, who, like Stalin, scans and controls its political environment). Eventually this alien force is defeated, but the film ends with the implication that the danger is still clear and present. More ambiguous and threatening is the justly famous and still effective *Invasion of the Body Snatchers* (1956), Don Siegel's portrait of a small town that on the surface appears normal, but a local doctor and his woman friend discover that local people are not themselves anymore, having lost essential American characteristics. They find that they are being "replaced" by duplicates grown in seedpods from outer space (making them, of course, into "vegetables," without human feeling). These transformed beings that are taking over the metaphorical American village claim to represent a higher order without individuality, emotion, or "humanity," their final goal being world domination. Yet the doctor sees them as not superhuman but rather subhuman, regimented, uniform, and amoral. Everyone is converted to the new order save him (his lovely woman friend is changed into a sexually frigid totalitarian woman worthy of Orwell's "Junior Anti-Sex League" in the novel, *1984*). He must flee to warn the rest of America of "the malignant disease spreading out all over the country" but finds that no one will believe him. In the end, a psychiatrist fortuitously discovers evidence of the pods, and calls the FBI; but at this point, the subversion may have spread beyond official cure. Even though this ending was tacked on at studio request, it still leaves things hanging as to whether the aliens will succeed or not.

    Invasion of the Body Snatchers has been interpreted as a straightforward tale of the fear of communist takeover and conversion. The aliens do display some of the traits we associated with a subversive party--secrecy, infiltration, unity of purpose, the subordination of the individual to the group, the resort to any means to triumph. Further, they want to create an America, and world, that coincided with our fears of Soviet ambitions, one that was characterized by the kind of collectivism and robotic conformity and dreary sameness we associated with the Soviet bloc. But there are alternative interpretations. It may well be the case that *Body Snatchers* was about something less specific and even more subtle: rather than fearing that they would make us over to resemble them, that we were instead making ourselves over to be like them, in effect subverting ourselves. The town of the film changes into a place of ideological and social conformity, with the betrayal of fellow townspeople, the persecution of individualists, the willingness to purge or punish those different among us, and the suspicion of intellect. *Body Snatchers* made the demand for "consensus" and the then current theory that the United States and Soviet Union were "converging" systems into something sinister. The growth of a "mass society" of "other-directed" and anxiously conforming people made us afraid of what we were becoming as a nation, a puerile society with paranoid fears about ourselves and the world. We had become the agent of our own alienation, destroying the older American political tradition for a new and complacent order that was rationalized and predictable, and which excluded alternatives and possibilities. The doctor of the story is the last American individualist escaping what was now a domestic American nightmare, evil lurking not in the unfamiliar but in the familiar.

This latter concern also emerged in thematic form in the "corporate" films of the 1950s (*Executive Suite*, 1954; *Pillow Talk*, 1958; *Patterns*, 1956), which took recognition of the new corporate order that seemed so central to post-war American life, and at the apex of the Eisenhower consensus between the public and private orders. But the same concerns that gave thematic direction to *Body Snatchers* were also interwoven into films about corporate settings--the extent to which the new corporate order was transforming life, creating a new style of American character devoid of the "inner direction" and moral core of heroic tradition. The Fifties was haunted by this transformation, with much discussion of the new "organization man" whose fluid loyalties and moral standards devoted him to a pragmatic "social ethic" of group adaptation and often cynical opportunism. It was feared that the conformism and exploitation symbolized by corporate life was serving as a model for what the nation, and its politics, was becoming--sterile, valueless, and easy, corrupt beneath the facade of organizational power and private affluence. This politically significant theme was treated most adequately in Billy Wilder's *The Apartment* (1960), a story of a quintessential Fifties junior executive on the make who becomes involved in a corporate corruption scandal that makes him into a conspirator and then a victim of a system that virtually excludes the possibility of decency. *The Apartment* depicts a thoroughly manipulative society at work and play, with overlapping power and sexual games enacted with duplicity and cold self-interest. Life in the large insurance firm is anxiety-ridden, devoid of joy or certitude, not really much different than *The Crowd* of the Twenties, and certainly bereft of the democratic leadership and moral purpose of the Forties war film. But as a portrait of what many critics thought of "the enormous file" of Fifties corporate life, and what they thought American political culture was becoming, *The Apartment* speaks volumes.

There were other visions of a "dark underside" of American life that remained important for understanding the political *ethos* of the Fifties. As *The Apartment* suggested, the "consensus society" of the Fifties had scarcely hidden aspects about it that were in uncomfortable contrast to the official public view of mass happiness and progress. Critics talked of "the lonely crowd" in individual pursuit of their own loneliness, of the emptiness of the "perfected" life in the new planned suburban Utopias, of an "other America" of poverty and exclusion that was denied. In the midst of political self-congratulation for our post-war economic achievement, there was little official attention drawn to the social costs borne by such innovation. The price of the consensus was the maintenance of a "patina of normalcy" that made social problems either disappear or render them nonpolitical, beyond the care or agenda of the political system. But neglect did not make them go away, and some sly or daring filmmakers dealt with these nagging fears and failures. Three films are representative: Hitchcock's *Rear Window* (1954), Ray's *Rebel Without a Cause* (1955), and Kramer's *The Defiant Ones* (1958). Alfred Hitchcock believed that normal order was a veneer at best, and that just beneath the surface were irrational forces bound by social convention wishing to be loosed. In *Rear Window*, a photographer immobilized by a broken leg amuses himself by using his telescopic lenses to survey the lives of his neighbors. What he sees is a portrait of Fifties society in microcosm, the product of individualism in a mass society, people who are lonely, bored, inconstant, shallow, unsuccessful, alcoholic, suicidal, and murderous. The "complacency" of the Fifties comes out as an individual indifference to the fate of anyone else, neurotic self-absorption and isolation, with desperate attempts to escape one's fate of social entrapment, and a real lack of progress in solving human relations (it is not clear at the end whether the hero and heroine have now solved their differences, and the murderer who killed his nagging wife is "succeeded" by newlyweds wherein the bride has become a nagging wife). The hero is a voyeur who can see the awful truth of what we had become behind the curtains, but has not the legitimate power (or even the interest) in interfering in other people's lives except in the most extremely threatening circumstances. All are discrete individuals in a mass society of private hells, a society held together by the flimsiest form of consensus, a tacit Hobbesian agreement to let each other alone, with freedom defined as the absence of community.

Another area of Fifties society that suggested latent dissatisfaction with the normalised state of things was among alienated youth. The appearance of alienation at a time when widespread prosperity was supposed to have resolved social conflict was profoundly unsettling, especially when it involved rebellion or rejection by the most privileged heirs to affluence, middle-class youth. It was one thing to witness on screen or streets the behavior of "juvenile delinquents" (cf., *The Wild One*, 1953; *Blackboard Jungle*, 1955, but it was quite another to see respectable youth in extremely comfortable circumstances (most notably, in *Rebel without a Cause*, 1955) so completely alienated from the major domestic creation of postwar American political economy (when asked where she lives, a girl sighs, "Who lives?"). The teenage trio that forms a temporary empathic community in *Rebel* have no political but they convey a political message by simply knowing what they are against: an overly rationalized world of stultifying comfort and sex roles reduced to male emasculation and female bitchery. What they are symbolically for is something else: a world of tolerance, affection, and fun, something sneered at by both adults and their peer delinquents. When the world will not let them alone, and the most disturbed among them becomes potentially violent, the leader (James Dean) must assume a role of social leadership that attempts to reconcile the alienated with authority, with pathetic results; nevertheless, he and his now equally matured girl friend must assume a wiser adult responsibility, one that transcends the social and political stagnation that the "placid" Fifties had become, and one that presages the youth rebellion of the Sixties. These kids were "private" rebels against a world they never made, remaining essentially unrevolutionary seekers without a cause; in the succeeding decade, their successors would become political rebels with a cause.

Another disturbing unresolved violation of the consensus myth was the question of racial justice, a matter that no amount of official indifference or hostility could ignore with the advent of the civil rights movement. As we noted, the question of race began to appear in the "social problem" films of the late Forties (Intruder in the Dust, 1949; Pinky 1949). The Fifties continued, although often in oblique and justificatory ways, the theme of racial differences and conflicts although without much direct reference to the civil rights struggle or possible political solutions. Perhaps the most direct confrontation, and special pleading, on the issue was Stanley Kramer's The Defiant Ones (1958), a story of a prejudiced white prisoner who escapes from a Southern prison chained to a black prisoner. So "joined" in a project of escape, they are forced to confront each other as individuals separated by a system of segregation but connected by common exploitation, making injustice something they share that transcends race. The film offers no clear political solution, but it did offer the most direct "liberal" statement of the times of the problem and the hope that racial contact would bring understanding and tolerance.

It is worthwhile noting that racial and ethnic differences, often connected with class differences, is a theme much more prevalent in the films of the Fifties than is often recognized. Films as diverse as Giant (1956), Imitation of Life (1959), West Side Story (1961), and To Kill a Mockingbird (1962) all included the theme of racial prejudice. This theme was to emerge in the work of even some of Hollywood's more traditional directors. Perhaps the more subtle, and enduring, treatment of the subject was John Ford's The Searchers (1956), arguably his greatest Western, but certainly a movie that raised all the disturbing questions about the psychosexual, and ultimately political, roots of racism in the

American experience, in this case Indians rather than blacks. This was John Wayne's most complex role, displaying the possibility that American male heroism has a demonic side that includes exclusionary racial hatred so intense and thorough that it is destructive to both the white and Indian communities when the racial code is violated. Ford's film was not so much a plea for racial tolerance as it was an examination of the roots of racism in the very fabric of American history and the assumptions of legitimate violence against alien peoples in the pursuit of a righteous empire. Although set in the heroic frontier setting of the Far West, *The Searchers* was both about the sad and self-destructive legacy of a racial code enforced by the dominant white community, and the immediate conflict about segregation by race that was one of the outcomes of that institutionalized prejudice. *The Searchers* pointed up for 1956 the agony of the American political dilemma, the possibility that a nation which is officially committed to liberty and equality but which practices exclusion and discrimination contains the seeds of self-hatred and self-destruction. *The Searchers* was to have great subsequent influence on young filmmakers, and acquire wider relevance with the war on an alien people in Vietnam, but at this time this film seemed concerned with what was happening in Montgomery and Little Rock, and whether traditional political authorities, be they Wayne or Eisenhower, could accept the inclusion in the American Dream of those of another culture or race who were so different as to be potentially threatening. *The Searchers* saw our political culture as put to a test, a test of tolerance that it by no means assures us that we will pass.

As the Fifties progressed, there were glimmerings of understanding of the importance of political television. In different ways, two films of the period are worth examination because they begin to understand the power of this new political instrument: Ford's *The Last Hurrah* (1958) and Kazan's *A Face in the Crowd* (1957). *The Last Hurrah* was an elegiac look at the passage of urban machine politics, in its populist and anti-establishment ethnic roots. It emphasizes the functional and humanitarian aspects of such a machine (presumably Boston, with Spencer Tracy as a nicer version of Boss Jim Curley, a combination of McGinty and Gettes). But the film is not only about the passing of the urban machines, it is also about the eclipse of community. The old city machines built bonds between people, and promoted social camaraderie; now the communal politics they represented are replaced by television candidates who are photogenic and facile, unconcerned with the individual concerns of the machine's personal welfare but rather with the communication of an image that, as the dying political boss says, makes politics "all TV." *A Face in the Crowd* originates in rural populism but sees the same emerging power of television. An itinerant country-and-western singer/commentator becomes through television a national celebrity, and an advisor to a wealthy and ambitious would-be president who turns to him to understand the use of the new medium. What is memorable is the pervasive cynicism which television fame and candidacy seems to promote, similar to the vacuous "family" candidate of the Boston establishment in *The Last Hurrah*, and the power of the medium to both create and destroy political celebrities on the irrational and fickle whim of a thoroughly debased public. Indeed, here the public seems for the first time to be identical to the TV audience, a political assumption that would give impetus to the growth of more sophisticated, but no less manipulable, television managers of "national morale" in the future, and to the advent of television celebrities who would understand the power of political entertainment. In both films, the consequences of political television is the replacement of a political agenda by an image, and that political success becomes defined by mastery of media technique, themes that would appear again as television's curious power became increasingly pervasive.

As the decade of the Fifties came to an end, another form of technological power was to continue to haunt us: the great Faustian power of the atomic bomb made all the more threatening by the advent of accurate and long-range missiles that deliver them to targets quickly. Such a possibility obviously gives credence to apocalyptic thinking and imagery, as we saw in the sci-fi films. But finally one film dealt with the worst case: Kramer's *On the Beach* (1959). In the near future, World War III has ended, and everyone lost. The survivors in Australia face their imminent death with admirable stoic resolve, and indeed even enter into a suicide pact to avoid the agony of death by radiation poisoning. Despite the melodramatic touches and preachments ("There is still time brother"), the point is made: The atomic bomb could kill everyone. After a decade of rhetoric about "massive retaliation" and the "nuclear umbrella," *On the Beach* really broke a political taboo in Hollywood, and was to begin a cycle of nuclear war films that would examine more boldly the nuclear assumptions of the Cold War, and what the possibilities were that it would literally get "hot" very fast.

The long decade of the 1950s began in the breakdown of the political agenda and projects of one age and created the post-war world, including the norms of domestic life, the expansion of the consumer economy, and the illusion of consensus at home, and the fear of external Soviet hostility and expansionism abroad. Like every political era, it went as far as its own assumptions would take it, and dissipated or evolved into something else. It was "placid" or innocent and peaceful only in retrospect, but the myth of its superiority to subsequent times was forged in comparison. A glance at television reruns of family situation comedies set in the Fifties gives a clue of our devotion to it, and the extent to which we feel we have "fallen" from it. But the movies of that time remind us that it was no such thing; that certain things were very much at issue, and very much unresolved, and that both society and politics operated in a milieu of contention. It is true, as our movies reveal, that certain political themes, and social discontents, could only be dealt with in oblique ways; but it is our task to use those films to understand the political conduct, and subsequent influence, of a decade that was haunted then, and still haunts us now.

Chapter Six

The 1960s: From Holding the Line to Coming Apart

Like any other political time, the 1950s was a period that achieved its own self-definition as it went along, and by the "high Fifties" of Eisenhower's second term had achieved both the thrust and limits of its own politics that invited both continuation and supercession. Political decades are at once continuous and discrete, acquiring the measure of distinctness that makes them identifiable from what precedes and what supercedes. The paradox that the past is never really past reminds us that the Fifties was to survive as both memory and model, for many a prelapsarian age from which we have fallen, whether one thinks we should have or not. The admirers of the Fifties often do so, not only because of the myth of consensus on values and practices that were supposed to have obtained them, but also because it provides a reference point for guidance in a contemporary and perhaps "fallen" world. In this view, the future after the Fifties did not complement its achievements so much as violate them, and much subsequent political effort was undertaken to try to reverse or redirect the energies unleashed by the 1960s. Others thought that the astonishing political and social developments of the Sixties were a logical outgrowth of the contrived normalcy and social neglect of an age content to "hold the line" by denying the legitimacy, or even the existence, of turbulent social forces and energies just beneath the surface. The institutionalization of anti-communism had done the same for the willingness to fight World War III, a sword of Damocles that hung unconsciously over everyone, as well as the willingness to maintain a level of military preparedness and interventionist strategy that made the maintenance of peace into a virtual and constant state of warfare. Too, the Fifties completed itself with the assumption that the shape of American society, as symbolized by the ever-expanding suburbs and the lifestyle it entailed, was becoming a universally accepted way of life so fraught with moral and material prosperity that everyone would find it irresistible, and that such acceptance made the shape of American life and thought, as well as politics, predictable for the foreseeable future. By the end of Eisenhower's terms, there was confident talk about "the end of ideology," the permanent growth of capitalist middle-class democracy as a model for the emerging new nations, the integration of all into the canons and benefits of the American achievement, and the benevolent conduct of the Pax Americana that would complete the American Dream. At least on the surface, America entered the Sixties with confidence that the past had defined the continuity of domestic life, and that American power would remain a benign and unchallengeable force in the world.

It would always remain a difficulty for historians to know what to do with the "brief, shining moment" of the Kennedy Era. In many ways, Kennedy was essentially an extension of the Fifties with added glamor and energy. The assumptions and goals of the Cold War were now to be solved by the application of technocratic intelligence and flexible responses to differing circumstances. The "New Frontiersmen" were committed to an ideology of pragmatism that would apply American "commitment" and power around the globe to the extent of "bearing any burden" to prevail in the perceived competition for influence with the Soviet Union and international communism. In that sense, Kennedy was only a stylistic addition to the national security state, with notions of countering third world insurgencies with a military "Special Forces" and a civilian "Peace Corps." Similarly, the marginal domestic agenda that quickly stalled seemed only an incremental program of piecemeal reforms that were mild to the point of timidity. Kennedy's difference was intangible, a matter of youth, a new start, liberal politicians and intellectuals who believed once again in American mission, something that the Right could only quibble about. In death, Kennedy has achieved a kind of popular apotheosis as the Arthur of an American Camelot, the keeper of the flame of a myth that if he had lived, we would have prevailed in some sense and would have avoided the travails and abominations that were to follow. In a mythic sense, Kennedy still presides over a liminal age between the past and the present worlds. Golden Ages are to be fallen from, and succeeding political eras and figures have had the considerable difficulty of trying to rule in the shadow of perfection. (In this regard, consider how many subsequent films with a nostalgic search for innocence in a "better time" have been set in the Kennedy Era: *American Graffiti, Dirty Dancing, Tin Men, Eddie and the Cruisers, Little Shop of Horrors, Hairspray,* and *Stand by Me.*)

Despite Kennedy's continuity with the political preconceptions that immediately preceded him, the movies of the period began to display a new boldness about political themes, although couched in the same ambivalence that characterizes the popular art of all times of change. Rather than perfection, the films of the early Sixties display political doubts and confusions, structures of feelings that were to become salient in the political opposition to Establishment assumptions that were to be at the core of the sustained revolt of the time. For example, two films with Henry Fonda as a liberal political hero appear tame enough at first glance but more challenging on reflection. In *Advise and Consent* (1962), Fonda is the president's choice for secretary of state, a New Deal intellectual with ideas about disarmament and dealing with the communists. But he is opposed by Southern conservatives and the Right, supported by a fanatical Senator who leads a disarmament movement (and has political ambitions of his own), and is considered for office in an atmosphere of controversy. Although quite similar to the obstructionist congress during Kennedy's tenure, the political conflict of the film left the impression that the fate of the world in a nuclear age was in the grip of an Establishment of old men playing a political game in an institutional interior where the issue of human survival was secondary to the maintenance of senatorial rituals. The liberal hero, and presumably the ideal of disarmament for which he stands, is diverted from power by procedure and then succession, suggesting that institutions take precedence over ideals, and that a Senate that had resisted the perorations of the Depression Era Mr. Smith was still very much fiddling while Washington faced a nuclear burn. Similarly, Fonda played the liberal candidate-hero in *The Best Man* (1964), who is faced with a convention challenge from another political barnacle from the Fifties, an unscrupulous but popular McCarthyite who rode to fame on the bogus exposé of a preposterous collusion between the Reds and the Mafia. The plot revolves around the rather sordid political maneuvering at the convention, but, like the aborted climax in the Senate of *Advise and Consent*, the contest between liberal intellectual and conservative populist is averted by the liberal withdrawing in favor of an unknown but safe candidate. In both cases, not only is the (presumably good) liberal hero sacrificed to institutional power, but also both desirable political resolutions are thwarted in favor of less desirable ones. In odd ways, both films were celebrating institutions of the inherited "System" vaunted to work so well in the political science textbooks, yet both demonstrated quite clearly that the institutions in question produced either no result or less than the best result. As many in the Sixties were to conclude, the advice and consent of the senate was less than worthwhile, and the best man does not always win.

The heritage of the anti-communist crusade and policy of the 1950s began to undergo more satirical treatment, in films that suggested the struggle was not in the realm of political realism so admired in policy circles but rather comic insanity. Billy Wilder's *One, Two, Three* (1961) is set in divided Berlin, and is unsympathetic to the East German regime, contrasting it with the prosperous West; yet the capitalist ambitions of the Coca-Cola executive to "conquer the East" with Coke seem an equally ludicrous imperialism of the soft drink executive. Both sides are caught in an absurd cycle of suspicion and deception that has very little to do with ideology and a great deal to do with personal motives and systemic corruptions. More complex than that is

John Frankenheimer's *The Manchurian Candidate* (1962), a critical
and intelligent Cold War political melodrama that makes the
Soviet-American conflict so absurd as to be comic. An American
patrol is taken prisoner during the Korean war; when they escape,
one of their members is awarded the Medal of Honor. But patrol
members are plagued by bad dreams. What unfolds is a complex
tale of communist conspiracy in league with a McCarthyite
senator, confirming the liberal fantasy of the Fifties that such
figures were political opportunists willing to do anything for
power. The film takes the "communist conspiracy" seriously, but
at the same time makes the figure of the Chinese psychologist
engaged in engineering brainwashing and murder a sophisticated
and charming character. But *The Manchurian Candidate* is not
mired in the political *ethos* of the waning decade; rather like
Wilder's film, it sees the East-West conflict, and the "normal"
conduct of national politics in such circumstances, as insane, a
tangled web of dark motives and ambitious plots so irrational as to
be comic. It unwittingly anticipates much of what the Sixties was
beginning to believe about politics: that the postwar struggle
between the Great Powers had become so portentous and self-
important as to render itself absurd and idiotic, destructive of the
ideals and even the interests of both "sides" to a seemingly endless
and expensive struggle. The outcome of the story could not be
more symbolic: the innocent who is sacrificed by both sides for
their own purposes revenges himself by the destruction of the
authority figure who represents conspiratorial betrayal, so
duplicitous as to render the "ideological" and political war between
democracy and communism both ridiculous and contemptible. In
that sense, *The Manchurian Candidate* transcends the assumptions
of the Fifties, and gives impetus to the darkly comic view of
politics that was to become such an imaginative force in the
perspective of the Sixties. The film would be pulled from
circulation, particularly because of its assassination theme, and
finally in re-release became one of the big retrospective hits of
1988, perhaps because of the reprise of the Cold War in the 1980s
and the bleakly comic view of such a latter-day revival.

Something of the same process happened to the image of
the American military, which had been virtually immune from
critical or negative examination by the movies during the postwar
period, basking as the Pentagon did from the victory of World War
II and the maintenance of "peace" by achieving instantaneous
poise for righteous intervention and even justified annihilation
(there were a few exceptions, such as *Attack!*, 1956). But with the
growth of the influence and budget of the Pentagon, the growth of
the sophistication and destructive power of nuclear war, and the
occurrence of superpower standoffs (the Berlin crisis of 1961, the
Cuban missile crisis of 1962), critical or suspicious attitudes

appeared and were given horrific dramatic shape in the movies. In 1964, three popular films appeared that spoke to these discontented feelings. Frankenheimer's *Seven Days in May* (1964) let audiences play with something that before the long and elaborate struggle with the Russians would have been unthinkable: a military *coup d'état* that replaced presidential and congressional authority with the top military commanders. Although such generals as McClellan and MacArthur had their supporters in the past, the tradition of civilian control of the military was always firmly entrenched. However, the power of the military by this time had never been stronger, engendering fantasies of a new kind of conspiracy, one among soldiers that challenged the wisdom of the rule of civilian politicians. By 1964, the military seemed for some a force capable of such a challenge. In the film, the issue that fomented the revolt was a disarmament treaty with the Russians, something that the Right had opposed throughout, and which directly challenged both the privileged position and reason for being of a powerful military Establishment. This movie suggested not only military culpability in opposing a peaceful resolution to the arms race, but also in an effort to become the very kind of dictatorial and aggressive authority they were created to oppose, another implicit challenge to the very premises of the highly militarized conflict.

Similarly, in *Fail Safe* (1964), military technology, backed by the intellectual formulations of governmental nuclear theoreticians, went awry. Rather than generals becoming power-mad and attempting the overthrow of the government, the foolproof system of nuclear protection they devised proved to be an unsafe failure. But the fault here is systemic, the product of mutual distrust that has developed from the reinforcing systems of reprisal and destruction on attack. Technology had made this by now such a complex hair-trigger operation that something went wrong, and the president and the Soviet premier on the "hot line" had to agree upon a tradeoff of limited destruction of such heinous proportions that one could only wonder how either could survive politically given the decision that they made. In any case, *Fail Safe* was a serious attempt to face how political limits might be imposed after a technological failure of military hardware, with the agonizing possibility that politicians were more and more becoming prisoners of the military-technological systems they had arranged to protect us with. Yet, as in *Seven Days in May*, responsible elites were able to avert military disaster through rational action. More in the tradition of *The Manchurian Candidate*, and the emerging spirit of the Sixties, was Kubrick's *Dr. Strangelove* (1964), which takes the same plot complication as *Fail Safe*--a system of nuclear deterrence that manages to outwit itself-- and elevates the entire military-political enterprise of nuclear "defense" to the level of insanity, rendering it amenable only to satire. The massive system of technocratic and bureaucratic power amassed around American nuclear capability is such that not even presidents or generals can understand or control it. As they sit in "the war room" bickering over culpability and strategy, it becomes clear that human response time is inadequate to stop the demonic power they have created. The movie is imbued with the new sensibility of the Sixties--irreverence, skepticism, refusal to trust the solemn assurance of authority. The war comes about not because of an accident alone, but also because of the lunacy of a general driven mad by paranoid distrust of the enemy and thus by extension distrust of the unwillingness of civilian powers to fight the war that to him seems the logical outcome of the military buildup that pointed to a day of reckoning with the Soviets. But questions of political lunacy and sanity quickly become irrelevant, since the system of power itself is revealed to be insane, leaving decision makers helpless before the obligatory fatalism of suicidal technology. *Dr. Strangelove* was to seem prescient in the years of the Sixties, a film that placed the blame for the insanity of war, or for that matter other ills, at the top among elites trapped in the hermetic isolation of executive palaces and towers, whose strange love of war is revealed as a childish game played within those who have lost contact with rational humanity. *Strangelove* offers no hope of escape from our political self-destructiveness, in whatever form that may take, a clear break with sacrosanct arguments of the postwar period, not only of the "necessity" of nuclear armament and the willingness to fight a nuclear war in an instant, but also that all problems or challenges are soluble by the application of technology, which assures progress. The Sixties did not see nuclear war, but it did see "limited" war fought with these confident assumptions, and many began to think that the war machine's ability to do things was limited in focus to mere means, without thought given to the inhumanity, or even the political logic, of the ends sought. For *Strangelove*, war was the ultimate triumph of political power taken over by the mechanisms of power, so that humankind, and the politicians that lead us, become powerless before the logic of the techniques of destruction they have loosed. Such a film gave credence to the Sixties view that institutionalized power as such was hopeless to reform, so the only viable alternative was either to oppose or destroy it.

Perhaps the central political theme that ran through the important political films of the 1960s was the idea, that was to reach extreme and violent form, that freedom was something that could only be realized in opposition to established authority. In recurrent ways, resistance to authority and the "way things are" was unstable, unsure of alternatives, and even doomed to failure. Freedom was associated with, and much the concern of, the young, the famous "baby boom" generation suspicious of the political "realism" of their elders and attracted toward a new version of political romanticism that included visions of idealistic reform and peace, but also individualistic visions of rebellion that ranged from the instinctive to nihilistic. We were drawn to these images of reform and rebellion for a variety of motives, not the least of which was to seek forms of action that provided escape from social and political traps--the obvious traps of responsibility and even respectability that by the mid-Sixties more and more of the young were coming to resist. As usual, the movies at first were cautious in developing themes subject to political criticism, but the discovery of the salience of contemporary themes and subsequently an audience for them helped them overcome their natural timidity. *A Hard Day's Night* (1964), for example, convinced the purveyors of popular culture that there was a segmented and identifiable "youth culture" out there interested in play-forms of the celebration of life that expressed their resistance to the adult world. As that culture grew in adherents and controversial activities--bizarre dress, rock, drugs, resistance to the draft, political activism--Hollywood gingerly began to participate in the upheavals of the Sixties, and was quickly affected by the changes in popular attitude and behavior that would appear in the movies, and record the political *ethos* that was to characterize the most explosive, and creative, decade of this century. As the decade progressed, the movies became more bold in the frankness, and political awareness, of theme and language. By the mid-Sixties, many movies were highly politicized in that they were made with political intent and partisanship in the loose sense of taking sides or stating a politically potent theme. If it is fair to term the Sixties a "liberal" decade, that liberalism in the movies often took the polarity of pitting those who advocated, or symbolized, the value of social change against those who stood, unwisely or irrationally, against such much-needed change. In retrospect, the rapidity of change, no matter how much resisted, was breathtaking in its scope, although much of that change was unsponsored and diffuse, taking time to really sink in. The sexual revolution, for instance, was restricted to the young and experimental. But the young were perceived to be the "carriers" of change, and for their admirers became the repository of virtue that would create a new world in the morning which would transcend the ancient habits and conflicts of the present. It is likely that after the impact of the Sixties many Americans were in some sense freer (although not necessarily happier), and political and social authority weaker and less reverential. Much subsequent American politics has been an attempt to put the political genii loosed by the furious Sixties back into the bottle, but it is likely that much of what is wrought cannot be undone short of draconian enforcement by reactionary authorities armed with an iron doctrine that would involve unprecedented controls on individual and political behavior. We still look back on the Sixties with a sense of awe that so much creative and destructive energy could coexist at the same time, and search for popular evidence of its vitality and impact in the movies.

The initial political movie strategy was to imbue change with the blessing of a recognizable liberal social authority in accord with the agenda of President Johnson's Great Society. Such a representation would give legitimate approval to elite-sponsored change. This was most apparent with the political effort to win mass acceptance of civil rights as the logical and legitimate completion of American consensus. Everyone would be made middle class and respectable through reform efforts, "integrating" the excluded into the acceptable conventions and comforts of white society. So taken was the liberal elite that sponsored such a change with both the justice of and ease with which racism, inequality, and deprivation could be overcome that they underestimated the resistance and the "backlash" that was eventually to frustrate, and then undermine, the officially sanctioned movement. The difficulties involved are both avoided in, and suggested by, Stanley Kramer's *Guess Who's Coming to Dinner* (1967), a film about racial tolerance and acceptance that states an uncomfortable premise (interracial marriage) but then so stacks the cards in favor of it that grounds for objection become, from the perspective of civil rights advocates, without merit. A wealthy old liberal couple are challenged in their beliefs when their naive but colorblind white daughter suddenly falls in love with a black man, planning a hasty and moonstruck marriage. The pro-civil rights parents are put to the test, and hesitate, a hesitation reinforced by the objection to the marriage by the black bourgeois parents. But not only are the couple "in love" or somesuch, the would-be black groom is represented as extraordinary to the point of being superhuman, with a string of achievements in medicine, education, and international humane services that qualifies him for the Nobel Peace Prize! Further, the objections to a quick romantic marriage are transferred from a racial to a generational conflict, making both sets of parents seem less residual racists than unromantic old fogeys who have forgotten what it means to be in love. At last, the sponsoring white liberal male sees the light, and lectures the group not about civil rights but romantic love, making the case for interracial understanding and even marital union as one founded not on rational principles of justice but rather on the legitimacy of succumbing to waves of emotion. The young black man's rage seems ill placed as such a ringing success (occurring at the same time as riots in American cities by young blacks lashing out at their exclusion and marginality), and his quick entry into intimate acceptance by a white elite makes power sharing by a new group clamoring for a share seem deceptively easy. But the moral authority of a rather patronizing elite dispenser of wisdom and justice (Spencer Tracy) offered confident hope that racial division could be immediately transformed into personal and social union.

In the film *In the Heat of the Night* (1967), the competent and clearly superior black man (again played by Sidney Poitier) is the moral authority pitted against a corrupt and entrenched political authority in the metaphorical South, a country that is violent, prejudiced, and exclusive. The black "Mr. Tibbs" is a detective of Holmesian intellect and adherence to the norms of a professionalism thrust into a society where traditional authority, and even the raw and cynical power of the sheriff, are not only prejudiced against racial difference but also against truth, the truth of entrenched local corruption in "nice" society and the virtue of authority embodied in a figure that society has prejudged but who converts, or at least wins the respect of, the prejudicial. The hopeful thrust of these two films obviously made the civil rights struggle easier and simpler than it was in Selma or Cicero, making it a matter of determination and the triumph of evidential good sense, but the earnestness of both show throughout, resolving on screen what was not so easy to resolve in a world of racial tensions. Yet in the anti-black backlash that one can witness so uncomfortably in the movies of the 1970s, such films did record Hollywood's brief venture into the advocacy of racial tolerance and unity.

The various rebellions and movements of the Sixties were to affect the moviemaking art as much as any other form of popular expression, and in their own way, daring moviemakers were to join, and admittedly capitalize on, the new *ethos* of the time, although not without trepidation and constraints, nor curious depictions and surprising hits among those who dared. The year 1967 is again axial: Hollywood began to address the unfolding perspective of youth, from the milder forms of rebellion against the prospect of bourgeois stupefication to more daring and dangerous forms of violent and antisocial action. In *The Graduate* (1967), a new college graduate wanders through his parent's affluent world with little more ambition than to make his life different. This might seem a narcissistic conceit in the year of draft resistance to the raging Vietnam conflict, the Detroit riots, and civil rights agitation, but nevertheless the times did bring about a value crisis for many young individuals of which *The Graduate* struck a responsive chord. For all the somberness involved both in the political turbulence and individual agonies of choice, the movie worked by finding a representative character and situation altogether rather comic. The graduate is thrust into a structured world of planned expectations for him (marriage to the "right" girl, graduate school, predictable career and private life), is urged to go into "plastics," the substance of the world around him. He is prevented from forming a relationship with a lovely young woman by her mother, who gives herself to the young man in a hopeless affair presumably to prevent their union, which she senses would constitute a new generational coalition superior to her own corrupted and mindless generation. Social power conspires to prevent the newly innocent coalition, and she is only rescued from a Sixties fate worse than death--bourgeois marriage into a vacuous normality--at the end, at which point neither of them in the new and rebellious coalition have a clue as what to do. There is no talk of political rebellion, but it is clear that by rejecting adult rituals and habits they have chosen to cling to youth, a stance against the awesome power the adult world exercised for repression, and which now would make their lives different from parental, and political, authority. Although they join the rebellion, they have no known cause other than a negative desire for freedom from the pathologies of their elders, the underpinnings of a world that seemed to those who shared the hopes and illusions of youth in 1967 to have produced horrible results.

The refusal of youth to accommodate to the prevailing norms and expectations of society reached more extreme, and shocking, form in Arthur Penn's *Bonnie and Clyde* (1967). Ostensibly based on the popular legend of romantic "Robin Hood" criminal-rebels of the Thirties (*You Only Live Once* drew on their story), this film was very much about violence and rebellion, and questions of social and individual violence. The shooting spree of the kid-rebels is comic and anarchic, a freedom that is both exhilarating and hopeless, since the power of social violence is eventually more ruthless and efficient. Yet *Bonnie and Clyde* was not a diatribe against rebellion, nor did it depict family or police as trustworthy or helpful social institutions. This film flirted openly with nihilism as a viable, if doomed, alternative to complicity in the sanctioned violence of the authorities. In that sense, its complex message was implicitly radical, but a radicalism only of anarchic individualism as an often outrageous stance outside of the ken of a discredited social order more violent than they. Their eventual confrontation with destruction by authority is one that is inevitable not only by their lawlessness but also by the ethic of "doing your own thing" that is implied, and the perception of institutional power feeling the necessity of destroying freedom. As in *The Graduate*, we see the absence of a viable political cause as a positive alternative, and simply the representation of either moderate or extreme rebellion as a kind of romantic negation of the negation, removing oneself from allegiance from both the cultural and political bond of American life.

The same dialectic is present in subsequent films that are more openly radical in their orientation, although just as ambiguous or self-defeating in their resolutions. The kids in search of something different could have wound up in the commune of *Alice's Restaurant* (1969), a not altogether totally sympathetic view of an alternative experimental life outside of the mainstream, but certainly one that views the forces of social discipline and responsibility (police, draft boards) as comically absurd and hopelessly unsympathetic, but yet finds only faint hope in the "natural religion" and sexual freedom of the new communal arrangement. The central project of "the kids" and their adult earth mother and father sponsors is to be different, but that difference implies only the vaguest political agenda. However, their persecution is minimal compared to the more threatening bikers on the road of *Easy Rider* (1969), who face hostility and violence from police and backwoods yokels, yet acceptance at the homestead of an independent rancher with a large family and an even larger "family" in an operative, happy, and sexually liberated commune wherein the members have decided to "make a stand." But the bikers have chosen the freedom simply to roam an American road (West to East, the opposite of the usual trek) that is no longer songful nor open, constricted by hateful authorities and ignorant locals who become vengeful and murderous when reminded of the unfree sterility of their own lives. Here perhaps more than in any "youth culture" film of the period is the vision of America as a "culture of death" that must destroy whatever defies it, both abroad (Vietnam) and at home (reformers and activists), juxtaposed with the attempts of youth to transcend or escape it. Before their martyrdom, the thoughtful biker concludes that they "blew it," a sentiment applicable to various quarters of a very divided society in which both young and old, the powerless and the powerful, seemed at the time to many to be beyond either political or moral redemption. A sense of "lateness" seemed to pervade the late Sixties, a foreboding either of failure of the outburst of energy that gave the movement of the time its force, or perhaps a more general sense that American political culture in general was losing its vitality. It is interesting to note how many youth-oriented films then end with death that destroys beautiful rebellion or independence: *Cool Hand Luke* (1967); *Midnight Cowboy* (1969); *Butch Cassidy and the Sundance Kid* (1969); *Harold and Maude* (1970); *Joe* (1970); and *Medium Cool* (1969). In *Medium Cool*, for instance, a TV photographer takes documentary footage of real participants in the 1968 Chicago Democratic convention conflict, interspersed with a story of the photographer's involvement with a woman and their political polarization. The film ends with their deaths in a car crash, apparently for no other reason than to participate in the cycle of doomed heroes who become the victims of violence that imbued these movie expressions with a curious sense of the rebellion's ingrained fatal flaw. Such movies seem to say self-destruction before powers they have challenged but can neither control nor defeat is the fate of rebellious youth.

It was indeed the political question of violence that was to haunt the late 1960s: did the Vietnam war and domestic violence--including that of the New Left revolutionary groups and itinerant groups such as the Manson gang--demonstrate that the fond hopes of humankind moving to a new plane of peaceful and ecological existence in harmony with nature were ill-founded? The world seemed to have descended into a violent place, with violence visited on the just and the unjust, the innocent and damned, those who loved it and hated it. The disturbing questions about the necessity, inevitability, and even the beauty of violence were raised by Sam Peckinpah in two films, *The Wild Bunch* (1969) and *Straw Dogs* (1971), and by Stanley Kubrick in *A Clockwork Orange* (1971). *The Wild Bunch* is virtually a celebration of the aesthetics of violence, a vision of a world in which violence is an integral and ineradicable part of life, a bloody feast that can only be enjoyed. Further, in *Straw Dogs*, the director forces us on the defensive, urging our sympathies with a mild and peaceable mathematician whose life is invaded and abused by thugs; when he finally responds, his ruthless use of violence transformed him so that we can only conclude that successful violence is character-building. Finally, in *A Clockwork Orange*, humankind's brutality is so ingrained, so much a part of not only some kind of bestial nature but also of cycles of aggression and revenge, as to be hopelessly beyond the reform of moral authorities or the control of behavioral scientists. These films indicate that at this late point in the history of the Sixties there was much doubt and despair about the ability of humankind to transcend ancient impulses and divisions, and to achieve a higher state of being without divine guidance. In this regard, perhaps the fascination audiences held for Kubrick's *2001: A Space Odyssey* (1968) was a counterpoint to these bleak musings about violent human nature, since in that film humanity's destiny is set by a divine, or at least intergalactic, superintelligence that guides technological man towards a predetermined goal that will lead us to a state of transcendence in spite of ourselves, a reassuring and even inspiring future hope occurring in the midst of so much immediate bloodshed and conflict.

Hollywood was reluctant to touch the Vietnam conflict directly, but eventually the political controversy it engendered was to come to the screen in one direct treatment, and several oblique ways. In John Wayne's *The Green Berets* (1968), the war is "located" as not only an extension of America's postwar commitment against Asian communism, but also in more mythic terms as a quasi-Western defense against barbarians on a new frontier in the jungle (a Special Forces camp is called "Fort Apache"). But by this time, the Western metaphor was not fully appreciated or accepted, and indeed the idea that this was a continuation of a struggle of the cavalry against the "Indians" ignored the fact that by 1968 there was not only doubt about the morality of the current struggle but also in some quarters sympathy for the enemy, or at least the victims of the savage fighting. Another "revisionist" Western, *Little Big Man* (1970), turned the Western metaphor on its head, and used the generic formula to cast the Indians as virtuous and "native" victims of a rapacious and aggressive white American society, represented most viciously by the U. S. Cavalry. For director Arthur Penn and the admirers of the film, *Little Big Man* draws very different lessons from our "Western" experience and myth: Vietnam is the logical outcome of the imperial and racial assumptions of American interventionism. In *Little Big Man*, a white moves back and forth between Indian and white society, discovering that the former is what the Sixties wanted society to be--peaceful, mystical, natural, tolerant, communal, and sexually liberated. By stark contrast, white society is repressed, destructive, greedy, and hypocritical, with every hero (Custer, Wild Bill Hickok) an egoist or fraud, and every institution (family, church, town, business, military) corrupt and untrustworthy. *Little Big Man* made it clear that the Vietnam experience was not only rending the country asunder, it was also destroying the continuity of traditional popular myth, making American power seem a dark uncivilized force that eradicates alien cultures and innocent peoples. Other revisionist Westerns of the time (*Tell Them Willie Boy is Here*, 1969; *Soldier Blue*, 1970; and *McCabe and Mrs. Miller*, 1971) also undermined the mythic traditions of the Western that had previously justified righteous empire or community.

As the politics, and movies, of the late Sixties grew more somber, they were bound to invite political satire, either of the pretensions and fears of the powerful, or of the similar self-delusions of the youthful who felt so superior and the righteous wave of the future. In the former case, *The President's Analyst* (1967) manages to satirize about everything, including the secret operation of the national security state, international espionage stemming from the Soviet-American rivalry, conspiracies hatched in the most surprising and seemingly innocuous institutions (TPC), deep pathologies in the presidency itself, and indeed the perception that the conduct of high-level politics in the American superstate was not heroic but preposterous. In the latter instance, the madly satirical *Wild in the Streets* (1968) is both a "youth-exploitation" film of the period but also a sharp parody of a youth

culture coming to believe the myth of its own superiority and
destiny, and the willingness of politicians to pander to that myth.
In the movie, a popular rock singer manages to have the voting
age lowered to fourteen, which is passed when the legislators are
under the influence of LSD; the singer then becomes president and
puts everyone over 35 into "Paradise" concentration camps,
instituting a kind of teenage rock fascism, although hoping to
create "a purely hedonistic society." But the dictatorship of the
young is undermined by time, as the new power is to be challenged
by the very young, who vow at the end "to put everybody over ten
out of business." These two films reminded us of the impudence of
both the power establishment and some of those who challenged
it, and that the more they sought power, the more likely they were
to display the very excesses of powerholding or powerseeking that
were subject to ridicule.

With the advent of the Nixon Administration and the
creation of "the silent majority," time began to eclipse the spirit,
and the salience of the issues, that had given impetus to the
political Sixties and the "political Hollywood" that had responded
to it. As the force went out of the movement, a sense of
resignation and political impotence crept into late-Sixties movies.
In films such as *Getting Straight* (1970), *The Strawberry Statement*
(1970), and *Zabriskie Point* (1970), the youth revolution is a revolt
against caricatures, and romantic involvement is a result of, and
substitute for, political activity. Campus authorities and cops are
either brainless or brutes, and youth, although confused, is a bit
too earnest and virtuous to be believable. Such films had the smell
of formulaic stagnation about them, suggesting that belief in
generational succession leading to a higher political order was
waning and that a reaction was setting in. Indeed, at the same
time that the last of such defenses of the youth movement were
appearing, films that captured something of the new force of
reaction against, and desire to punish, the Sixties and all that it
represented began to appear. In the wake of Kent State, Nixon's
attack on students, and "hardhat" working class attacks on
demonstrators, a movie named *Joe* (1970) appeared that perhaps
represents best the depth of hatred and fear amongst both
established elites and ignored working people upset by both the
contempt in which they were held, and the extraordinary sexual
freedom and personal irreverence the young flaunted. The sage of
Easy Rider had warned that if people who are powerful or
powerless were reminded that they really aren't free, they can
become hateful and murderous, and *Joe* seemed to confirm it. In
this movie, a universally prejudiced workingman seething with
rage against virtually everything that has happened in the Sixties
meets by chance an advertising executive who has just murdered
his "hippie" daughter's drug dealing boy friend. Joe praises him

and becomes his ally, and a friendly coalition blossoms, united by their shared hatred of the aspirations of the young, and by extension the disadvantaged and peaceful youth championed. In the end, the new coalition of establishment and working class is moved to vigilante and revengeful wrath, attacking a hippie commune with rifles. The stunning climax reminds us that the upheaval of the Sixties was an internecine war, a "gap" that divided more than generations, but was symbolized in the movies and in political life by the possibility that by destroying established authority, we destroy the moral and political base of "law and order," and by destroying the hopes and ideals of a suddenly energized and involved youth we risk killing our future.

The Sixties may forever defy complete explanation, but it seems clear in retrospect that it was a time of sudden and explosive energy that the movies, like all other popular art, could only partially understand and depict. The politics of the time was so at war with itself that it risked denying the past and refusing the future. The political reaction since then might lead one to think that the "conservative" forces of established order and tradition won against a feeble protest over the gigantic goals of empire and the sterile prospect of bourgeois life. Perhaps it is the historical case that the Sixties were the last gasp of American reformism and vitalistic rebellion before we settled into the corruptions and cynicism of a polticial Silver Age that augurs not only our refusal to live up to our political ideals but also our slow descent into the inevitabilities of political entropy and the shift of imperial power and will elsewhere. But there is also a sense in which the "spirit of the Sixties" was to have a very real cultural impact, long-term effects of much more import than simply the elegiac celebration of past hopes in nostalgic movies (*Four Friends* (1982); *The Big Chill* (1983); *Return of the Secaucus Seven* (1980). No amount of subsequent political victimage and denial of what the Sixties wrought can ever undo the cultural storm it unleashed, nor undermine the models of idealism or simply raw freedom that it gave us as a legacy, nor stop its most important discovery, that cultural expression may well be the true popular source of change that is worthwhile and liberating, and while political power may content itself to celebrate the pre-Sixties past, popular culture, including the movies that the Sixties so revolutionized, is much more daring, and at its best it continues to give us visions of the political present and future that reveal and admit much more of our cultural truth than presidential politics since the Sixties has ever been willing to face. The thesis could be argued that national politics since the Sixties has been an exercise in denial. If that is the case, it can also be advanced that the movies since the Sixties, however conservative or reactionary they may be argued to be in tone, still have not escaped the orbit of the Sixties since they too have felt the impulse toward frankness, and perhaps also complication and ambiguity, that has characterized American political culture ever since. It is easy enough to demonstrate that the Seventies were a political decade in many ways derivative from the Sixties, and the astonishing movie creativity of that decade one that had benefitted from its explosive predecessor. But it is also likely the case that the Eighties, for all of its vaunted rewriting of the past and contempt for what the Sixties represented, were conducted in the shadow of what they could not as much as the powers that be might have wished, undo. Ronald Reagan was no less a creation of the Sixties than Woodstock Nation, the rock revolution, and the new filmmakers that invaded Hollywood in the Seventies; but it is still an unanswered question of American political history as to whether political reaction or cultural innovation will in the long run have the most influence on the way we live.

Chapter Seven

The 1970s: A Political Time in Search of Itself

At this early retrospective date, the 1970s have acquired, it is probably fair to say, a bad reputation. Historical periods, like figures, are subject to revisionism, and maybe in the fullness of time the Seventies will not be regarded so harshly. In a political sense, there were notable achievements. It was a period, some economists have argued, of greater economic growth than the much heralded Eighties; the Constitution and Congress survived the greatest threat to their power ever in Watergate; the war in Vietnam collapsed of its own unsustainable delusions with the fall of Saigon; and there were steps toward normalization of relations with Russia and China and peace in the Middle East. Yet it is hard to escape the conclusion that the Seventies were politically unsatisfying, inheriting the frustrated hopes and agenda of the Sixties and accumulating a sense of incompletion and drift. With the stalemate of the Iranian hostage "crisis" in 1979, the demand for imperial reassertion and revenge against those deemed culpable for our perceived low and humiliated state was to bring about the Presidential election of a figure who promised to undo the previous two decades in both political and cultural innovations and "turn the country around." Running against the upsetting Sixties and the confusing Seventies had its appeals, since the "fallout" from the Sixties had done so much to undermine American political myths of a domestic bourgeois community of peaceful consensus, and international myth of righteous empire as "leader of the Free World." Self-appointment as the powerful and virtuous center of the political universe is a difficult role to abandon, and perhaps it is useful to view the Seventies as a search for a way past a disillusioned political doldrums wherein the country was in the grave danger of achieving political maturity by recognizing the harsh changing realities of environmental, economic, and political limits. Such talk is dangerous for a country imbued with a belief in its own sanctioned mission and ascendancy, so it was perhaps inevitable that the "spiritless" Seventies had to be defeated, or more accurately, superceded by something more reassertive and mock heroic.

It is likely, then, that the 1970s will always be seen as a "liminal" age in that it was "in between," a transitional decade that defies definition since it really had none, persisting in memory and meaning as a passage from one strongly defined period to another. The Seventies had no sense of political identity, but rather served as a period for the obliteration of one identity and for the recreation of another more venerable and familiar political identity in the Eighties. It was this lack of identity or direction that gave support to the retreat of the individual into "self," searching for meaning in areas of self-concern and self-development that gave rise to characterizations such as "the age of privatism," "the culture of narcissism," and "the me decade." The fashionable social activism and radical stances of the Sixties disappeared, much to the chagrin of those truly committed to heartfelt social causes. There were glimmerings of a "new conservatism" that was to flower as part of the Reagan victory, and a return to religion that was to give force to a new and aggressive Christian political fundamentalism. Perhaps it was the case that the history of the Seventies was essentially a slide from complexity to simplicity, from the future to the past, from a search for solutions to a search for certainty. In any case, history did not turn out as the idealists and dreamers of the Sixties had hoped and even expected, and the Seventies ended fittingly with the triumph of a presidential politician pledged to "right" the mistake of historical change, the reform impulse, and the spirit of experimentation that had so unsettled the predictable world of the imaginary Fifties. We now can see not only the confusions and internal contradictions of the Seventies in the movies, but also the seeds of what was to become the Eighties as the decade struggled toward symbolic resolutions. It did not anticipate the Eighties but it was also a necessary precedence to that time that succeeded and resolved the temporal "suspension" of the Seventies. Even though the 1970s are usually belittled, in the long run they may be recalled as historically and politically important, although not so much as the genesis of a recrudescent conservatism that augured a renascence of "the American Century" as much as one that dimly understood the terms of national political and economic decline. The Nixon Administration in that perspective will be remembered not so much for scandal as for its institutionalization of the management of imperial decline, and its identification of a nationalistic and social "conservatism" as an individual political defense against the terrors of change that threatened from both domestic and foreign forces that would do such things as redistribute wealth, either through social welfare or engineered oil embargoes. To understand both the advent of the Eighties, and the long-term role of the decade of the Seventies in American political history, we must again turn for popular evidence in the movies.

We noted in the previous chapter that by the late Sixties and early Seventies, a notable political reaction had set in against challenges to power and authority. Social and political rebels in popular culture came increasingly during this period to be portrayed as pathological or wrong-headed, fools or villains rather than heroes. Those who had so recently been heroes--youth, blacks, liberals--became social threats in a movie world that was portrayed as precarious and dangerous, a world desperately in need of the reassertion of strong social authority. With the success of the Nixon Administration in garnering supporting amongst Middle Americans, and with the fragmentation of the issues and impulses that had held the Sixties attention, Hollywood, ever sensitive to changes in political mood and audience expectations, portrayed the shift. Two early Seventies films are representative: *Patton* (1970) and *Dirty Harry* (1971). *Patton* appeared as both the Vietnam war and the debate over it were raging, and added fuel to the fiery political dispute. *Patton* was ostensibly the war biography of the great World War II general, with all of his warrior ethic (and strangeness), but at this later moment he was for many, including President Nixon, a model of American will, embodying heroic resolve, belief in national mission and the functions of social discipline, and the efficacy of military solutions, as exemplified by the mythic setting of the American "crusade in Europe" against the Nazi evil. Nixon himself identified much with the maligned and frustrated Patton attempting to "fulfill his destiny," which the president likely equated with the national interest and historical teleology. Patton was represented as such a complex character that   antiwar sympathizers could argue that war attracted leaders with pathological ambitions and self-images, such as belief in reincarnation and divine destiny. Patton was, however, given most praise by those, from Nixon on down, who saw us as a nation in yet another great "test" not only of our power, but of our "will" and "character" that undergirded that power, and seemed quite willing to put ourselves under the command of a determined, charismatic, and unconventional leader if he could successfully prosecute the war at any cost to a victorious end and restore respect for authority at the expense of liberty at home. Such a fantasy might have remained ideal political talk if the movie had not inspired, and then reinforced, Nixon on his course of action about the war, especially his disastrous decision to invade Cambodia in April, 1970, watching the film to "steel himself" for what he thought was in the "true American spirit" of Patton rather than those who doubted both the myth of Patton and the mission in Vietnam. In the subsequent fire-storm (including students shot by the National Guard at Kent State), Nixon may have found identification with Patton useful, convincing him that they had both stood for the right military course in a hostile and weak-willed world. Nixon's eventual--and largely self-willed--political fate, and the resolution of the Vietnam war now make all this attempt at national bravado appear pathetic and maudlin, an effort to shore up faith in American mission by reference to the rogue heroism of a cinematic creation, as if the last desperate recourse of Washington was an appeal to Hollywood.

In some measure, what *Patton* represented for those who dreamed of undoubted American will at work making the world over into our own image or whim, *Dirty Harry* meant for the changing imagination of the domestic scene. Here the youthful social rebel is merely sick and murderous, offering no idealistic hopes nor example of the tenacity of freedom. Rather the repulsive killer simply takes advantage of Constitutional restraints on legal procedure as proof of civilization's unwillingness to defend itself. Yet "law and order" conservatives who defended this film's reassertion of the power of the police to restrain the perceived advancing threats to social order and decency were forced in the odd position of virtually defending extra-legal and supra-Constitutional action by the very government that was supposed to be the bastion of political rectitude and civilized behavior. Once that was abandoned, one is beginning to see the political seeds of the "Watergate mentality," justifying extraordinary governmental action against social and political enemies as a necessary measure against advancing and threatening evils. Like *Patton*, social wars can only be won by a rogue hero who is almost as independent of civilized restraint as the enemy; indeed, society comes near to defeating itself by restraining the extraordinary hero who understands that means must be equal to the gravity of the threat. A rogue cop like Harry Callahan must defy instituted authority as well as legal and Constitutional rules in order to become an agent of social revenge on those who have brought us close to anarchy. Thus in a perverse sense, official power is reasserted through the independent action of someone at odds with sponsoring governmental authority. It is only a small step after such toleration of, and success by, a Dirty Harry to the wink-and-nod justifications of Watergate, and eventually, Irangate. But at that time, officialdom, in the police and mayoral authorities, is helpless before the onslaught of a mad serial killer, yet feel constrained to thwart the avenging will of Harry's modernized frontier justice. *Dirty Harry* represented the emergent sensibility of the precariousness of ordered social life, with change that had only yesterday seemed so welcome now thought to be threatening to the point of justifying aggressive retribution. Harry destroyed social evil for a world that seemed oddly indifferent to it, and indeed patently undeserving of his effort. He was little more than a vigilante for a society incapable of caring for its own defense, suggesting an unsung hero who strikes out at evil as a matter of personal rather than political, revenge, since he alone understands the immensity of the demonic force and the necessity of its destruction. But *Dirty Harry* did strike a political chord: at the end, he kills the malefactor and throws his badge away, signifying not only the felt necessity of direct action independent of institutions no longer capable of adequate self-defense, but also the power to take necessary and just actions--vengeance, for example--which could no longer be trusted to such "normal" means of instituted authority. After *Harry*, the Seventies would play with two alternatives: the individual avenger who would take action in government's stead, and the more disturbing idea of vigilante government itself.

The figure of the individual violent avenger was not new in American popular culture, but what was new was the story that he (and sometimes she) acted as an agent of vengeance without hope of social redemption, indeed opposed by the corrupt or stupid powers that be who cannot see the decaying social order around them. Besides *Harry*, this could take the form of rogue cops, such as the harassed rural sheriff of *Walking Tall* (1974). But most remarkably, the claim that vengeance is mine was made by fictional private citizens. We have already noted the emergence of this in *Joe* (1970), with the attack on the counterculture, and their equally vigilant defense by a mythic suprafigure in *Billy Jack* (1971), as well as the perhaps quasi-fascist theme of the rediscovery of ennobling primitive masculine forces of individual power through violent defense of home and wife in *Straw Dogs* (1971). But maybe the most astonishing of these films is *Death Wish* (1974), in which a former conscientious objector (shades of Sergeant York!) is converted into a vessel of wrath after a vicious attack on his wife and daughter, killing one and rendering the other catatonic. But unlike York, he acts not to make the world safe for democracy but to make the prototypical mean streets of the city safe from muggers, without real hope that they ever will be, or that political institutions such as the mayor and the police will take his cue and simply shoot them down as they commit antisocial acts. The startling reception to *Death Wish*--cheers from urban audiences as the former pacifist kills repulsive nighttown creatures--climaxed a mood, a discomfiting popular assertion that the explosive thrust of the Sixties had resulted in social chaos, turning freedom into license and rights into a procedural dodge for criminals, and rendering institutions helpless before these darker Hobbesian powers that control the streets. Yet these vigilante movies tended to see the action of their vengeful hero as a hopeless gesture, simply striking out at contemptible social objects without any more of a political agenda than scorn and hatred of those different or deranged, and suggesting that the only solution to social problems was to kill the most visible manifestations of them, a theory of domestic deterrence worthy of Dr. Strangelove.

More insidious was the view that governmental power dare not be constrained by civilized and constitutional norms of political conduct. As the Nixon Administration expanded its powers of surveillance and its aggressive condemnation of dissent, criticism, and reportage, it asserted the authority to act above or outside the law, and seemed determined to be at war with elements of the very society it was pledged to protect and defend. But the political assumptions of the age were now very different than the one that had preceded it, stressing the power of executive suppression as a malevolent necessity independent of law, and even justifying the idea of government itself as a kind of secret vigilante that protected us from ourselves. Our only hope was to put ourselves under the auspices of a protector who would use aggressive power to guard us from a threatening world, asking only in exchange our obedience and acquiescence in this bold and expansionary exercise of executive authority. The movies began to search for metaphors for this assertive theory of power, placing it in other genres where it was oblique but recognizable. Nixon himself mused on the exercise of power by John Wayne in *Chisum* (1973), in which it is suggested that the only way to avoid the horrors of an outside world rent with anarchic and hostile forces was to place oneself under the protection of a strong, if slightly illegitimate, leader who when need arises is as ungoverned by the rules of civilized response as those who threaten life and property (see also his *Big Jake*, 1972). But clearly the most remarkable film that touched on this theme was *The Godfather* (1972), and to a lesser extent, *The Godfather, Part II* (1974). For his social "family," the Mafia Godfather provides the functions of a vigilant leader in a hostile world, and dispenses justice that is nothing more than revenge on those who have wronged someone friendly to the Family. The political inference was clear enough: the price of protection from harm involved the surrender of independence and choice, placing oneself in the care of those equal to dealing with implacable hostility. At the time, the idea seemed to fit the garnered power of the Nixon Administration in its approach to domestic suppression and the invitation to become part of the political umbrella of the "silent majority" that would silently consent to the silencing of opposition, which was often equated with treason. The Nixon White House convinced itself that the situation was so grave as to justify vigilante government that was more similar to the steely operation of the Godfather than anyone cared to admit. This theory nicely punctuated when Nixon, in his revealed secret tapes, spoke enviously and wistfully of the free hand the Mafia had in its dealings with the external world.

This theory of government broke into the open with the Watergate scandal that so dominated the early 1970s, and was to play an important role in supporting the cynicism and political paranoia of the time. For the assertion of supralegal powers by a government that admired criminal illegality and secrecy inevitably led to the contrary idea that government now was a conspiracy of an elite that has arrogated to itself great power against the citizenry. Conspiracy has always been a popular motif in the American popular mind, and in the Seventies the idea of conspiracies within the government took on a wide variety of forms. The revelations of Watergate and of illegal FBI and CIA domestic activity made such a widespread view more plausible, and made movie audiences receptive to conspiratorial themes in films that accused elements of their own government, or elite groups, of webs of intrigue, hidden agendas, and secret actions that explain events as the result of "wheels within wheels" turning behind the scenes. Conspiracy became a Hollywood staple that explained everything from the Kennedy assassination (*Executive Action*, 1973) to the operation of the international oil industry (*The Formula*, 1980) and international banking (*Rollover*, 1981). In *The Parallax View* (1974), assassination is covered up by the usual elite commission evasions, and the truth disappears with the mysterious death of witnesses. The investigative reporter (a popular hero of the Seventies) infiltrates a shadowy corporation, and in the end himself becomes the political victim of this ominously powerful force that manipulates events in order to prevent worthwhile political innovations. Even those "inside" the overwhelmingly powerful System can become victims as the CIA researcher of *Three Days of the Condor* (1975) discovers when he ventures into knowledge he doesn't need to know, namely that the inner sanctum of conspiratorial government itself, the intelligence community, has been "taken over" by an even more mysterious hidden force, a force so powerful it might even be able to prevent *The New York Times* from printing news deemed by the conspiracy as unfit to print. In *Twilight's Last Gleaming* (1977), a maverick general seizes and threatens to use nuclear weapons to force the President to reveal the true reason for fighting the Vietnam war, which was the "doctrine of credibility," to prove to the Soviet Union that the United States will senselessly sacrifice lives in war, thus demonstrating that we are crazy enough to fight a nuclear conflict! But the general and President are silenced by the conspiracy internal to the government, and the truth remains concealed in the inner sanctum of the military-industrial complex. In *The China Syndrome* (1979), the nuclear power magnates are willing to risk a major accident, and intimidate employees and press, in order to maintain profits and power. In virtually all of the Seventies conspiracy movies, the truth does not come out, heroic action is largely futile, and the conspiracy is of such immense, if covert, power that those who challenge it usually fall victim to it. This was not, to be sure, a healthy view of government, but after what had transpired and been revealed, not an entirely unjustified one either.

Those films loosely associated as "Watergate" movies were not exactly upbeat either, but even though only one of them was directly inspired by the Watergate scandal, they offered the most insightful and lasting examination of the meaning of such concentrated elite power. The story of how the political reporting of the *Washington Post's* young team, Woodward and Bernstein, broke the Watergate story was told in *All the President's Men* (1976). Washington is portrayed as a dark, foreboding place under the spell of some kind of unseen power that makes information unreachable, knowledgeable people afraid and mute, and the truth something hinted at in telephone conversations and whispered in the darkness of underground parking lots. Even truth agreed upon in the bright lights of the newspaper office is easily undermined and attacked, and everywhere else in official Washington it is concealed and denied. The two reporters are tenacious and curious holy innocents who are guided by their shadowy mentor, Deep Throat, through the awesome caverns and corridors of power, pursuing a slender thread in the political darkness that eventually unraveled the garment of Presidential power. The film ends with the image that the pursuit of journalistic truth will triumph, yet the impression left of Washington is one of systemic closure, of an undemocratic and monumental imperial city dominated by brooding forces that are virtually impenetrable, and when the belly of the beast is entered reveals a malignancy at the very core of the system, in Presidential power itself. In retrospect, *All the President's Men*, while quite topical, did point to the historical development that increasingly important executive actions were submerged in a twilight world hidden from scrutiny and protected by the encompassing rationale of national security.

Two other films of the period, *The Conversation* (1974) and *Chinatown* (1974), pursued the same general theme: that conspiratorial government was no paranoid delusion, and that the heart of darkness was at the top of the pyramids of power. *The Conversation* follows the activities of a professional eavesdropper, a part of the "security" industry that became famous with Watergate. He is familiar with the need for information on the part of powerful clients, and absolves himself of moral responsibility for the uses to which that information is put. Yet he becomes involved in interpreting the meaning of a recorded conversation, and the corporate intrigues, including murder, that it entails; to his horror, he only interprets it correctly too late, and realizes that he has been used in a corporate-political intrigue, preventing him from any moral recourse. The film ends with the master bugger himself bugged, with the dark message that seemed to resonate so much from the world of Watergate: "We'll be listening." In *Chinatown*, the searcher for truth is not a reporter or wiretapper but a private detective. His search reveals not only political and moral corruption at the apex of power, but also that even the most seemingly innocuous and natural elements--water-- can itself become a political commodity inspiring the most heinous actions. As in the other "Watergate" films, the politically powerful operate in a morally open universe for their own aggrandizement and without regard to notions of the public interest, capable, as the patriarch remarks to the detective, "of anything." These two films in particular suggest one major reason for the apolitical, and indeed antipolitical, stance that developed with many people during the 1970s: those granted a glimpse at what was essentially conspiratorial, self-serving, and evil in purpose were repelled at what they saw, so that the wise person was one who chose, in the phrase of the disillusioned Watergate witness who was asked what advice to give those interested into going into government, to "stay away." *The Conversation* and *Chinatown* stand as reminders of the extent to which the powerful force of the imperial presidency and national security state seemed to be a byzantine maze of lies, secrets, and alien purposes that suggested the metaphor of Chinatown, where "nobody knows what's going on."

Such a political state of affairs also implied to people that nobody knew what to do. The country seemed adrift at best, and in the grip of fools and madmen at worst. There seemed to be a radical disjunction between power and justice, and with the spread of disillusionment with politics and other areas of elite leadership, the expression of a kind of cynical outrage--cynicism about the motives and efficacy of those in power, and outrage that things had turned out so badly for the country. In the movies, this general sense took various forms, perhaps most notably in such varied films as *One Flew Over the Cuckoo's Nest* (1975), *Shampoo* (1975), *Nashville* (1975), and *Network* (1976). All these films share in common the Seventies perspective that powerful elites possess no saving grace that gives them the right to rule, and the Watergate films to the contrary, we can see clearly into the paucity of their lives and transparency of their exercise of power to the extent that their unfitness or pettiness is revealed. In *One Flew Over the Cuckoo's Nest*, the authority figure in the mental hospital rules her ward with a subtle venality that relies upon the lack of self-esteem among the inmates;·the implication is that political rule depends upon the acquiesence of the many in their own oppression by an elite that is narrow and stupid, and is threatened by assertions of freedom, independence, or sensuality. The system's final indignity spurs the cynical antihero to blind rage against authority's hypocrisy, at the price of the destruction of his own rebellious rationality and wit. In *Shampoo*, the Hollywood social elite gathers to celebrate Nixon's victory in 1968 and listen to the litany of political hypocricies about traditional values, while their actual lives are parodies of all an exemplary elite is supposed to stand for. Through the hair stylist-gigolo who serves the women of this thoroughly corrupt community, we see that those in charge or with wealth are no mystery, and they do not deserve to rule. *Nashville* examines another media community, and finds that the expressions of piety and patriotism among both the visible popular music elite and an unseen presidential candidate devoid of roots and meaning. The famous and powerful display their self-importance and utter vacuity, traits pathetically shared by those "little people" who adore them, want to desperately succeed in Nashville or in love, or even kill their heroes. Emptiness of purpose pervades the films, with everyone both absorbed in themselves and consumed with odd ambitions. *Nashville* depicted a non-community of exploitative isolates, who do not touch except to use, and whose two figures that "reach out"--the country music queen and the politician--are destroyed or unseen. The film ends with a disrupted political rally on the steps of the Nashville replica of the Athenian Parthenon, where democracy was born and where now its popular simulation, destroyed by the cynicism of the age, continues as entertainment devoid of substance or direction. *Nashville* is a maddening movie, but it did grasp where our own disbelief in anything save ourselves might lead us. Finally, perhaps the mood of impotent disillusionment was best captured in *Network*, a fantasy about a television network that builds a news show around a deranged newsanchor-prophet in a totally cynical media world of manipulated audiences, corporate takeovers, and the eclipse of journalistic values(UBS would tolerate noWoodward and Bernstein). But the "mad prophet of the airways" articulates a popular rage among the powerless witnessing the disarray of things, a rage manipulated into a harmless channel of protest by elites with a stake in such diversion of political discontent. The "Howard Beale Show" mobilized the many who were mad as hell, and cynically betrayed them by convincing them that through Beale they were not going to have to take it anymore. But now the audience was part of the manipulation, and when their champion became a bore, like everything else on TV or in politics, he became quickly dispensable. These films all shared the politically charged sense of authoritative structures in eclipse, collapsing by their own abandonment of value, leaving a world of mutual manipulation that offers the rest of us only the cold comfort of sharing the cynicism inherent in maintaining relationships that are reduced to mere appearances.

Even those sincere and strong enough to participate in politics ran the risk of being consumed by it. In *The Candidate* (1972), a handsome young lawyer for the poor, and son of a former governor, is talked into running a hopeless race against the incumbent California Senator with the proviso that he can say what he wants. But soon he is caught up in the transformation of political discussion into media image management, and as he sees the campaign take off and that he has a chance to win, the lure of power is too much and he is thoroughly compromised, made into an attractive media personage comfortable with the sixty-second spot and staged appearances. If the candidate ever had moral or political weight, the system of winning elections breeds it out of him, and in the end he is as evanescent and facile as the opponent he held in so much contempt, reduced to asking his media "handlers," "What do we do now?" What, indeed? In *The Seduction of Joe Tynan* (1979), an equally liberal and attractive senator tries to do the right thing while making the necessary compromises, but he too is seduced, both politically and sexually, by these who tell him that he's got the power, the political magic that makes ambitious politicians convince themselves that they're different. But here again the lure of power--the senator is bitten by the presidential bug--leads him into a tangled web of broken promises, familial neglect, and an ego-enhancing extramarital affair. In both films, powerseeking is the demon of political life, and those drawn into politics risk a Faustian bargain with power that costs them their soul. Both senators seem refugees from the Sixties who have become so compromised by "the system" that their integrity is irrecoverable, and their capacity for accomplishing good minimized by the inherent corruptions and intractabilities involved in playing the political game. In the Seventies, sincerity was not good enough to cope with what seemed unregenerate.

In an important sense, Hollywood treated Vietnam as a disaster, something that symbolized what had gone wrong with America in the recent past. After the fall of Saigon in 1975, moviemakers felt freer to meditate on the meaning of the Vietnam experience, something that was to continue into the 1980s. Two complementary themes emerged immediately: first, that Vietnam was a domestic disaster, one that had such disruptive effects on American life that the war was by implication not worth the price we had to pay when we brought its impact home; and second, that Vietnam was an imperial disaster, one that immersed us in an Asian other-world to the extent we forgot who we were and why we were supposed to be there. In the former case, most obviously, is *Coming Home* (1978), Jane Fonda's antiwar statement, that juxtaposes her with two veterans, one a husband who represents the moral bankruptcy of militarism brought home; although physically healthy, the contradictions wrought in him have destroyed him, and when he learns of his wife's infidelity with an antiwar paraplegic, the implied impotency and rejection spur him to suicide. The paraplegic physically disabled by the war grows in political value, recovers his sexual potency through her, and apologizes for the war to high school students. The movie associated the "proper" political stance with reintegration into civilized society, but militarism is self-destructive and antisocial. More complex and controversial was *The Deer Hunter* (1978), which Fonda condemned without seeing, and which won the Academy Award for Best Picture (presented by John Wayne) amongst heated critical debate and even demonstrations. Yet *The Deer Hunter* remains of interest to the student of Seventies movies precisely because it does contain many of the contradictions and experiences that did make "coming home" more agonizing and varied than the simple dichotomy of Fonda's film. *The Deer Hunter* suggests that the war had not only policy but also popular roots, in ethnic patriotism; male bonding and machismo as expressed in drinking, hunting, cursing, and the exploitation of women; and in the belief, learned from popular creations such as the war movie, that war is a great adventure that vindicates masculinity. The war itself is treated as an unmitigated horror, in which Americans who were part of the domestic community are subjected to the cruel disregard for life attributed to this alien Asian culture (director Cimino was accused of racism in his portrayal of the Vietnamese). Yet most of the film concerns how what transpires in Vietnam affects the working-class social group back in Clairton, Pennsylvania, and how the war destroys the integrity of those relationships.   But the physically and emotionally mangled survivors of the war and their friends do not grow in political awareness, and in the end, after the failure to extricate the gentle Nick from captivity in the Asian game of ultimate chance, the ones in mourning can think of nothing more profound than a guarded affirmation of faith in country, something that the very national affirmation of power and willingness to fight in both policy and popular circles had just done much to undermine. The meaning of American entanglement in such an Asian quagmire was explored in   Coppola's *Apocalypse Now* (1979), which uses as format Conrad's famous meditation on evil and empire in a jungle setting, tracing the search "upriver" for an officer who has founded his own "state" off the map of civilization, as exemplified by the American Army. The trip reveals the war as an absurd and idiotic undertaking devoid of meaning, climaxing with the discovery by the emissary-assassin of the other-world ruled by a mad genius who has abandoned all pretense to civilized "rules of war" or national purpose, brooding on "the horror" of the war. But upriver, the war had disappeared, and American authority was left with facing the descent of our purposes into madness, a madness the Army wanted to deny by destroying, refusing to admit that the consequences of warfare the emissary had just witnessed were continuous in malignant effect with the out-of-control officer who had to be eliminated for carrying unbridled warfare to its logical conclusion, the creation of a death culture. *Apocalypse Now* was an ambitious and uneven film, but at least it attempted to portray the extent to which a political war can plunge us into dark horrors that we ourselves entangle ourselves into, revealing aspects of our national soul we really don't want to believe are there.

There was one major domestic variant on the dark characterological flaws in us that many came to think Vietnam revealed in the film by Martin Scorsese, *Taxi Driver* (1976). The antihero here is a Vietnam veteran living a lonely and pathetic existence in the urban hell of the decaying city, the asphalt jungle similar to Vietnam in its violence and degeneracy, the bleak image of a civilization in chaos and ruin. Taxi driver Travis Bickle (Robert De Niro) cruises a world not unlike "upriver," revealing the nightmarish absurdity of the urban nighttown, a world that maintains the illusion of sanity and beauty, as exemplified by Senator "Palatine" (reminiscent of the Palatine Hills, the residence of the Roman elite as the city decayed and fell), the presidential candidate, and the lovely but icy girl whose life Travis briefly touches. But they are part of a world of illusion that makes them incapable of caring or understanding; driven mad, he can only wreak revenge on the society that is responsible for his madness and indeed the network of madness it sustains. He sees himself as no less a rational assassin than the emissary gone upriver after the official, a disciplined warrior on a secret mission no more or less insane than Vietnam. But rather than killing the consequences of war, Travis wants to kill the consequences of politics, a world no less hypocritical and insane that ignores the very "people" with which it wants so much to identify. Denied that, he ironically becomes a hero lionized by the power structure he wanted to lash out against, but was diverted into destroying sleazy masters for the underworld he occupies. But his own sense of "apocalypse now" drives him to the position that many Americans wished someone would take, that here was someone who would not take it anymore. Yet he becomes a socially sanctioned hero by striking at illegitimate and street-level power rather than legitimate and suite-level power. The powers of the "upper world" are sanctimonious and remote, protected from contact from the democracy of degraded souls they would champion but remain fearful of. *Taxi Driver* is many things, including a portrait of a society characterized by extreme political polarization, not over ideology or even class, but rather by an unbridgeable gap between those few who run society and the rest who are victimized by it. Travis Bickle is in one sense the ultimate victim of Vietnam, bringing the war home and realizing that home was a war too, a society, like his personality, so close to disintegration that no one seemed to notice, with violence now the norm of a barbaric world. Travis was for that time the madman on the periphery who could see the emptiness at the center.

So this was the depths of the Soporific Seventies as Hollywood and many people imagined it. After the tremors of Watergate, the OPEC oil embargo, and the fall of Saigon, it was easy to believe in the common vision of a decaying and drifting society over which no one had control. There was much talk of limits to growth, the shift of power elsewhere, environmental depletion, and dinosaur technologies; Presidents Ford and Carter gained probably the undeserved reputations as inept bunglers. The movies had done much to sully the exercise of uncomplicated heroism leading to the defeat of evil, making it difficult to recognize who was who and what values remained. In the late Seventies, there were two movie trends of interest, since they both suggest a mass yearning for heroic reassertion at, first, the level of interpersonal stability and achievement; and second, at the level of social leadership that used heroic powers to advance American values and interests. In the former case, there was in the late Seventies a renewal of concern over the stability of the family, as if that were a microcosm of the larger society that could be salvaged at the base. But implicit in these "pro-family" films that persisted into the Eighties (*Ordinary People, The Four Seasons, Tootsie, An Officer and a Gentleman, On Golden Pond, Terms of Endearment, The Big Chill,* even *Hannah and Her Sisters*) is something rather "conservative": that social and political order is based on the correct relationship between man and woman in a familial bond, and that variations or failures threaten that order. It is easy to see in a film such as *Kramer vs. Kramer* (1979) an undercurrent that finds the woman "searching for identity" who leaves husband and child to be at fault, and that the true American "family" would abandon now discredited notions of "liberation" in exchange for social stabilization. While not reactionary, such films did augur a change in the political climate: films such as *Looking for Mr. Goodbar* (1977) and various horror films had warned of the punishments for female sexual independence (cf., *Dressed to Kill,* 1980) and began to reassert normalcy in the terms of endearment of the private lives of ordinary people. This is not to say that there were not still images of strong and working women (*Norma Rae,* 1979; *Julia,* 1977), only that there appeared complementary, and sometimes contradictory, images of women, and familial happiness, that suggested the reassertion of the nuclear family as a political, if not totally realizable, norm. Similarly, during the late Seventies there was a revival of what we might loosely term norms of individual ambition in the appearance of "achievement" movies, although often in "non-business" settings (*Rocky,* 1976; *Saturday Night Fever,* 1977; *Fame,* 1980). But such films augured the reawakening of notions about individual achievement as another redeeming form of behavior at the base, a norm that was to give increasing credence to the label attributed to the "me decade" and "the culture of narcissism," and would lead to the rediscovery of business as theme and setting in the 1980s.

There was also a yearning during this period for the reassertion of cultural heroism with somewhat more traditional and uncomplicated traits and satisfactions than those of the deeply antiheroic Seventies. The signal event in the movies was the release of *Star Wars* (1977), a mythic fantasy offering "A New Hope" against the evil Galactic Empire by a coalition of heroes of true comic book proportions--the earnest kid out to prove himself, seek revenge, and discover his roots; the devil-may-care sidekick; the beautiful and feisty princess fighting for democratic values. Their heroism is childish but effective in a political universe without ambiguity or nuance, or for that matter, the possibility of failure. They ground heroic militarism in a mystical "Force" that lets them serve "The Alliance" while maintaining their individual identity but enjoying the plaudits of military achievement. *Star Wars* was a mythic mishmash that conjured up heroic memories from a variety of popular sources, reviving our hopes of politico-cultural vindication through heroic action. It was no accident that it was followed by a cycle of superhero films drawn from sword-and-sorcerer origins, comic heroics, and of course, the movies. *Superman* (1979) revived one of the venerable emerges of godly heroism and American male "nice-guy" acceptability as a vehicle of community protection. Similarly, *Raiders of the Lost Ark* (1981) brought back the American adventurer as someone able to defeat evil forces abroad without the taint of imperialistic motives. These very old heroic figures were self-confident, light-hearted, and undaunted by the political tremors that had undercut political faith in the Seventies. They sought no political power, but they took it upon themselves to exercise heroics, reasserting the undemocratic idea that everything depends upon one charismatic leader with power far beyond those of mortal men. Like *E. T.* (1982), their power is extraordinary but benevolent, eliminating any suggestion of self-interest or will to power. They are monomythic figures reviving the hero's quest, a quest that apparently we desperately wanted to see undertaken again, in both the movies and politics, with all of the dangers to our lives and political traditions that such a quest seems to entail. Our political need was such that we were not willing to contemplate the dark side of the Force, the possibility that heroic redemption has a price in critical repression and political subjugation.

The Seventies ended with the Iranian hostage stalemate, a new form of the old captivity folktale in a newly hostile setting. It seemed to symbolize to many Americans our new political impotence, an unheroic state that had to be superceded, even if that meant appeal to the lotusland of fantasy itself, Hollywood. The merger of Hollywood and Washington in 1980 not only ended the Seventies, it also ended the notion that we would accept gracefully the conditions of political decline, or enter with resignation an era of political maturity. For good or ill, the eclipse of the Seventies reminded us that the American will towards political belief in our own heroic mission and destiny is not the palest of the gods, and that we are willing to accept leadership that believes simply in its own heroism, and by extension, the heroism of the country. Perhaps the Eighties was to divide us between those who thought this assertion juvenile and pernicious, and those who thought it hopeful and necessary. But certainly the political transformation into the Eighties did suggest that political learning from the movies is not neatly static nor cumulative, and can draw on more archaic and primitive sources of cultural depictions and tales in order for people to renew their grip on political hope for a future over which those in whom they invest so much power will have control.

Chapter Eight

The 1980s: The Politics of Renewal and Decline

The 1980s was a political period deemed to be governed by a "new conservatism," and there was much official breastbeating about "American Renewal," "standing tall," "New Beginnings," and other rhetorical investitures. The president who presided over this political "movement" reassured us through his very physical longevity and folkish memory that we were to enjoy not only political and cultural continuity into the future, but also fulfill our self-defined national destiny. If there was renewed optimism and sense of purpose in the land, clearly the corollary to that was a massive denial of the recent past, and also a refusal to admit the possibility of anything less than a grandiose future of expansionary capitalism and benevolent empire. The elections of 1980, 1984, and 1988 were won on the basis of claims to represent a kind of militant positivism about national values and destiny that was at once metapolitical and monarchial. The presidency became an office that was "above politics" in the sense of contempt for the process (Reagan left office condemning the politics of Washington as if he had never been president). But he left a legacy for an imperial presidency known only through staged appearances in ritual settings or dramatic formats of foreordained heroic actions that his successor would attempt to emulate. In an odd sense with which historians will long grapple, the Reagan presidency was both a success and a failure, on the one hand achieving popularity and promoting its agenda, but on the other failing to make a dent in the political establishment for which it had so much contempt, nor solving, or often even admitting, the problems that were to be magnified years later by their denial and neglect.

There is something even more politically fundamental about the history of the 1980s that will be the stuff of historical debate. Like the 1950s, there was a good bit of political reassertion through military expenditures, and appeal to cultural normalcy and complacency as a prerequisite for economic mobility. And like both the Fifties and the Twenties, individualism was extolled as necessary for capitalist expansion, with government playing again the helpful role of encouraging private exploitation of markets and resources. But for all of the military theatrics of the Eighties, it was dubious that American political will would be more heeded in the world, and indeed it might even have been the case that all of this political assertion resulted from chronic political frustration that power was drifting elsewhere and that we were being ignored or defied. Easy targets like Grenada and Libya defined the extent of American military intervention during the period, and the rest of the world, from Nicaragua to South Africa, seemed determined to go its own way without asking us. Too, for all the self-congratulation about our economic "recovery"--from what was never clear--the American economy was very uneven in performance and outcomes, and economic initiative had simply shifted elsewhere. Nor was there much evidence that an increasingly diverse people accepted the cultural norms and lifestyle requirements of old rich white men of World War II vintage, symbolized by the ambitious but highliving young urban professionals ("Yuppies") who became entrepreneurial heroes of Eighties conservative apologists. There was a sense, then, in which Reagan's power was elegiac, presiding over a mythical country with histrionic grace but unable to enforce a "conservative" agenda (on abortion, for instance), and unwilling or unskilled in fighting for draconian measures against a Congress and a good part of the country that would resist or defy such efforts. It was true that there emerged in the Eighties conservative organizations with money and influence, but it was also true that in both politics and culture their impact was limited, and the decade ended without any clarity as to whether they were somehow going to "turn the country around" (to what was never clear). What was clear was that the politics of the decade did not escape the critical eye of popular culture, and if the New Right had dreams about reshaping popular creativity and consumption into something "supportive" or "uplifting," they must have been sorely disappointed. Hollywood could not bring itself to join wholeheartedly in an ideological drumbeat, nor even propagandize for the regime of one of their own, since they knew audiences would have found such fare to be patently silly. Even if there were concessions to the new political *ethos* (e.g., promoting the Soviets to the status of international villains), there was in no way the possibility of reimposition of some sort of cultural consensus that would have turned movie fare into puerility. Perhaps Hollywood, more than anyone, had reason to know that Reagan's power was essentially illusory, the stuff that dreams are made of, and that elegiac politics was unlikely to attempt a politico-cultural agenda beyond its capacity.

There was not, then, in the 1980s a merger of Hollywood and Washington beyond the mythic, and below this metapolitical level it was very much politics as usual. It likely can even be argued that American political and economic power actually declined during the Reagan ascendancy, and that all the posturing about American political centrality and destiny had more to do with the management of decline than the restoration of the American Century. George Bush's brave talk about a "second American Century," acclaimed well before the completion of the first one, was met with amusement and disdain in the new foreign capitals of power and wealth, as they continued to treat the United States as an economic market rather than a political model, and much to our anxiety, bought up more and more of our property and perogatives. For all of the Reaganesque self-congratulation that characterized the Eighties, there were disquieting undercurrents of doubt and fear--doubt that our national self-assertion amounted to anything more than the defiant cries of a musclebound giant helpless to defeat the armies of change, and fear that our mad search for national self-vindication would have apocalyptic consequences in war, economic collapse, or more insidiously, temporal eclipse as the sun of power shines elsewhere. In the Eighties, the more power had to be asserted the more it became difficult to exercise, since much of the country, and the rest of the world, resisted the consequences of American aggressiveness and self-willed right to rule. With Reagan, we were content with the ritual celebration of power, since such a restriction contained power to military theatrics and rhetorical apologetics.

The merger of Hollywood and Washington was often heralded as a triumph of style over substance, but it is more accurate to say that it was a triumph of our movie-educated imaginations over the recalcitrant realities of the new global economy and world powers. In a sense, Hollywood in the Eighties became more than ever a bastion of our political consciousness, acutely aware of the shifts and subtleties of public opinion during the period that was to give the 1980s the overlay of optimism and pride, but also the undercurrent of anxious discomfort with our renewed fantasies of innocent and destined national power. The official doctrine of the age was alleged to be a "new conservatism," although critics argued it was a conservatism that conserved nothing, threatening limited government and civil liberties, the social "safety net" and the tradition of government altruism, and the international role of America as a benevolent and peaceful force. More deeply, there were those who maintained that Reagan had eradicated our historical memory and the hard lessons of our recent past in favor of movie-made memory that was more pleasant and conflict-free, reassuring us of personal and national happy endings foreordained by the mythographers who write our scripts. In the Eighties, it was difficult for political opponents and critics to oppose and criticize a collective solipsism that desired for the moment the joys of political irresponsibility, basking in the warmth of a metapolitical present vindicated by the glory of our cinemaphotogenic past. But, curiously, it was not difficult for the movies to retain critical and even oppositional faculties, and in any case to dance around the political assertions and consequences of the Reagan years without altogether wholehearted enthusiasm.

In that regard, Hollywood responded to the revival of "capitalist values" with the advent of the Reagan Right in ways that were not totally supportive. There was a tendency to treat capitalism as a not totally unalloyed blessing, and that capitalist success did not necessarily confer heroic status. Oddly, the decade even began with a reminder that the United Stated had a reform tradition of the Left, in Warren Beatty's epic rendition of the political and personal lives and adventures of John Reed and Louise Bryant in *Reds* (1981). *Reds* was something of a *Gone With the Wind* for the Left, with its hero and heroine suffering through sweeping events (the Russian Revolution) but enjoying intense love. The oddity was, however, that they were American political radicals dedicated to the demise of capitalism, unlikely heroes for a political age that extolled the virtues of capital investment (including backing popular movies like *Reds*). *Reds* softened the radical politics of Reed and Bryant through their romantic love interest, intellectual independence as journalists, and witness to grand historical events and personages. Yet like so much in the 1980s, *Reds* was elegiac, as if the American reform tradition, including the New Deal and the radical movements of the Sixties, was now safely behind us, a curiosity of history. *Reds* was viewed at the White House with the calm assurance that for whatever minor disturbance the people depicted (and the surviving "witnesses") might have caused, the progress of bourgeois democracy and corporate capitalism was now safely beyond their criticism or mass appeal.

The extraordinarily ambivalent, and largely comic, attitude the movies took toward the alleged "capitalist revival" of the Eighties suggests an underlying reluctance to fully accept the consequences of the system's "accumulative justice." The Reagans symbolized the advent of a new "Gilded Age" complete with the opulence and vulgar display of ostentatious wealth worthy of the robber barons of old. Like so much else of this archaic leisure class, their untrained incapacity across class, racial, or gender lines limited not only their empathy but also their generosity. But they served as a model and rationale for many among the young who sought justification for their pursuit of wealth to the exclusion of social consciousness or even consequences, and their emulation of conspicuous consumption in fashionable lifestyle. Yet neither the gerontocratic elite led by Reagan nor the speculative entrepreneurial class that they admired as heroes escaped the critical attention of the movies. As always, Hollywood did not directly attack capitalism itself, but it did distinguish between good and bad capitalists, and depicted the silliness and venality that the popular mind believes characterizes the excessively wealthy. Perhaps this was captured best in *Trading Places* (1983), a prince-and-the- pauper fantasy that switches a black derelict with a white Yuppie commodities trader as a cruel experiment by arrogant and aged wealthy brothers. The movie contrasts the lives of the opulently wealthy with hardscrabble street people, leading eventually to a joint capital venture for revenge by the ruined trader, his replacement, and the inevitable whore with a golden heart that gives the brothers their well-deserved comeuppance, providing that the "best way to hurt rich people is to make them poor people." But it does not condemn capitalism, only an archaic form of "old money" amongst a Scroogean elite who can and should be replaced by younger and more deserving, indeed more "liberal," capitalists who can combine the wisdom of streets and suites. Indeed, in the tradition of Renoir's *Boudu Saved from Drowning* and *My Man Godfrey, Down and Out in Beverly Hills* (1986) brings together a rich and vacuous family in crisis with a homeless and impoverished man whom they save from a suicide attempt in their swimming pool, but upon whom they become dependent to reform their lives. Here the union of the hapless and empty rich and a streetwise companion and mentor is complete, with the family regressing to their previous state of psychic disorders without him, finally begging him to return so that he can continue to "give them what they want," which is apparently an advisory ability on how to cope with the burdens of wealth. Both in the marketplace and at home, the impact of capitalism on our lives had to be amended to include individual, but not social, justice in order to include the excluded.

There was even in the Eighties some reflection on what capitalism does to us when we are lured into its practice and experience its benefits. In *Risky Business* (1983), the teenage hero left alone at home parlays his rudimentary knowledge of enterprise from a "Junior Achievement" project into a thriving, if illegal, prostitution business, one that leaves him broke, threatens his life, but ironically leads to his admission to an elite school and thus entry into an elite safe from the "street capitalisms" which had taught him so much. Indeed, those who sought mobility up the corporate ladder were indeed involved in risky business, since achievement in such a world requires unethical and illegal behavior. In *The Secret of My Success* (1987), the young mail room clerk acts out a fantasy of instant hierarchical power, eventually bringing him into the comforts of the boardroom and stretch limousine by brash, unscrupulous, and helpful actions that earn him entry into the citadel of power and wealth. But Hollywood's glimpses into those citadels were not very reassuring. In *Wall Street* (1987), the young protégé of a big-time financial operator becomes corrupted by his ambitions and admiration for his charming and demonic mentor, who exemplifies the moral price of a fluid and cunning economic world. The "inside traders" are brought to justice, the young man has learned his lesson, and the "good capitalists" are once again in charge on the Eighties street of dreams. In a wide variety of period films (*Beverly Hills Cop, Robocop, Aliens*), big business people are engaged in enterprises that are illegal and immoral. Even the much-vaunted Yuppies were rarely depicted as heroes; quite the contrary, they were constantly being degraded as unable to cope without their possessions or outside their haunts (aside from *Trading Places*, there were such films as *The Money Pit, Lost in America, Something Wild, After Hours*, and *Desperately Seeking Susan*).

This is not to say that the movies of the Eighties indiscriminately attacked the structure and conduct of American society as it was being practiced, but they often did find that the present did not compare favorably with the past. Part of Reagan's success stemmed from his longevity, reminding us of a golden past that he would represent and revive in the "fallen" present. This prelapsarian myth took many forms, including placing wisdom and feistiness in gerontocratic leaders, much like Reagan himself, from which the present could learn much (*Cocoon, On Golden Pond, Tough Guys, 18 Again, The Color of Money*). If there was, for all the national self-congratulation about "standing tall" again, a lingering sense that the present was past redemption, then either times or voices from the past were important to heed or even return to. The past was used as a nostalgic setting to re-enact the past or re-think the present, from the Forties (*Radio Days*) and the Fifties (*Hoosiers, Diner, Back to the Future, Peggy Sue got Married*), to the very point of the perceived Fall from grace, the happy "Camelot" days of Kennedy before the complications that led to the present (*Dirty Dancing, Tin Men, Little Shop of Horrors, Hairspray*). But we were in the Eighties also self-conscious about our dimished state, something that endeared us to Reagan all the more as he told us of our shameful condition. Indeed, in the movies, we were constantly being visited by outside observers innocent of our grotesque ways that were superior if sympathetic to our plight (*E. T., Cocoon, Starman, Tough Guys, Crocodile Dundee, Coming to America*). Like Reagan, such figures from "outside" the present were both more innocent and more powerful, able to exercise both contempt for and mastery of the American present.

There was even the suggestion in the virtually idolatrous allegiance to Reagan that somehow the postlapsarian past could be denied or altered so that the revitalizing force of the values and practices of the past could inform the present, and restore the continuity of American mythic history into the Hollywoodish happy ending of the future. In *Back to the Future* (1985), the present life for young Marty McFly is disillusioning, with a rundown town and unhappy and unsuccessful family. But he vows that "history is going to change," and returns by time machine to

1955, a time of social prosperity and peace. But he cannot transport that into the Eighties; rather, he alters the basis of his parental relationship (the father stops aggression through counter-violence, gaining the respect of his wife-to-be and his own self-respect), which when he returns to the present has borne fruit in their private happiness and success, although it has not altered the decay of the community. Thus we could restore private virtue through individual achievement, but could ignore as impossible the restoration of social prosperity and justice (the present has abandoned stores, homeless street people, even terrorists), since the former took precedence over the latter in the "new beginning" of an America sustained in its illusions. As the "public household" of the country was being abandoned, the private household was celebrated with sanction and traditional structure, sustaining the distinction between the legitimacy of private power and the illegitimacy of community power in the solution to our historical disintegration. It was a popular and diverting solution, but one whose comforts might not outlast the eventual realization of the consequences of social neglect for private prosperity. (By contrast, in *Peggy Sue Got Married*, 1986, the heroine discovers on return to the Fifties that its romantic charm and social superiority are an artifice of the politics of the Eighties, an illusion imputed from the present to the past. Rather than altering her past, she accepts it as a necessary preface to a not altogether pleasant future; nevertheless, it is still a private solution coping with an individual disillusionment now of both past and future, reconciled for her own personal, if not the country's, political history.)

This play with the past in the 1980s culminated in *Field of Dreams* (1989), in which ancient lapses (the Black Sox scandal, a metaphor for our many failures out of greed and pettiness) and recent aberrations (the rebellion of the Sixties) are forgiven in a reconciliation of generations, experiences, and ideology. The elysian baseball field at the metaphysical core of the American heartland represents both our link with our past selves and the divine blessing that now Americans once again can come and give thanks for. Here is a vision of a politics of reconciliation at the end of the Eighties that brings together divergent past political stances in a fantasy of transcendent union, appealing to a fundamental faith in the American Dream, and as with Reagan, American dreamers. The magical field reminds us how much we wish to believe in our own national timelessness and cultural union, and how easily we seem to be able to forgive ourselves for past political and personal divergences from the true faith. By making peace with our pasts, we restore faith in our individual and national future, a fantasy that might not insure our actual political future but certainly renewed our faith in the magical power of movies to appeal to the cultural bases of American innocence and rectitude that underwrite political power.

There was in the 1980s movies very little direct treatment of Reagan, but there was an implicit theme of heroic leadership through a public automaton who is controlled or informed by hidden managers directing the words and actions of the performer. We assume again that moviemakers were grinding no political ax, but the cluster of such films was too large and recurrent to be entirely accidental or apolitical. In *Broadcast News* (1987), for instance, the articulate and handsome television news reporter is a "mouthpiece" for the much smarter hidden producer backstage who guides the public performer. Reagan's presidential career was characterized by praise for his public demeanor, tempered by the evidence that he was a compliant and "easily handled" figure who saw his role as playing president. With the premium on performance, we became used to the idea that Reagan was not a free agent, and were satisfied with the quality of the political simulation of presidential greatness manipulated by his team of media managers. This theme of collaboration on the creation of a public automaton took many forms in the movies, but in all cases represented something very much in the backs of our political minds (*Innerspace*, *No Way Out*, *Roxanne*, *Making Mr. Right*, *Mannequin*, *Power*, and *Without a Clue*). An interesting variant on this theme was *My Favorite Year* (1982), in which an aging movie idol in the new age of television brings his movie-mythic heroism to bear on a semi-fictional (and televised) situation after much coaching and reassurance that we need him to act for us since we "need him to be larger than life." Even though his heroic intervention is in a sense a mediated contrivance, nevertheless with such a star we "forgive a lot." Reagan, as we have noted, successfully cast himself in the mold of Hollywood heroes who were both ordinary and extraordinary, combinations of democratic commonality and epic adventurous spirit, represented in the Reagan era perhaps most fully by the Indiana Jones movies, with the political inference that not only democratic but extraordinary heroism is possible, but it can be undertaken as a virtually neo-imperial venture without reservations about American intervention in foreign, and specifically Third World, settings. The comic-book heroics of an Indiana Jones sustains the impression that things done by popular-political heroes can be done easily, without cost or danger, and with the assurance of American victory in a simplified world of the discovery and defeat of identifiably nefarious villains of equal comic-book stature.

It was in this political atmosphere that Reagan was able to revive something of the glory days of the Cold War by conjuring up one of the more venerable popular images of villainy, the

Russians. The Russians have since World War II served as a significant and largely negative political Other, and in the new milieu of American nationalist reassertion, served once again as a convenient political villain not only responsible for much of the world's ills but also as a political projection of virtually every negative attribute that we seem to fear about ourselves--aging, incompetence, aggressiveness, stupidity, the possibility that we have become a political dinosaur like them, locked in a mortal combat that is destroying both. In a wide variety of movies, we vicariously defeat the Russians, stealing their airplanes (*Firefox*), escaping from their evil clutches (*White Nights*), or defeating their inhuman but super-trained athletes (*Rocky IV*), in all cases reassuring ourselves that they are committed foes who we are certain to best in whatever endeavor. Their image as stolid and unattractive bunglers was shaken by the advent of the Gorbachevs, and the uses of rage against "the evil empire" began to play itself out as Reagan himself made the popular and expedient transition from warmonger to peacemaker. With the decline of the Soviet villain in the late Eighties, Hollywood searched for new villains with which American heroes could contest, using Third World dictators, terrorists, and drug dealers, but none measured up to the Soviet colossus that in two political periods of moviemaking gave us the most satisfying foreign foe, combining fear about their superhuman and subhuman status. But for movie audiences before Reagan's conversion, there were delicious moments of cinematic revenge against the hapless Russians. In *Red Dawn* (1984), a group of teenagers fight a guerilla action against Russian and Cuban invaders who have communized Colorado's franchise foods. The invaders take over a woefully unprepared and compliant populace with disconcerting ease, leaving the defense of the republic in the hands of teenagers who revert to barbarism and sexual denial, straining our credulity enough, but who acquit themselves well against alien troops and targets. Yet the invasion fantasy did not enjoy quite the vogue that refighting, and often revenging, Vietnam enjoyed, offering us a vicarious victory over the Communists. But such films as *Invasion, USA* (1985), *The Hidden* (1986), *Alien Nation* (1988) and *They Live* (1988) played again with the consequences of alien infiltration and attempts at control, and indeed in *No Way Out* (1987) a trusted American naval commander turns out to be a Russian mole in the Pentagon who disrupts military policy. However, if the astonishing turnabout in Soviet-American relations was anything more than Reagan's sense of theatrical climax, then negative images of the Russians may disappear from the movies for awhile.

One of the most remarkable sidelights of the nationalistic ferment that Reagan stirred was the refighting, revenging, and for many perhaps even resolving in their minds the Vietnam War. What was recrudescent in the popular mind was a clear sense that the war was not so much "lost" as unresolved, which became symbolized by the fantasy that there were still American MIA's being held against their will in Indochina. This was the latest version of the captivity narrative so imbedded in American culture, but it served the immediate purpose of letting us win one last vengeful and liberating victory over the enemy we could not actually defeat. This cycle was begun by a surprise 1983 hit, *Uncommon Valor*, beginning the very contemporary notion that an aggressive leader (in this case a Vietnam-era colonel fed up by reluctant State Department bureaucrats) must act independently of established governmental rules in order to achieve worthy goals. This kind of paramilitaristic action against America's foes was continued in such films as Chuck Norris's *Missing in Action, I* and *II*, but most notoriously and successfully in *Rambo: First Blood, II* (1985), in which a virtually sociopathic veteran, jailed for savaging a town (*First Blood, I*), is sent on a rescue mission to Vietnam, but even though he finds MIA's, he is almost betrayed again by his own government, and on return destroys government computers in a rage, as if the rationality such machines represent were the domestic enemy that prevented us from winning there. Audiences "got into" *Rambo* as a kind of ritual catharsis, although the movie was roundly condemned by veterans and critics as perpetuating a fantasy of rescue and the preposterous fear that the Vietnamese, like the Indians of old, were still holding our children in ignominious captivity. The figure of Johnny Rambo was an icon of a muscle-bound superpower lashing out at foreign and domestic enemies in rage and futility, seeking quick revenge without official sanction as an agent for all of those who wish we had won and want to demonstrate that superior warrior unrestrained by political cowards still could defeat an "inferior" and "barbaric" enemy and his Soviet masters. For many observers of the popular response to *Rambo*, we were glimpsing a highly irrational political pathology. But as an expression of the political *ethos* of the Eighties, *Rambo* also involved our ambivalence about government and our inability to do very much that decisively affected the conduct of world economic and political affairs, and the drift of power away from the United States, symbolized by Japanese acquisitions in the United States and the open defiance to American will by Third World leaders. Reagan enjoyed the complicit vigilantism of *Rambo*, casting himself throughout his term in office as someone who shared Johnny Rambo's contempt for government rules and political constraints on the tough actions of rugged individuals acting alone but for their country. This formula reaffirmed in an age of the decline of our power to affect things and a sense of the loss of individual power that heroic action, even if limited to the role of violent avenger, was still possible to realize rough justice against irredeemable foes. But it was movie politics, since such films enjoyed a vogue while real American hostages languished in Beirut and the real Vietnam maintained its independence. There were other military movies that exploited this latent desire, such as *Iron Eagle, Top Gun, Heartbreak Ridge* (all 1986), and *Death before Dishonor* (1987), all of which dealt with a strong patriotic military man forced to take independent action in order to deal our enemies a fatal and well-deserved blow. *Heartbreak Ridge* climaxes with the invasion of Grenada and the triumph of a grizzled veteran Marine over the pettiness and unwillingness to take risks of military bureaucrats, a stance that Reagan associated himself with. Yet the admiration of paramilitary circumvention of bureaucracy inspired Oliver North, whose zeal in actually attempting to enact in real politics the heroic adventures and vigilante justice of such films led, ironically enough, to the Iran-contra revelations that did much to puncture the Reagan bubble.

These films were vaguely associated with the New Right, although it can be much debated as to whether movies that envision political virtue in paramilitary action and defiance of instituted authority are truly "conservative." In some ways they were often more survivalist in tone, in which a remarkable individual such as Rambo learns to distrust not only the country's enemies but also his own government, from local to federal. Reagan, after all, swept into office on the notion that government was the problem, had botched everything, and should be gotten off our backs; and he left office still running against the government he ostensibly had headed. Films associated with the political Right tend to validate the myth of individual efficacy, but extending this to an attack on the very authority that heroes have traditionally defended was an odd, if characteristic, expression of patriotism. Oliver North's clear contempt for legislative and bureaucratic constraints was echoed in the movies. But what was remarkable about this period in American political history was that the same anti-government feeling was pervasive in films that had a liberal, radical, or pacifist bias and theme. Films appeared that were critical of American policy in Latin America, but they shared with the right-wing films the depiction of the U.S. Government as venal, stupid or incompetent. In *Missing* (1982), a family searches for a son who disappears during the anti-Marxist *coup d'état* in Chile. But evil is not confined to quasi-fascist generals, rather it also resides in the U.S. embassy, where the family learns that not only does their own government engineer right-wing coups, but it also lies to its own citizens, refuses to help Americans abroad with the wrong politics, and sees its role as defending big business. In *Under Fire* (1983), CIA agents are unrestrained and murderous, and in *Salvador* (1986) American culpability extends to unsympathetic U.S. immigration officials.

Despite their policy differences with the current American regime, these films all shared the view that one cannot trust one's own government any more than alien governments, since governments all possess the same attribute of hostile intentions toward the individual. Thus disparate "ideological" movies all wind up envisioning a political theme consistent with the *ethos* of the age: that the individual is alienated from government; heroic actions for worthwhile values or causes are taken with the active hostility and interference of government, and thus must be defied or circumvented; and thus, as Reaganites argue, virtue and initiative resides in the individual, who rightfully must fend for himself or herself in order to achieve justice. What tended to distinguish the "left-wing" movies was that government was more powerful than the individual, and justice was not done. This was clear enough for those with unconventional political views, as with the radical retrospective on the Rosenberg case and the persecution of the Old Left in the 1950s in *Daniel* (1983). But it also applied to cases of good American capitalists, such as *Tucker* (1988), who tried to build an innovative new car after World War II, but in the film is thwarted by a conspiracy of Detroit and Washington. Similarly, a cluster of films about women being treated unjustly by a hostile and insensitive legal bureaucracy (*A Cry in the Dark; The Accused*; and *The Good Mother*, all 1988) expressed the same liberal pessimism about a government bureaucracy which was mired in deadly procedures and disinterest in the truth that would serve justice. Something of the same theme persisted in films about ordinary individuals who become victims of organizational power. In *Silkwood* (1983), an employee at a nuclear production plant becomes a union activist who is suspicious of plant safety. She and her house are apparently contaminated by the company, and when she takes evidence to a reporter, is murdered, becoming a martyr for anti-nuclear forces. In two of the "save-the-farm" movies, the heroic resistance of small farm families and their rural allies wins temporary respites but the powerful forces pitted against them remain. In *Country* (1984), the Department of Agriculture representatives could not be less helpful, and the film ends with foreclosure still on the horizon. In *The River* (1984), state government and agribusiness are in league against small farmers, and even though the family farm is saved from destruction, the powerful remind the powerless that in the long run those with power will win, hardly a heartening prospect after so much resistance.

The interplay of such themes across the ideological and social spectrum suggests that in the Eighties there were many different kinds of political fears and doubts, unrelieved by popular reassurances in the movies that one's own government was either sympathetic or helpful. A sense of alienation is the breeding ground of populist resentment against authorities and enemies, often seen as one and the same. The movies can exploit these resentments by depictions in which heroes fight back, lashing out and besting stereotyped social foes. Two movies from this period are of comparable interest, since they represent the desire for resentful action that punishes not only political and social opponents, but authority in general, since the distinction between good and bad authorities has collapsed. The first of these is *Aliens* (1986) in which an intelligent and liberated woman is betrayed by her corporate employers and failed by a military force to the point that she must take action herself to defeat an alien race and prevent their use as a military weapon by the corporation. In the process she becomes an androgynous superbeing who not only defeats a threatening alien and her offspring (justifying a kind of "liberal genocide" in defense of Earth and motherhood) but also proves that women can be hardline feminists as capable of "rational" violence as men, and as willing as men to act upon their loathing of both alien threats to maternal power and domestic threats from stupid, weak, or venal men. The second movie is *Die Hard* (1988), involving a policeman who stumbles into multiple alien threats, a party wherein Japanese corporate executives are taken hostage in their high-rise headquarters by German terrorists. The policeman defeats them, of course, but in the process expresses much working-class male rage against his feminist wife who left him for a career, snobbish Yuppie executives, the police and television news, and contemptible foreign terrorists and our new Japanese masters. This film's orientation is vaguely "right-wing," but in effect it shares with *Aliens* an enormous sense of resentment against the world with which both hero and heroine are forced to deal, in particular against those who represent arrogant or manipulative power. But it is the universality of that resentment that is remarkable, suggesting that underneath the overlay of normalcy and niceness to which the Reagans appealed were dark and raging emotions unfulfilled by the largely symbolic gestures of the Administration. Indeed, by the late Eighties, there was the reappearance of Everyman, superceding the Superman of "the Rambo impulse," often unable to control evil forces around himself or herself, and often exposed to a dark underside of society hidden from respectable view or official recognition. This collective act of denial or association, preserving the facade of polite society, can be easily violated by a wrong turn or a random meeting, and the hero subjected to a sense of helplessness (as in films such as *D. O. A.* and *Frantic*) or degradation by remorseless denizens of the social underworld (as in *Something Wild, Lethal Weapon*, and *Blue Velvet*). If the movies at that time were beginning to capture a sense that superheroics was ludicrous and that the persistence of social evil made ordinary and unthreatened life problematic, then we might have been witness to a subtle but significant change in popular attitude.

Something of the same process appears to have gone on in those mature films of the late 1980s that tried to come to grips with some unsavory aspect of the recent American past, a past that it had been the fashion to either deny or denigrate. Most notable at the time was the attempt to deal with Vietnam in ways other than fantasies of revenge and rescue. These films--*Platoon* (1987), *Full Metal Jacket* (1988) and *Hamburger Hill* (1988)--shared with *Rambo* our interest in what went wrong in Vietnam, but unlike the rectification of history into myth that *Rambo* implied, they suggested that war was not a romantic adventure but rather an existential nightmare, made all the worse by the confused purposes and insane logic of the Vietnam war in particular. If *Rambo* tried to rescue the American heroic self and bring it home in self-respect and glory despite our own government, these films in one way or another expressed a deep split in ourselves, and that duality meant that we were at war with ourselves as to what we were doing in this alien land. *Platoon* was directed by a Vietnam veteran with clear antiwar sentiments, yet the film is not only about the horror of war, but rather more about having to fight without clear social support or military unity and purpose. But at least the soldier-protagonist who is divided between the good and evil sergeants learns from the experience, returning home with hope that the division in the American soul has now been resolved through learning, rather than some fantastic hope of returning to Vietnam to unlearn, and undo, what happened there before the Fall. He now can return home with his soul cleansed and united, with the murderous or restrained victims of the contradiction left behind dead. Yet *Platoon* at least holds out the possibility of reason learned by and from survivors of the war; *Full Metal Jacket* denies even that possibility. The Marine trainees of that movie have entered a "death culture," a disciplined tribe dedicated to dehumanized violence. But to become efficient killers, they have to abandon not only the possibility of reason but also hope. Vietnam becomes the forum for a savage heroism freed from the civilized part of the American Self, but once we have descended into such hellish expression, there is no return to either individual or social redemption. Whereas *Rambo* suggested that we were victims of some sort of elite betrayal, and *Platoon* that there was a moral and political lesson learned of never again, *Full Metal Jacket* said that we were not victims but perpetuators, had learned nothing from the war, and that in a sense we were still there and not even really looking for a way out. With the possibility that Vietnam could be interpreted as the emblem of a national descent into nihilism (the conclusion from *Hamburger Hill* was that "It don't mean nothing"), it was no wonder that great political effort was undertaken to give meaningful credence to the Vietnam effort, since future Third World interventions held the danger of comparison. In any case, it was clear that Vietnam continued to remain an unresolved wound in the popular mind, and Hollywood found it a setting and reference for a wide variety of experiences (cf. *Good Morning, Vietnam; The Killing Fields; The Iron Triangle; Lethal Weapon*).

The other unresolved war much on the mind of the Eighties was one not yet fought: World War III. With the return of clear bellicosity to Washington, expressed as a willingness to fight a nuclear war on the fantasy that it could be limited and winnable, popular fears about the possibility of such a catastrophe were given cinematic form. Hollywood's imagination of the ultimate disaster took two broad narrative strategies either depicting the danger of nuclear war as something clear and present but averted at the last moment by heroic intervention, or showing what responses were made after the disaster occurs. The latter was more satisfying than the former, and there really was only one post-nuclear film of note that focused on the immediate personal aftermath of a nuclear war, the restrained *Testament* (1983), wherein a mother and her children await with stoic resolution their death from radiation poisoning. This movie had plenty of pathetic touches, such as abandoned and dying children, to underscore its anti-nuclear point of view, but it insisted on depicting such thoroughgoing bourgeois responsibility (maintaining neighborhood norms of cleanliness and neatness) in the face of slow death that it strained credulity. Like *On the Beach*, the post-nuclear fantasy of *Testament* was oddly non-apocalyptic, with most people accepting their fate as victims in much the same way they accepted the existence of nuclear weapons before they were used. Hollywood and audiences were much more taken with fantasies of the ultimate disaster averted, since they could play with a primal fear but leave the theater reassured that somehow it won't happen. Various agents of nuclear mercy, such as James Bond (*Never Say Never Again*) and clairvoyants (*The Dead Zone*), prevented us from experiencing the worst. But clearly the most perceptive of the doomsday thrillers was *War Games* (1983), a tale of a boy and his computer who break in NORAD and begin a nuclear conversation and game with the defense supercomputer, triggering a countdown to nuclear launch. After much trepidation, the teenager finally convinces the authorities to let the computer stop the madness by learning the futility of playing, with the computer finally expressing the moral lesson of the nuclear game, that the only winning move is not to play. The ingenious young man who both precipitates and resolves the crisis is a kind of Sorcerer's Apprentice who learns the folly of fooling around with computer science. But we all learn the folly of war games themselves, with the NORAD headquarters as a theater of the absurd, wherein the fate of humankind becomes an arcane game remote from the existential realities of life, with its own internal logic devoid of reference to the real American world it was ostensibly designed to protect. In *War Games*, the disaster is averted, and the teenager becomes a hero to the military and technocrats who control the system; but once he is gone, and we are satisfied by the aversion, the controllers return the nuclear deterrence system to "normal," and we are left with the nagging question of whether someday heroic intervention that stops a system of death from doing what it is designed to do will not happen in time.

     With the possibility of nuclear holocaust still quite on our minds, film-makers of the Eighties envisioned an apocalyptic future that was either post-nuclear or more broadly "post-civilizational." These ranged from depictions of a kind of "urban Gothic" future of ruined cities and decayed civilizations to "desert worlds" of bleak countrysides peopled by desperate and predatory groups struggling to survive. Indeed, one of the darkest undercurrents imagined by popular films in the Eighties was this pessimistic and often dystopian view of the future. It was virtually impossible to find a futuristic film that offered an optimistic vision of things to come. The "urban Gothic" movies (cf., *Escape from New York, Blade Runner, Brazil, Robocop, The Running Man*) gave us a glimpse of a future city in decay and ruin in the wake of some sort of holocaust that left an urban hell that was either partially or completely ungovernable. If there is government, it is not legitimate nor effective, since it is involved in exploiting an environment that is anarchic and reduced to barbarism. Those with power in such a world--corporations, television networks, paramilitary police, street warlords--are completely cynical and manipulative. They certainly have no illusions about the restoration of political civility and benevolent rule; their ambitions might be totalitarian, but their capabilities of control are limited. The state that most resembles Orwell's model of a future totalitarian order from *1984* is depicted in *Brazil* (1985), yet it too rules without any hope of order triumphing over chaos. Rather it is a comic Orwellian state, whose pretensions to total control render it absurd and bungling, as grotesque in its gigantism as its hapless functionary-victim is in his pathetic desires for freedom and happiness. There was a rather faithful movie version of *1984* out in 1985, but *Brazil* was much more imaginative, capturing not only Orwell's original point about the demonic logic of totalitarianism, but now also our doubts about the rationality of large governments in general, and the somewhat more comedic and contemptuous attitude we entertain towards administrators and politicians. *Brazil* shared with the other "urban Gothic" films, and for that matter many other politically relevant movies, the recurrent sense that the powers that be in the "post-modern" world are either indifferent and incompetent or downright malignant and manipulatory. The decayed cities of these films are futuristic nightmares of the lack of control, in which governments, public or private, are either at war with their own subjects or attempt to divert them through the circus of entertainment. What is strikingly absent is any belief in progress toward either mastery of the future or the reinstitution of political benevolence, as exemplified by the decline of the city into irredeemable and neglected ruin. Similarly, the desert worlds of the many "warriors of the wasteland" films (most notably, the *Road Warrior* series) were survivalist in tone, with a reversion to barbarian cultures struggling for existence in worlds of ecological and political scarcity, without any hope given for the restoration of civilization as we have known it.

There was also no dearth of images of political elites that showed them to be out of touch with the realities of life outside of their palatial courts and protected illusions as to the way the world works. Perhaps one of the most prescient films of the period was *Being There* (1979), in which a mature simpleton whose life had been restricted to working as a gardener for a wealthy protector and whose education consisted solely of watching television is thrown into contact with a wealthy industrialist and then his friend the U.S. president. His television-trained manner and simple talk of the cycles of the garden impresses them into thinking he is a man of rare bearing and wisdom, demonstrating their own inability to distinguish truth from cliché as well as their desire to believe in optimistic metaphors that validate their own hopes and position. *The Last Emperor* (1987) depicted a ruler who lives in the majestic isolation and splendor of a court that is radically separated from, and irrelevant to, the political turmoil outside the palace. *Empire of the Sun* (1988) shows an elite living in a splendid dream world with little knowledge of or interest in the turbulence outside their protection. In these and many of the films we have already discussed, elites recurrently appear as arrogant and remote, secure and privileged within their penthouses and pleasuredomes, but without a clue as to the conditions out on the street or farm. In some measure, their sensibility characterized the Eighties because of the "imperial presidency" and the opulent lifestyle of the rich and famous, but also because of a more general feeling that not only were elites not capable of or even interested in coping with the growing problems that beset our lives, but that change for the worse was something beyond their comprehension and control.

If this is a correct assessment, it helps explain why the Eighties included filmic stories about individual rage or anomie to the point of nihilism.   The rage of a disillusioned and spiteful veteran or policeman was recurrently directed at a variety of social types against whom neglected or abused heroes might hate-- feminists, drug dealers, terrorists, bureaucrats, street gangs, and so on.   While such hostile outbursts may be cathartic, other film images dealt with the inability of people to find an easy way to express their fury and confusion.   In *Alamo Bay* (1985), hard-pressed Gulf Coast fishermen are incensed at the encroachment of Vietnamese fishing boats as competition, and turn to the Ku Klux Klan as a violent and nativist solution.   Similarly, in *Betrayal* (1988), Midwestern farmers are drawn into the conspiratorial fantasies and vigilante outrages of neo-fascist survivalist groups. But perhaps the lingering sense of thwarted rage and anomic existence was best expressed in *Talk Radio* (1989), a movie about an insult-the-caller late-night radio talk show host whose jeremiads against the conditions of the country are interspersed with his banter with a depressing variety of lonely and other pathological callers.   Most of them treat it as "tabloid radio," an outlet for their frustrations by either identifying with or expressing their hatred of the host.   But the conspiratorial Right takes him seriously, and indeed he begins to feel himself a spokesperson for some sort of mass rage and frustration that no one else is articulating or acting upon.   But only the lunatic fringe is capable of caring about what is said, and the film ends with his callers still talking into a night, and a country, without meaning.   The anomic and drugged young people in *Less Than Zero* (1987) and *River's Edge* (1987) are both nihilistic and soporific, unable either to comprehend or respond to moral or political choices.   They seem unable to locate themselves in time, or care much about a future.   If they are representative of the American future, then there likely won't be one at least in the way we might want it to be.   In any case, the persistence of this pessimistic strain in American film reminded us that the official gloss of rosy expectations and self-congratulation might well be just an overlay that ignored a thousand points of blight beneath.

The persistence of social divisions that tended to be ignored during the 1980's was nowhere better illustrated than in Spike Lee's *Do The Right Thing* (1989).   This film concerned itself with race relations in an inner-city setting, centering around a pizzeria owned by Italian-Americans catering to a largely black clientele.   Tensions mount on a blistering hot day, and the neighborhood's seething racial hatreds are revealed.   The poor blacks resent Italian pride, symbolized by the pictures of famous Italian-Americans on the wall (DiMaggio, Sinatra, Marciano) and the refusal of the owner to put up pictures of prominent blacks to please black customers.   They also resent the Korean immigrants who run a successful inner-city store, and the police that contemptuously patrol their neighborhood. The feeling among those resented is mutual, all coming to a climax with a racial confrontation in the pizzeria, a riot in which a black youth is killed by the police, and then the torching of the restaurant. This apocalyptic ending conveyed the black director's feeling that race relations in Eighties America were that bad, and getting worse because of a decade of malign neglect and a growing gap between not only rich and poor, but also white and black. *Do The Right Thing* was a view of American society from the bottom, a point of blight that conveyed a sense of hopelessness as to the resolution of a racial crisis that lurked beneath the purview of official optimism and elite opulence.

As the Eighties ended, there was no clear resolution of the political agenda that had originally given it a "conservative" thrust. Throughout, Hollywood continued to make films that had clear antiwar or progressive sentiments attached. Even during all of the renewed militarism and war talk of the early 1980s, a movie about *Gandhi* (1982) won the Academy Award for best picture, treating with reverence the memory of the great advocate of non-violent resistance, and associating itself as inspiration for the anti-nuclear movement. A little film entitled *Amazing Grace and Chuck* (1987), about a small boy and a professional basketball player who led an anti-nuclear movement, became something of a cult film in anti-nuclear circles. Robert Redford's *The Milagro Beanfield War* (1988) suggested that an established ethnic community rooted in the traditions of the soil could successfully resist the encroachments of superimposed upscale development that destroys community and environment. Too, there was considerable cinematic interest in the radical and liberal traditions of the American past, traditions that filmmakers and audiences did not reject as devoid of meaning nor impossible to revive. *Matewan* (1988) dealt with a classic labor struggle. Beginning with *Mississippi Burning* (1989), there were a series of films exploring the conflict over racial integration and civil rights that agitated the South, and eventually the entire country, in the 1950s and 1960s. Indeed, at safe distance, movies began to look at the social conflicts of the Sixties (cf., *Running on Empty* and *1969*, both released in 1988) with none of the nostalgia and resignation of *The Big Chill* (1983) but rather with the implicit hope that the Eighties could learn something from the vitality and commitment that gave that period its exciting flavor and receptivity to change. If there was a kind of retrospective idealism running through such films, it did not seem to stem from a complete sense that the American future was to be a hopeless descent into political stagnation and reaction.

In any event, the movies of the Eighties demonstrated that it was a somewhat more complex and multi-directional era than the political personage who presided over it might have wished. At its conclusion, there was not even much consensus as to whether we were freer, safer, or even richer because of what has transpired. Some films did join and exploit the conservative tide, but others expressed contrary and oblique political communications, ideas and images that resisted the urge toward simplicity and single-dimensionality. In an ironic way, political Hollywood flourished during the ascendancy of one of its own, but without returning to some kind of movie-made Golden Age, either on screen or off, that made the older myths about America it had given cinematic life to coincide with the contemporary American condition. The movies of the Eighties expressed what we were at the time, which was the sum of all that we had been, but to which we added what it is that we are becoming now.

Afterword

It is the stated purpose of a filmography to provide readers with a sketchy map of the territory they are attempting to encompass. Since political movies do not constitute a clearly defined genre, they can be viewed on our imaginary map as something that are not a sharply recognizable feature of the cultural atlas. But even if they are not easily seen, the interplay of political and cultural dynamics is strong enough for us to discover that the relationship between what's going on in politics and what's appearing on the movie screen is worth knowing. But now that we have traversed the contours of the map, it is worthwhile for us to reflect on our travels, however exploratory.

It seems clear enough on reflection that Hollywood approaches politics as a topic for the movies with its usual caution, but it is unfair to say that commercial moviemakers have always avoided political controversy. As we have seen, they will often come to political subjects in ways that do not directly and immediately confront an event or process that is currently part of the political environment. Yet for all of Hollywood's claim that they are not political, it seems clear from our filmographic tour that they have always been aware of politics, incorporated politics into their movies, and if anything, have become more openly political over the decades. If there is merit to our broad and speculative approach to politics in the movies, then the reader should take away from this work the conviction that politics is interwoven into the fabric of movies even if the intentions of the moviemaker and the content of the film are on face patently apolitical. This is not to say that all films are political, but it is to say that many films are much more amenable to political interpretation than we might think at first glance. Some of the movies we have discussed above were neither "ideological" nor propaganda, nor made the slightest direct reference to politics, but in our terms they were political because we can learn much of the political *ethos* of a time by examining what they were about. Our effort has been to place films in some kind of very real temporal context, without unduly burdening them with an inclusive and abstract theory that predetermines their participation in a political time. If we had a guide for our journey through uncharted territory, it was not Marx nor Freud but rather Machiavelli.

Reliance on Machiavelli allows us to take an "agnostic" approach to the movies and politics. Rather than prejudge the nature of politics, we took his rather abductive perspective, asking instead what the political situation is, how and by whom power is

being exercised, and what the imagined outcomes to power
struggles might be. Considering these questions grounds us
solidly in the warp and woof of politics as it unfolds in time, and
reminds us that at the core of politics is the dynamic process of
communication. Political communication includes the
manipulation of appearances and the mobilization of opinion. But
how we understand the ebb and flow of ongoing communication is
often difficult and subtle. What has motivated our inquiry here is
the idea that forms of popular communication, occurring in a
given political context, may offer us a key insight into the
interplay of art and experience. Moviemaking and moviegoing is
an endless dialectic, but it is always an aesthetic creation that is
directed toward popular audiences who want to be entertained and
edified. But if the mutual process of learning by the parties to the
transaction does take place, then movies do become important
artifacts of political communication worthy of serious study. As
the bibliography that follows attests, more and more scholars are
beginning to take this hypothesized relationship seriously.

Our claims here are rather modest, but now it is clear that
students of politics and the movies must move beyond this
perspective for more ambitious theoretical constructions than
simply the relation of film to political time and place. Some of
these efforts might include the placement of the movies in theories
of American culture, or in the more arcane and exalted theoretical
perspectives that abound. It might be worthwhile for us to
conclude our inquiry by stating one hypothesis about the movies
and politics that deserve investigation.

For reasons of convenience and insight, we divided our
inquiry up into rough decades as periods characterized by an
identifiable political *ethos* that the movies help us understand.
But obviously there are politically powerful themes that transcend
decades, and indeed may become cumulative over time. This
"transperiodical" viewpoint is more ambitious and sweeping than
what we have attempted here, involving the identification of
recurring or accumulating themes in the movies that offer us
popular evidence of where the political culture is going in time. To
be sure, certain themes that are rooted deeply in national
mythology--such as the belief in national mission and the fear of
alien captivity--recur in politics and the movies. But it may be the
case also that thematic changes over time take on a pattern that
cannot be discounted as simply characteristic of a particular
period that will disappear in due time. The movies may record
political sentiments and thoughts that persist even through
periods of political renewal or decay, revealing an aesthetic
imagination of a political and cultural trend that transcends a
particular time.

Many things have changed with the movies since their inception. The movies quite obviously demonstrate the expansion of tolerance and choice as to subject matter, imagery, and language. Many older Americans are upset that the movies include shocking themes and are not uniformly "uplifting," although it is a myth that they ever were that puerile or uncritical. But it is generally true, I suspect, that the movies are willing to probe aspects of society and politics that many would prefer to remain untreated and unrevealed, and that as time goes on they have repeatedly focused their aesthetic imagination on the downward trends and changes of American political culture.

Since the 1960s, the movies seem to be less optimistic about the American future and more suspicious of American institutions and activities. The general tenor of so many of the films we discussed above suggests the development of what we might call the "imperial theme," the vaguely understood consciousness that the United States has passed some kind of political and historical threshold that cannot be undone or recovered from. Many observers have noted the extent to which Americans tend to think in terms of "lapses"--states of grace or innocence from which we have fallen. Political rhetoric often points us toward the rediscovery or recovery of something we have lost but will regain. Reagan was only the latest success in the recurrent announcement that he would "make us great again," defying once more the drift or indifference of the world. Yet Hollywood, the popular institution that spawned Reagan and much of the national imagery he utilized, did not uniformly share in any renewed euphoria or resurgent will to power. Quite the contrary, if we take the long view of political trends in the movies from the Sixties on, it is striking as to the extent to which they support the view that America is an empire in slow but sure decline from the apex of its power after World War II and during the *pax Americana* of the 1950s. They may do this quite unwittingly, but nevertheless many of the classic themes of imperial decline are there, offering aesthetic recognition of changes, and worries, in the popular imagination about the fate of the nation.

In movies of the last thirty years, there has been a growing sense that the American historical moment is slipping away. The many films set in a more innocent era (with the Kennedy years of 1962-1963 being one of the favorite cutoff dates) suggest a lingering nostalgia for a past that is perceived to be better than the present or future. There was even the idea that we can use that past in order to help rectify the present, but primarily in a private rather than political sense. In the curious "bodyswitching" movies of the 1980s, there were symbolic mergers of aged wisdom and youthful vitality in a mythic hope of achieving some continuity in political culture over time. During this entire period, there was the transformation, and then virtual disappearance, of our fundamental heroic story, the Western. We did compensate for this in some measure with heroics placed in other mythic settings, such as space and the exploits of superheroes, but such actions seemed more elegiac than exemplary. It was true that we witnessed many examples of what we might call praetorian daring, with paramilitary or military heroes who embodied heroic virtues from a bygone age engaging in clashes with alien foes on behalf of our government. Yet these reassertions of heroic potential seem to revolve around a desire for a renewed individual rather than political power. If there were celebrations of military adventure, they tended toward spectacle rather than victory, reasserting the scope of imperial interest rather than the magnitude of victorious intervention. Indeed, both the Western and the Vietnam war movie became vehicles for doubts about the efficacy and the righteousness of imperial intervention. And those very films that depicted praetorian daring, even those involving fantasies of revenge against past foes, had such a comic air about them that it was difficult to believe that audiences took them seriously as a parable justifying an imperial future. Periods of imperial decline seem to vacillate between support for and doubt about the burdens of empire, with the awareness that for all the display of militaristic might the ability to control history continues to slip beyond our grasp.

The sense that the United States no longer could exercise the kind of heroic power that extended righteous empire abroad was accompanied by the loss of confidence in the American domestic future. In stages of imperial decline, the authority and legitimacy of power itself is questioned. In the movies, this political self-doubt took many forms, not the least of which was the interest in elite intrigues, conspiracies, the private lives of those in palaces of wealth and power, and either the stupidity and ineptitude or the mendacity and decadence of established elites. Such a recurrent theme in the movies gives notice to the "late-empire" feeling that elite and mass life is radically separated, and that life at the top is a corrupt concentration of power devoid of merit or morality. There is afoot the assumption that everyone is out for himself or herself, and that expressions of public function or interest is a guise for self-aggrandizement or cynical manipulation. Such depictions in the popular arts do not only reveal the loss of *civitas*, or republican public spirit, but also *gravitas*, the ability to take public affairs and civic responsibilities seriously. A sense of both cynicism and absurdity pervades the arts, making facetious satire a modal form of comedy and indeed political rhetoric. But such an attitude makes the institutions of such a society seem all the more monumental and clumsy, and invites serious praetorians to attempts in militarizing the State, thereby restoring attention to imperial rule and discipline through the increasingly uncaring or alienated populace. Finally, if the arts capture a popular climate of hopelessness, with visions of the future that are bleakly "post-imperial," then they both understand and support resignation as to the inevitable decay and decline of gigantic but superceded power. An absence of optimistic images of the future suggest a real decline in the faith that the structure of power is equal to the task of ruling over vast space and time. The appearance of apocalyptic and death imagery in the arts offers confirmation of the pervasiveness of a "deluge mentality" that expects the worst and finds power unable and unwilling to cope with the historical abyss that lies just ahead.

In different ways, many of the imperial themes we have summarized, culled from different political visions, have appeared in American films over recent years. If it is the case that their appearance is not accidental, and they do constitute popular evidence of a growing awareness of America as a declining empire, then the movies may serve future historians, of, say, the twenty-seventh century, in attempting to understand the causes and consequences of the historical passage of a major twentieth-century political entity, one that went the way of all empires, but in this case recorded it on film.

SELECTED BIBLIOGRAPHY

General Works

Buscombe, Edward, "America on Screen? Hollywood Feature Films as Social and Political Evidence," in M. H. Clark ed., *Politics and Media.* Oxford: Pergamon Press, 1979.

Carroll, Noel. *Mystifying Movies.* New York: Columbia University Press, 1988.

Christensen, Terry. *Reel Politics.* New York: Basil Blackwell, 1987.

Coover, Robert. *A Night at the Movies.* New York: Linden Press/Simon & Schuster, 1987.

Davies, Philip and Brian Neves, eds. *Cinema, Politics, and Society in America.* Manchester: Manchester University Press, 1981.

Durang, Christopher. *A History of the American Film.* New York: Avon Books, 1978.

Eberwein, Robert L. *Film and the Dream State: A Sleep and a Forgetting.* Princeton: Princeton University Press, 1984.

Edelman, Rob. "The Politician in Films," *Films in Review,* November 1976.

Genovese, Michael A. *Politics and the Cinema: An Introduction to Political Films.* Lexington, Massachusetts: Ginn Press, 1986.

Jacobs, Lewis. *The Rise of the American Film.* New York: Harcourt, Brace, 1939.

Jarvie, I. C. *Movies as Social Criticism.* Metuchen, NJ: The Scarecrow Press, 1978.

Jarvie, I. C. *Movies and Society.* New York: Basic Books, 1970.

Jarvie, I. C. "Seeing through Movies," *Philosophy of the Social Sciences,* Vol. 8, no. 4, December, 1978.

Jowett, Garth and James M. Linton. *Film: The Democratic Art.* Boston: Little, Brown, 1978.

Kaminsky, Stuart M. *American Film Genres.* Chicago: Nelson-Hall, 1985, 2nd. ed.

McConnell, Frank. *Storytelling and Mythmaking: Images from Film and Literature.* New York: Oxford University Press, 1979.

Maltby, Richard. *Harmless Entertainment: Hollywood and the Ideology of Consensus.* Metuchen, NJ: Scarecrow Press, 1983.

Mellencamp, Patricia and Philip Rosen, eds. *Cinema Histories/Cinema Practices.* Frederick, MD: University Publications of America, American Film Institute monograph, Vol. IV.

Monaco, Paul. *Ribbons in Time: Movies and Society since 1945.* Bloomington: Indiana University Press, 1987.

Nimmo, Dan and James Combs. *Mediated Political Realities.* New York: Longman, 1990, 2nd ed.

O'Connor, John E. and Martin A. Jackson, eds. *American History/American Film: Interpreting the Hollywood Image.* New York: Frederick Ungar, 1988, 2nd ed.

Ray, Robert B. *A Certain Tendency of the Hollywood Cinema, 1930-1980.* Princeton: Princeton University Press, 1985.

Roffman, Peter and Jim Purdy. *The Hollywood Social Problem Film.* Bloomington: Indiana University Press, 1981.

Rollis, Peter C. ed. *Hollywood as Historian: American Film in a Cultural Context.* Lexington: The University Press of Kentucky, 1983.

Ross, Nathaniel Lester. "Portraying Presidents," *Films in Review,* Vol. XXIII, October 1972.

Ryan, Michael and Douglas Kellner. *Camera Politica: The Politics and Ideology of Contemporary Hollywood Film.* Bloomington: Indiana University Press, 1988.

Short, K.R.M., ed. *Feature Films as History.* Knoxville: University of Tennessee Press, 1981.

Sklar, Robert. *Movie-Made America: A Cultural History of American Movies.* New York: Random House Vintage Books, 1975.

Thompson, Robert. "American Politics on Film," *Journal of Popular Culture,* Vol. 20, no. 1, Summer 1986.

Thomson, David. *America in the Dark: The Impact of Hollywood Films on American Culture*, New York: William Morrow, 1977.

Thomson, David. *Suspects*. New York: Alfred A. Knopf, 1985.

Tudor, Andrew. *Image and Influence: Studies in the Sociology of Film*. New York: St. Martin's Press, 1974.

Movies of the 1910s

Barnouw, Erik. *The Magician and the Cinema*. New York: Oxford University Press, 1981.

Brownlow, Kevin. *The Parade's Gone By...* New York: Alfred A. Knopf, 1968.

Casty, Alan. "The Films of D.W. Griffith: A Style for the Times," *Journal of Popular Film and Television* Vol. 1, Spring 1972.

Everson, William K. *American Silent Film*. New York: Oxford University Press, 1978.

Fell, John L. *Film and the Narrative Tradition*. Berkeley: University of California Press, 1986.

Fishbein, Leslie. "The Demise of the Cult of True Womanhood in Early American Film," *Journal of Popular Film and Television*, Vol. 12, no. 2, Summer 1984.

Franklin, John Hope. "Birth of a Nation-Propaganda as History," *The Massachusetts Review*, Vol. 20, Autumn 1979.

Isenberg, Michael T. "The Mirror of Democracy: Reflections of the War Films of World War I, 1917-1919," *Journal of Popular Culture*, Vol. IX, no. 4, Spring 1976.

Kerr, Walter, *The Silent Clowns*. New York: Alfred A. Knopf, 1975.

Kepley, Vance, Jr. "Griffith's Broken Blossoms and the Problem of Historical Specificity," *Quarterly Review of Film Studies*, Vol. 3, no. 1, Winter 1978.

Maland, Charles. *Chaplin and American Culture: The Evolution of a Star Image.* Princeton: Princeton University Press, 1989.

May, Lary. *Screening Out the Past: The Birth, of Mass Culture and the Motion Picture Industry.* New York: Oxford University Press, 1980.

Merritt, Russell. "D. W. Griffith Directs the Great War: The Making of Hearts of the World," *Quarterly Review of Film Studies,* Vol. 6, Winter 1981.

Nye, Russell. *The Unembarrassed Muse.* New York: The Dial Press, 1970.

Rogin, Michael. "The Sword Became a Flashing Vision: D.W. Griffith's The Birth of a Nation," *Ronald Reagan, The Movie and Other Episodes in Political Demonology.* Berkeley: University of California Press, 1987.

Schickel, Richard. *D.W. Griffith: An American Life.* New York: Simon and Schuster, 1984.

Travers, Tim. "The New Consciousness and the Origins of Film," *Film and History,* Vol. XI, no. 1, February 1979.

Veblen, Thorstein. "The Breadline and the Movies," in *Essays in Our Changing Order.* New York: Viking Press, 1934.

Ward, Larry Wayne. *The Motion Picture Goes to War: The U.S. Government Film Effort during World War I.* Ann Arbor, MI: U M I Research Press, 1985.

Williams, Martin. *Griffith: First Artist of the Movies.* New York: Oxford University Press, 1980.

Movies of the 1920s

Durgnat, Raymond and Scott Simmon. *King Vidor, American.* Berkeley: University of California Press, 1988.

Eksteins, Modris. "War, Memory, and Politics: The Fate of the Film All Quiet on the Western Front," *Central European History,* Vol. 13, March 1980.

Fishbein, Leslie. "Dancing Mothers: Flappers, Mothers, Freud, and Freedom," *Women's Studies,* Vol. 12, 1986.

Isenberg, Michael. *War on Film: The American Cinema and World War I, 1914-1941.* East Brunswick: Fairleigh Dickinson University Press, 1981.

Mast, Gerald. *The Comic Mind: Comedy and the Movies.* Chicago: University of Chicago Press, 1979, 2nd ed.

Moews, Daniel. *Keaton: The Silent Films Close Up.* Berkeley: University of California Press, 1977.

Robinson, David. *Buster Keaton.* Bloomington: Indiana University Press, 1969.

Robinson, David. *Hollywood in the Twenties.* Cranbury, N.J.: Barnes, 1968.

Sloan, Kay. *The Loud Silents: Origins of the Social Problem Film.* Champaign-Urbana: University of Illinois Press, 1989.

Stewart, Garrett. "Keaton through the Looking Glass," *Georgia Review,* Vol. 33, 1979.

Movies of the 1930s

Affron, Charles. *Cinema and Sentiment.* Chicago: University of Chicago Press, 1982.

Arthur, Thomas H. "An Actor in Politics: Melvyn Douglas and the New Deal," *Journal of Popular Culture,* Vol. XIV, no. 2, Fall 1980.

Babington, Bruce and Peter William Evans. *Blue Skies and Silver Linings: Aspects of the Hollywood Musical.* Manchester: University of Manchester Press, 1987.

Basinger, Jeanine. "America's Love Affair with Frank Capra," *American Film,* March 1982.

Bergman, Andrew. *We're in the Money: Depression America and Its Films.* New York: Harper Colophon Books, 1972.

Bordwell, David, Kristen Thompson and Janet Staiger. *The Classical Hollywood Cinema: Film Style and Production to 1960.* New York: Columbia University Press, 1985.

Browne, Nick. "The Politics of Narrative Form: Capra's Mr. Smith Goes to Washington," *Wide Angle*, Vol. 3, no. 3, 1982.

Byrge, Duane. *A Critical Study of the Screwball Comedy Film.* Ann Arbor, MI: U M I Research Press, 1988.

Carney, Raymond. *American Vision: The Films of Frank Capra.* Cambridge: Cambridge University Press, 1986.

Cavell, Stanley. *Pursuits of Happiness: The Hollywood Comedy of Remarriage.* Cambridge: Harvard University Press, 1980.

Dooley, Roger. *From Scarface to Scarlett: American Films in the 1930s.* New York: Harcourt Brace Jovanovich, 1981.

Glatzer, Richard and John Raeburn (eds.). *Frank Capra: The Man and His Films.* Ann Arbor: U M I Press, 1975.

Karnes, David. "The Glamorous Crowd: Hollywood Movie Premiers between the Wars," *American Quarterly*, Vol. 38, no. 4, Fall 1986.

Karpf, Stephen. *The Gangster Film: Emergence, Variation, and Decay of a Genre.* New York: Arno Press, 1973.

Levine, Lawrence W. "Hollywood's Washington: Film Images of National Politics During the Great Depression," *Prospects*, Vol. 10, 1985.

Maland, Charles. *American Visions: The Films of Chaplin, Ford, Capra, and Welles, 1936-1941.* New York: Arno Press, 1977.

Maland, Charles. *Frank Capra.* Boston: Twayne, 1980.

Maland, Charles. "Mr. Deeds and American Consensus," *Film and History*, Vol. VIII, no. 1, February 1978.

McConnell, Robert L. "The Genesis and Ideology of Gabriel over the White House," in Richard Dyer MacCann and Jack C. Ellis eds., *Cinema Examined.* New York: Dutton, 1982.

Moore, James Tice. "Depression Images: Subsistence Homesteads, Production for Use, and King Vidor's Our Daily Bread," *Midwest Quarterly*, Vol. 26, Autumn 1984.

Phelps, Glenn Alan. "The Populist Films of Frank Capra," *American Studies*, Vol. 13, no. 3, 1979.

Raeburn, John. "History and Fate in I Am a Fugitive from a Chain Gang," *South Atlantic Quarterly,* Vol. 85, no. 4, Autumn 1986.

Richards, Jeffrey. "Frank Capra and the Cinema of Populism," *Film Society Review,* Vol. 7, 1972.

Roddick, Nick. *A New Deal in Entertainment: Warner Brothers in the 1930s.* London: British Film Institute, 1983.

Roth, Mark. "Some Warners Musicals and the Spirit of the New Deal," *The Velvet Light Trap,* Vol. 17, Winter 1977.

Sacks, Arthur. "An Analysis of the Gangster Film of the Early Thirties," *The Velvet Light Trap,* Vol. 1, 1971.

Shadoian, Jack. *Dreams and Dead Ends: The American Gangster Crime Film.* Cambridge: Massachusetts Institute of Technology Press, 1977.

Weales, Gerald. *Canned Goods as Caviar: American Film Comedy of the 1930s.* Chicago: University of Chicago Press, 1985.

Films of the 1940s

Bates, Robin. "Fiery Speech in a World of Shadows: Rosebud's Impact on Early Audiences," *Cinema Journal,* Vol. 26, no. 2, Winter 1987.

Baker, M. Joyce. *Images of Women in Film: The War Years, 1941-1945.* Ann Arbor, MI: U M I Research Press,s 1980.

Basinger, Jeanine. *The World War II Combat Film: Anatomy of a Genre.* New York: Columbia University Press, 1986.

Carringer, Robert L. "Rosebud, Dead or Alive: Narrative and Symbolic Structure in Citizen Kane," *Proceedings of the Modern Language Association,* Vol. 21, March 1976.

Conley, Tom. "Stages of Film Noir," *Theatrical Journal,* Vol. 39, No. 3, October 1987.

Davis, John. "Notes on Warner Brothers Foreign Policy, 1918-1948," *The Velvet Light Trap,* Vol. 17, Winter 1977.

Dick, Bernard F. *The Star-Spangled Screen: The American World War II Film.* Lexington University Press of Kentucky, 1986.

Doane, Mary Ann. *The Desire to Desire: The Woman's Film of the 1940s.* Bloomington: Indiana University Press, 1987.

Eco, Umberto. "Casablanca: Cult Movies and Intertextual Collage," *Travels in Hyperreality.* New York: Harcourt Brace Jovanovich, 1986.

Ewing, Dale E., Jr. "Film Noir: Style and Content," *Journal of Popular Film and Television,* Vol. 16, no. 2, Summer 1988.

Fyne, Robert. "From Hollywood to Moscow," *Literature Films Quarterly,* Vol. 13, no. 3, 1985.

Hark, Ina Rae. "The Visual Politics of The Adventures of Robin Hood," *Journal of Popular Film and Television,* Vol. 5 no. 1, 1976.

Harvey, John. "Out of the Light: An Analysis of Narrative in Out of the Past," *Journal of American Studies,* Vol. 18, no. 1., 1984.

Koppes, Clayton R. and Gregory D. Black. "Blacks, Loyalty and Motion-Picture Propaganda in World War II," *Journal of American History,* Vol. 73, no. 2, September 1986.

Koppes, Clayton R. and Gregory D. Black. *Hollywood Goes to War.* New York: The Free Press, 1987.

Lee, David D. "Appalachia on Film: The Making of Sergeant York," *Southern Quarterly,* Spring-Summer 1981.

Lingeman, Richard R. *Don't You Know There's a War On?: The American Home Front, 1941-1945.* New York: G.P. Putnam's Sons, 1970.

Maltby, Richard. "Film Noir: The Politics of the Maladjusted Text," *Journal of American Studies,* Vol. 18, no. 1, 1984.

Manvell, Roger. *Films and the Second World War.* New York: Dell Publishing Company, 1974.

Meerse, David E. "To Reassure a Nation: Hollywood Presents World War II," *Film and History,* Vol. VI, no.4, December 1976.

Poague, Leland. "All I Can See is the Flags: Fort Apache and the Visibility of History," *Cinema Journal,* Vol. 27, no. 2, Winter 1988.

Polan, Dana. *Power and Paranoia: History, Narrative, and the American Cinema, 1940-1950*. New York: Columbia University Press, 1986.

Renov, Michael. *Hollywood's Wartime Women: Representation and Ideology*. Ann Arbor, MI: UMI Research Press, 1988.

Shindler, Colin. *Hollywood Goes to War: Films and American Society, 1939-1952*. London: Routledge & Kegan Paul, 1979.

Simone, Sam P. *Hitchcock as Activist: Politics and the War Films*. Ann Arbor, MI: UMI Research Press, 1985.

Short, K.R.M., ed. *Film and Radio Propaganda in World War II*. Knoxville: University of Tennessee Press, 1983.

Sklar, Robert. "God and Man in Bedford Falls: Frank Capra's It's a Wonderful Life," in Sam B. Girgus ed. *The American Self*. Albuquerque: University of New Mexico Press, 1981.

Sochen, June. "Mildred Pierce and Women in Film," *American Quarterly*, Vol. XXX, no. 1, Spring 1978.

Tuska, Jon. *Dark Cinema: American Film Noir in Cultural Perspective*. Westport, CT: Greenwood Press, 1984.

Walsh, Andrea. *Women's Films and Female Experience, 1940-1950*. New York: Praeger, 1984.

Williams, Carol Traynor. *The Dream Beside Me: The Movies and the Children of the Forties*. Rutherford, NJ: Associated University Press, 1980.

Movies of the 1950s

Biskind, Peter. *Seeing is Believing: How Hollywood Taught Us to Stop Worrying and Love the Fifties*. New York: Pantheon Books, 1983.

Biskind, Peter. "The Politics of Power in On the Waterfront," *Film Quarterly*, Vol. XXIX, Fall 1975.

Ceplair, Larry and Seven Englund. *The Inquisition in Hollywood*. Berkeley: University of California Press, 1983.

Doherty, Thomas. *Teenagers and Teenpics: The Juvenilization of American Movies in the 1950s*. Boston: Unwin Hyman, 1988.

Dowdy, Andrew. *The Films of the Fifties: The American State of Mind.* New York: William Morrow, 1973.

Gabhard, Krin. "Religious and Political Allegory in Robert Wise's The Day the Earth Stood Still," *Literature/Film Quarterly,* Vol. 10, no. 3, 1982.

Gregory, Charles T. "The Pod Society Versus the Rugged Individualists," *Journal of Popular Film and Television,* Vol. 1, Winter 1972.

Henderson, Brian. "The Searchers: An American Dilemna," *Film Quarterly,* Vol. XXXIV, no. 2, Winter 1980-1981.

Hey, Kenneth R. "On the Waterfront: Another Look," *Film and History,* Vol. IX, no. 4, December 1979.

Johnson, Glen M. "We'd Fight...We Had To: The Body Snatchers as Novel and Film," *Journal of Popular Culture,* Vol. XIII, no. 1, Summer 1979.

Kaminsky, Stuart M. "On Invasion of the Body Snatchers," *Cinefantastique,* Vol. 2, no. 3, Winter 1973.

Leab, Daniel J. "How Red Was My Valley: Hollywood, the Cold War Film, and I Married a Communist," *Journal of Contemporary History,* Vol. 19, 1984.

Lenihan, John H. *Showdown: Confronting Modern America in the Western Film.* Urbana: University of Illinois Press, 1985.

Lucanio, Patrick. *Them or Us: Archetypical Interpretations of Fifties Alien Invasion Films.* Bloomington: Indiana University Press, 1987.

Macdonald, J. Fred. "The Cold War as Entertainment in Fifties Television," *Journal of Popular Film and Television,* Vol. 7, no. 1, 1978.

McGee, Mark and R.J. Robertson. *The J.D. Films: Juvenile Delinquency in the Movies.* Jefferson, NC: McFarland & Company, 1982.

Maland, Charles. "On the Waterfront: Film and the Dilemnas of American Liberalism in the McCarthy Era," *American Studies in Scandinavia,* Vol. 14, 1982.

Murphy, Brian. "Monster Movies: They came from Beneath the Fifties," *Journal of Popular Film and Television,* Vol. 1, Winter 1972.

Navasky, Victor S. *Naming Names.* New York: Penguin Books, 1981.

Noriega, Chon. "Godzilla and the Japanese Nightmare: When Them! Is Us," *Cinema Journal,* Vol. 27, no. 1, Fall 1987.

Palmer, R. Barton. "A Masculinist Reading of Two Western Films, High Noon and Rio Grande," *Journal of Popular Film and Television,* Vol. 12, no. 4, Winter 1984-1985.

Rogin, Michael. "Kiss Me Deadly: Communism, Motherhood, and Cold War Movies," *Representations,* Vol. 6, Spring 1984.

Sayre, Nora. *Running Time: Films of the Cold War.* New York: Dial Press, 1982.

Sobchack, Vivian. "The Alien Landscapes of the Planet Earth: Science Fiction in the Fifties," in *Science Fiction Films,* edited by Thoams R. Atkins. New York: Monarch Press, 1976.

Sontag, Susan. "The Imagination of Disaster," in *Against Interpretation.* New York: Farrar, Straus and Giroux, 1978.

Steffen-Fluhr, Nancy. "Women and the Inner Game of Don Siegel's Invasion of the Body Snatchers," *Science Fiction Studies,* Vol. 11, July 1984.

Strada, Michael J. "Kaleidoscopic Nuclear Images of the Fifties," *Journal of Popular Culture,* Vol. 20, no. 3, Winter 1986.

Tarrant, Margaret. "Monsters from the Id," *Films and Filming,* Vol. 17, no. 3, December 1970.

Quart, Leonard and Albert Auster. *American Film and Society Since 1945.* New York: Praeger, 1984.

Warren, Bill. *Keep Watching the Skies: American Science Fiction Movies of the Fifties.* Jefferson, NC: McFarland & Company, 1982.

Williams, Tony. "Female Oppression in Attack of the 50-foot Woman," *Science Fiction Studies,* Vol. 12, 1985.

Movies of the 1960s

Agel, Jerome. *The Making of 2001.* New York: Signet, 1970.

Baxter, John. *Hollywood in the Sixties.* New York: Macmillan, 1972.

Cawelti, John, ed. *Focus on Bonnie and Clyde.* Englewood Cliffs, NJ: Prentice-Hall, 1972.

Dickstein, Morris. *Gates of Eden: American Culture in the Sixties.* New York: Basic Books, 1977.

Doherty, Thomas. "The Exploitation Film as History: Wild in the Streets," *Literature/Film Quarterly,* Vol. 12, no. 3, 1984.

Herman, Gerald. "For God and Country: Khartoum (1966) as History and as Object Lesson," *Film and History,* Vol. IX, no. 1, February 1979.

Monaco, James. *American Film Now: The People, the Power, the Money, the Movies.* New York: Oxford University Press, 1979.

Nachbar, Jack, ed. *Focus on the Western.* Englewood Cliffs, NJ: Prentice-Hall, 1974.

Seydour, Paul. *Peckinpaugh: The Western Films.* Urbana: University of Illinois Press. 1980.

Movies of the 1970s

Berger, Arthur Asa. "Return of the Jedi: The Rewards of Myth," *Society,* Vol. 20, no. 4, May/June 1984.

Cagin, Seth and Phillip Dray. *Hollywood Films of the Seventies: Sex, Drugs, Violence, Rock 'n' Roll and Politics.* New York: Harper & Row, 1984.

Carpenter, Ronald H. and Robert V. Seltzer. "Nixon, Patton, and a Silent Majority Sentiment about the Vietnam War: The Cinemaographic Bases of a Rhetorical Stance," *Central States Speech Journal,* Vol. 25, Summer 1974.

Cawelti, John. "Pornography, Catastrophe, and Vengeance: Narrative Structures in a Changing American Culture," in Sam Girgus, ed. *The American Self* (Albuquerque: University of New Mexico Press, 1981.

Hellman, John. *American Myth and the Legacy of Vietnam.* New York: Columbia University Press, 1986.

Jameson, Frederick. "Class and Allegory in Contemporary Mass Culture: Dog Day Afternoon as a Political Film," *Screen Education,* Vol. 30, Spring 1979.

Kolker, Robert Phillip. *A Cinema of Loneliness.* New York: Oxford University Press, 1980.

Kuiper, Koenraad. "Star Wars: An Imperial Myth," *Journal of Popular Culture,* Vol. 21, no. 4, Spring 1988.

Miller, Martin and Robert Spritch. "The Appeal of Star Wars: An Archetypal-psychoanalytic View," *American Image,* Vol. 38, no. 2, Summer 1981.

Norden, Martin F. "The Disabled Vietnam Veteran in Hollywood Films," *Journal of Popular Film and Television,* Vol. 13, no. 1, Spring 1985.

Palmer, William J. *The Films of the Seventies: A Social History.* Metuchen, NJ: The Scarecrow Press, 1987.

Quart, Leonard. "Altman's Metaphorical America," *Film and History,* Vol. VII, no. 3, September 1977.

Roddick, Nick. "Only the Stars Survive: Disaster Movies in the Seventies," *Performance and Politics in Popular Drama,* eds. D. Bradby, L. James, and B. Sharratt. Cambridge: Cambridge University Press, 1980.

Roth, Lane. "Vraisemblance and the Western Setting in Contemporary Science Fiction Films," *Literature/Film Quarterly,* Vol. 13, no. 3, 1985.

Rushing, Janice Hocker and Thomas S. Frentz. "The Deer Hunter: Rhetoric of the Warrior," *The Quarterly Journal of Speech,* Vol. 66, no. 1, December 1980.

Shaheen, Jack, ed. *Nuclear War Films.* Carbondale: Southern Illinois University Press, 1978.

Shedlin, M. "Police Oscar: The French Connection," *Film Quarterly,* Summer 1972.

Symposium. "Four Shots at The Deer Hunter," *Film Quarterly,* Spring 1979.

Westerbeck, Colin L., Jr. "Beauties and the Beast: Seven Beauties and Taxi Driver," *Sight and Sound,* Vol. 45, Summer 1976.

Willson, Robert F., Jr. "On the Air/On the Line: Parallel Structure and Contemporary History in The China Syndrome," *Film and History,* Vol. IX, No. 3, September 1979.

Movies of the 1980s

Allen, Henry. "Remembering Vietnam: Art as Therapy," *The Wilson Quarterly,* Vol. XII, no. 1, 1988.

Caputi, Jane. "Films of the Nuclear Age," *Journal of Popular Film and Television,* Vol. 16, no. 3, Fall 1988.

Comber, Michael and Margaret O'Brien. "Evading the War: The Politics of the Hollywood Vietnam Film," *History,* Vol. 73, June 1988.

Glass, Fred. "Sign of the Times: the Computer as Character in Tron, War Games, and Sueprman III," *Film Quarterly,* Vol. 38, Winter 1984/1985.

Greenburg, Harvey R. "Dangerous Recuperations: Red Dawn, Rambo, and the New Decaturism," *Journal of Popular Film and Television,* Vol. 15, no. 2, Summer 1987.

Hoberman, J. "America Dearest," *American Film,* May 1988.

Johnson, Eithne. "The Business of Sex: Prostitution and Capitalism in Four Recent American Films," *Journal of Popular Film and Television,* Vol. 12, no. 4, Winter 1984/1985.

Schickel, Richard. "No Method to His Madness," *Film Comment,* June 1987.

Shelton, Robert. "Rendevous with HAL:2001/2010," *Extrapolation,* Vol. 28, Fall 1987.

Studlar, Gaylyn and David Desser. "Never Having to Say You're Sorry: Rambo's Rewriting of the Vietnam War," *Film Quarterly,* Vol. XLII, no. 1, Fall 1988.

Tomasculo, Frank P. "Mr. Jones Goes to Washington: Myth and Religion in Raiders of the Lost Ark," *Quarterly Review of Film Studies,* Vol. 7, Fall 1982.

Wachhorts, Wyn. "Time-Travel Romance on Film: Archetypes and Structures," *Extrapolation,* Vol. 25, Winter 1984.

Wood, Robin. *Hollywood from Vietnam to Reagan.* New York: Columbia University Press, 1986.

FILMOGRAPHY

The Accused. 1988. 110m. Director: Jonathan Kaplan. Cast: Jodie Foster(Sarah Tobias); Kelly McGillis (Katheryn Murphy).

The Adventurer. 1917. 2lm. bw. (silent) Director: Charles Chaplin. Writer: Chaplin. Cast: Charles Chaplin, Edna Purviance, Eric Campbell, Henry Bergman.

The Adventures of Robin Hood. 1938. 102m. color. Directors: William Keighley, Michael Curtiz. Writers: Seton Miller, Norman Raine. Cast: Errol Flynn (Robin Hood);Olivia de Havilland(Maid Marian); Basil Rathbone (Sir Guy of Gisbourne); Claude Rains (Prince John); Eugene Pallette (Friar Tuck).

Advise and Consent. 1962. 140m. color. Director: Otto Preminger. Writer: Wendell Mayes; based on the novel by Allen Drury. Cast: Don Murray (Sen. Brigham Anderson); Charles Laughton (Sen. Seabright Cooley); Henry Fonda (Robert Leffingwell); Walter Pidgeon (Sen. Bob Munson); Gene Tierney (Dolly Harrison).

After Hours. 1985. 97m. color. Director: Martin Scorsese. Writer: Joseph Minion. Cast: Griffin Dunne (Paul Hackett); Rosanna Arquette (Marcy); Verna Bloom (June).

Airport. 1970. 137m. color. Director: George Seaton. Writer: George Seaton;. based on the novel by Arthur Hailey. Cast: Burt Lancaster (Mel Bakersfeld); Dean Martin (Vernon Demerest); Jean Seberg (Tanya Livingston); Jacqueline Bisset (Gwen Meighen).

Alamo Bay. 1985. 99m. color. Director: Louis Malle. Writer: Alice Arlen. Cast: Amy Madigan (Glory); Ed Harris (Shang); Ho Nguyen (Dinh); Donald Moffat (Wally).

Alien Nation. 1988. 96m. color. Director: Graham Baker. Writer: Rockne S. O'Bannon. Cast: James Caan (Matthew Sykes); Mandy Patinkin (Sam Francisco); Terence Stamp (William Harcourt); Kevyn Major Howard (Kipling).

Alien. 1979. 124m. color. Director: Ridley Scott. Writer: Dan O'Bannon; based on a story by O'Bannon, Ronald Shusett. Cast: Tom Skerritt (Dallas); Sigourney Weaver (Ripley); John Hurt (Kane); Veronica Cartwright (Lambert).

All Quiet on the Western Front. 1930. 140m. bw. Director: Lewis Milestone. Writers: Milestone, Maxwell Anderson, Del Andrews, George Abbott; based on a novel by Erich M. Remarque. Cast: Louis Wolheim (Katczinsky); Lew Ayres (Paul Baumer); John Wray (Himmelstoss); George Summerville (Tjaden).

All That Jazz. 1979. 123m. color. Director: Bob Fosse. Writers: Robert Alan Arthur, Fosse. Cast: Roy Scheider (Joe Gideon); Jessica Lange (Angelique); Ann Reinking (Kate Jagger); Leland Palmer (Audrey Paris).

All the King's Men. 1949. 109m. bw. Director: Robert Rossen. Writer: Robert Rossen; based on the novel by Robert Penn Warren. Cast: Broderick Crawford (Willie Stark); John Ireland (Jack Burden); Mercedes McCambridge (Sadie Burke); Joanna Dru (Anne Stanton).

All the President's Men. 1976. 138m. color. Director: Alan Pakula. Writer: William Goldman; based on a book by Carl Bernstein, Bob Woodward. Cast: Robert Redford (Bob Woodward); Dustin Hoffman (Carl Bernstein); Jason Robards (Ben Bradlee).

All Through the Night. 1942. 107m. bw. Director: Vincent Sherman. Writers: Leonard Spigelgass, Edwin Gilbert; based on a story by Spigelgass, Leonard Ross. Cast: Humphrey Bogart (Gloves Donahue); Conrad Veidt (Hall Ebbing); Peter Lorre (Pepi); Kaaren Verne (Leda Hamilton).

Amazing Grace and Chuck. 1987. 115m. color. Director: Mike Newell. Writer: David Field. Cast: Jamie Lee Curtis (Lynn Taylor); Alex English (Amazing Grace Smith); Gregory Peck (President); William L. Petersen (Russell Murdock).

American Graffiti. 1973. 110m. color. Director: George Lucas. Writers: Lucas, Gloria Katz, Willard Huyck. Cast: Richard Dreyfuss (Curt); Ronny Howard (Steve); Paul le Mat (John); Charlie Smith (Terry); Cindy Williams (Laurie).

The Apartment. 1960. 125m. bw. Director: Billy Wilder. Writers: Wilder, I. Diamond. Cast: Jack Lemmon (C.C. Baxter); Shirley MacLaine (Fran Kubelik); Fred MacMurray (J.D. Sheldrake).

Apocalypse Now. 1979. 139m. color. Director: Francis Coppola. Writers: John Milius, Coppola. Cast: Martin Sheen (Capt. Willard); Robert Duvall (Lt. Col. Kilgore); Frederic Forrest (Chef); Marlon Brando (Col. Kurtz).

Attack! 1956. 107m. bw. Director: Robert Aldrich. Writer: James Poe; based on a play "The Fragile Fox" by Norman Brooks. Cast: Jack Palance (Lt. Costa); Eddie Albert (Capt. Cooney); Lee Marvin (Col. Bartlett); Buddy Ebsen (Sgt. Tolliver); Robert Strauss (Pvt. Bernstein).

Bad Day at Black Rock. 1955. 81m. color. Director: John Sturges. Writer: Millard Kaufman; based on a story by Howard Breslin. Cast: Spencer Tracy (John J. MacReedy); Robert Ryan (Reno Smith); Dean Jagger (Tim Horn); Walter Brennan (Doc Velie).

Battle Cry of Peace, The 1915. 9 reels. bw. (silent) Director: Wilfred North. Writers: Blackton, Stuart; based on "Defenseless America" by Hudson Maxim. Cast: Charles Richman, L. Rogers Lytton, Charles Kent, James Morrison.

Beggar on Horseback. 1925. 7 reels. bw. (silent) Director: James Cruze. Writer: Walter Woods; based on a play by George S. Kaufman, Marc Connelly. Cast: Edward Everett Horton (Neil McRae); Esther Ralston (Cynthia Mason); Erwin Connelly (Frederick Cady); Gertrude Short (Gladys Cady).

Being There. 1979. 130m. color. Director: Hal Ashby. Writer: Jerzy Kosinski; based on his novel. Cast: Peter Sellers (Chance); Shirley MacLaine (Eve Rand); Melvyn Douglas (Benjamin Rand); Jack Warden (President Bobby).

The Best Man. 1964. 102m. bw. Director: Franklin Schaffner. Writer: Gore Vidal; based on his play. Cast: Henry Fonda (William Russell); Cliff Robertson (Joe Cantwell); Lee Tracy (Art Hockstader); Margaret Leighton (Alice Russell).

The Best Years of Our Lives. 1946. 172m. bw. Director: William Wyler. Writer: Robert Sherwood; based on a novella "Glory for Me" by MacKinlay Kantor. Cast: Fredric March (Al Stephenson); Myrna Loy (Milly Stephenson); Teresa Wright (Peggy Stephenson); Dana Andrews (Fred Derry).

Betrayed. 1988. 123m. Director: Constantine Costa-Gavras. Writer: Joe Eszterhas. Cast: Debra Winger (Cathy Weaver/Katie Phillips); Tom Berenger (Gary Simmons); John Heard (Michael Carnes); Ted Levine (Wes).

Beverly Hills Cop. 1984. 105m. color. Director: Martin Brest. Writer: Story by Danilo Bach, Daniel Petrie. Cast: Eddie Murphy (Axel Foley); Judge Reinhold (Billy Rosewood); Lisa Eilbacher (Jenny Summers); John Ashton (John Taggart).

The Big Chill. 1983. 103m. color. Director: Lawrence Kasdan. Writers: Kasdan, Barbara Benedek. Cast: Glenn Close (Sarah); Tom Berenger (Sam); William Hurt (Nick); Jeff Goldblum (Michael).

The Big Heat. 1953. 89m. bw. Director: Fritz Lang. Writer: Sydney Boehm; based on serial in *Saturday Evening Post* by William McGivern. Cast: Glenn Ford (Dave Bannion); Gloria Grahame (Debby Marsh); Alexander Scourby (Mike Logana); Jocelyn Brando (Katie Bannion).

Big Jake. 1971. 109m. color. Director: George Sherman. Writers: Harry Julian Fink, R.M. Fink. Cast: John Wayne (Jacob McCandles); Richard Boone (John Fain); Maureen O'Hara (Martha McCandles); Patrick Wayne (James McCandles); Chris Mitchum (Michael McCandles).

Big Jim McLain. 1952. 90m. bw. Director: Edward Ludwig. Writers: James Edward Grant, Richard English, Eric Taylor. Cast: John Wayne (Big Jim McLain); Nancy Olson (Nancy Vallon); James Arness (Mal Baxter); Alan Napier (Sturak).

The Big Parade. 1925. 13 reels. bw. (silent) Director: King Vidor. Writers: Lawrence Stallings, Harry Behn. Cast: John Gilbert (James Apperson); Renee Adoree (Melisande); Hobart Bosworth (Mr. Apperson); Karl Dane (Slim).

Billy Jack. 1971. 112m. color. Director: T.C. Frank. Writers: Frank, Teresa Christina. Cast: Tom Laughlin (Billy Jack); Delores Taylor (Jean Roberts); Bert Freed (Posner); Clark Howat (Sheriff Cole).

Birth of a Nation. 1915. 12 reels. bw. (silent) Director: D.W. Griffith. Writers: Griffith, Frank Woods. Cast: Henry B. Walthall (Ben Cameron, the Little Colonel); Mae Marsh (Flora Cameron, the Little Sister); Miriam Cooper (Margaret Cameron); Lillian Gish (Elsie Stoneman).

Blackboard Jungle. 1955. 100m. bw. Director: Richard Brooks. Writer: Brooks; based on the novel by Evan Hunter. Cast: Glenn Ford (Richard Dadier); Anne Francis (Anne Dadier); Louis Calhern (Jim Murdock); Margaret Hayes (Lois Hammond).

Blade Runner. 1982. 114m. color. Director: Ridley Scott. Writers: Hampton Fancher, David Peoples; based on a novel *Do Androids Dream of Electric Sheep* by Philip Dick. Cast: Harrison Ford (Deckard); Rutger Hauer (Roy Batty); Sean Young (Rachael); Edward J. Olmos (Gaff).

Blind Husbands. 1918. 8 reels. bw. (silent) Director: Erich von Stroheim. Writer: von Stroheim. Cast: Erich von Stroheim, Sam de Grasse, Gibson Gowland, Francelia Billington.

Blockade. 1938. 73m. bw. Director: William Dieterle. Writer: John Howard Lawson. Cast: Henry Fonda (Marco); Madeleine Carroll (Norma); Leo Carrillo (Luis); John Halliday (Andre Gallinet).

Blue Velvet. 1986. 120m. color. Director: David Lynch. Writer: David Lynch. Cast: Kyle MacLachlan (Jeffrey Beaumont); Isabella Rossellini (Dorothy Vallens); Dennis Hopper (Frank Booth); Laura Dern (Sandy Williams).

Bonnie And Clyde. 1967. 111m. color. Director: Arthur Penn. Writers: David Newman, Robert Benton. Cast: Warren Beatty (Clyde Barrow); Faye Dunaway (Bonnie Parker); Gene Hackman (Buck Barrow); Estelle Parsons (Blanche).

Born Yesterday. 1951. 103m. bw. Director: George Cukor. Writer: Albert Mannheimer; based on a play by Garson Kanin. Cast: Judy Holliday (Billie Dawn); Broderick Crawford (Harry Brock); William Holden (Paul Verrall); Howard St. John (Jim Devery).

Boudu Saved From Drowning. 1932. 84m. bw.. Director: Jean Renoir. Writer: Renoir. Based on a play written by Rene Fauchois. Cast: Michel Simon, Charles Grandal.

Boy's Town. 1938. 96m. bw. Director: Norman Taurog. Writers: John Meehan, Dore Schary; based on a story by Schary and Eleanore Griffin. Cast: Spencer Tracy (Fr. Edward Flanagan); Mickey Rooney (Whitey Marsh); Henry Hull (Dave Morris); Gene Reynolds (Tony Ponessa).

Brazil. 1985. 131m. color. Director: Terry Gilliam. Writers: Tom Stoppard, Terry Gilliam, Charles McKeown. Cast: Jonathan Pryce (Sam Lowery); Robert DeNiro (Harry Tuttle); Michael Palin (Jack); Kim Greist (Jill Layton).

Broadcast News. 1987. 131m. color. Director: James L. Brooks. Writer: James L. Brooks. Cast: William Hurt (Tom Grunick); Albert Brooks (Aaron Altman); Holly Hunter (Jane Craig); Robert Prosky (Ernie Merriman).

Buck Privates. 1941. 82m. bw. Director: Arthur Lubin. Writers: Arthur T. Horman, John Grant. Cast: Bud Abbott

(Slicker Smith); Lou Costello (Herbie Brown); Lee Bowman (Randolph Parker III); Alan Curtis (Bob Martin).

Bullets Or Ballots. 1936. 68m. bw. Director: William Keighley. Writer: Seton Miller; based on a story by Martin Mooney. Cast: Edward G. Robinson (Johnny Blake); Joan Blondell (Lee Morgan); Humphrey Bogart (Nick Fenner); Barton MacLane (Al Kruger).

Bullin' The Bullsheviki. 1919. 4 reels. bw. (silent) Director: Frank P. Donovan. Writer: Frank P. Donovan; based on a play by Graham Moffat. Cast: Marguerite Clayton, George Ross, Olive Burke, Louise Fazenda.

The Candidate. 1972. 109m. color. Director: Michael Ritchie. Writer: Jeremy Larner. Cast: Robert Redford (Bill McKay); Peter Boyle (Lucas); Don Porter (Sen. Crocker Jarmon); Allen Garfield (Howard Klein).

Casablanca. 1942. 102m. bw. Director: Michael Curtiz. Writers: Julius Epstein, Phillip Epstein, Howard Koch; based on a play "Everybody goes to Rick's" by Murray Burnett and Joan Alison. Cast: Humphrey Bogart (Richard "Rick" Blaine); Ingrid Bergman (Ilsa Lund Laszlo); Claude Rains (Capt. Louis Renault); Paul Henreid (Victor Laszlo).

The China Syndrome. 1979. 122m. color. Director: James Bridges. Writers: Mike Gray, T.S. Cook, James Bridges. Cast: Jane Fonda (Kimberly Wells); Jack Lemmon (Jack Godell); Michael Douglas (Richard Adams); Scott Brady (Herman DeYoung).

Chinatown. 1974. 131m. color. Director: Roman Polanski. Writer: Robert Towne. Cast: Jack Nicholson (J.J. Gittes); Faye Dunaway (Evelyn Mulwray); John Huston (Noah Cross); Perry Lopez (Escobar).

Chisum. 1970. 110m. color. Director: Andrew McLaglen. Writer: Andrew Fenady. Cast: John Wayne (John Chisum); Forrest Tucker (Lawrence Murphy); Christopher George (Dan Nodeen); Ben Johnson (James Pepper).

Citizen Kane. 1941. 119m. bw. Director: Orson Welles. Writers: Herman Mankiewicz, Orson Welles. Cast: Orson Welles (Charles Foster Kane); Joseph Cotton (Jedediah Leland); Dorothy Comingore (Susan Alexander); Everett Sloane (Mr. Bernstein).

City Streets. 1931. 83m. bw. Director: Rouben Mamoulian. Writers: Max Marcin, Oliver Garrett; based on a story by Dashiell Hammett. Cast: Sylvia Sidney (Nan Cooley); Gary Cooper (The Kid); Paul Lukas (Big Fellow Maskal); Guy Kibbee (Pop Cooley).

Civilization. 1916. 7 reels. bw. (silent) Director: Thomas Ince. Writer: C. Gardner Sullivan. Cast: Enid Markey, Howard Hickman, J. Barney Sherry.

A Clockwork Orange. 1971. 137m. color. Director: Stanley Kubrick. Writer: Stanley Kubrick; based on the novel by Anthony Burgess. Cast: Malcolm McDowell (Alex); Michael Bates (Chief Guard); Adrienne Corri (Mrs. Alexander); Patrick Magee (Mr. Alexander).

Cocoon. 1985. 117m. color. Director: Ron Howard. Writer: Tom Benedek. Cast: Don Ameche (Art); Wilford Brimley (Ben); Hume Cronyn (Joe); Brian Dennehy (Walter); Maureen Stapleton (Mary).

The Color Of Money. 1986. 119m. color. Director: Martin Scorsese. Writer: Richard Price; based on the novel by Walter Tavis. Cast: Paul Newman (Eddie); Tom Cruise (Vincent); Mary Elizabeth Mastrantonio (Carmen); Helen Shaver (Janelle).

Coming Home. 1978. 126m. color. Director: Hal Ashby. Writers: Waldo Salt, Robert Jones; based on a story by Nancy Dowd. Cast: Jane Fonda (Sally Hyde); Jon Voight (Luke Martin); Bruce Dern (Capt. Bob Hyde); Robert Carradine (Bill Munson).

Confessions Of A Nazi Spy. 1939. 110m. bw. Director: Anatole Litvak. Writers: Milton Krims, John Wexley; based on a story by Krims and Wexley and articles by Leon Turrou. Cast: Edward G. Robinson (Ed Renard); Paul Lukas (Dr. Kassel); George Sanders (Schlager); Francis Lederer (Schneider).

The Conversation. 1974. 113m. color. Director: Francis F. Coppola. Writer: Francis F. Coppola. Cast: Gene Hackman (Harry Caul); John Cazale (Stan); Allen Garfield (Bernie Moran); Frederick Forrest (Mark).

A Corner In Wheat. 1909. Director: D.W. Griffith.

Country. 1984. 109m. color. Director: Richard Pearce. Cast: Jessica Lange (Jewel Ivy); Sam Shepard, Wilford Primley, Matt Clark.

Crossfire. 1947. 86m. bw. Director: Edward Dymtryk. Writer: John Paxton; based on a novel "The Brick Foxhole" by Richard Brooks. Cast: Robert Young (Finlay); Robert Mitchum (Keeley); Robert Ryan (Montgomery); Gloria Grahame (Ginny).

The Crowd. 1928. 9 reels. bw. (silent) Director: King Vidor. Writers: King Vidor, John Weaver, Harry Behn. Cast: James Murray (John Sims); Eleanor Boardman (Mary); Bert Roach (Bert); Estelle Clark (Jane).

A Cry In The Dark. 1988. 121m. color. Director: Fred Schepisi; based on a book by John Bryson. Cast: Meryl Streep (Lindy Chamberlain); Sam Neill (Michael Chamberlain); Charley Tingwell (Muirhead); Dennis Miller (Shirgess).

Daniel. 1983. 13m. color. Director: Sidney Lumet. Writer: E.L. Doctorow; based on his novel "The Book of Daniel." Cast: Timothy Hutton (Daniel Isaacson); Edward Asner (Jacob Ascher); Mandy Patinkin (Paul Isaacson); Lindsay Crouse (Rochelle).

The Dawn Patrol. 1938. 103m. bw. Director: Edmund Goulding. Writers: Seton Miller, Dan Totheroh; based on a story "The Flight Commander" by John Saunders. Cast: Errol Flynn (Courtney); David Niven (Scott); Basil Rathbone (Major Brand); Donald Crisp (Phills).

The Day The Earth Stood Still. 1951. 92m. bw. Director: Robert Wise. Writer: Edmund H. North; based on a story by Harry Bates. Cast: Michael Rennie (Klaatu); Patricia Neal (Helen Benson); Hugh Marlowe (Tom Stevens); Sam Jaffe (Dr. Barnhardt); Billy Gray (Bobby Benson).

Dead End. 1937. 93m. bw. Director: William Wyler. Writer: Lillian Hellman; based on a play by Sidney Kingsley. Cast: Joel McCrea (Dave); Sylvia Sidney (Drina); Humphrey Bogart (Baby Face Martin); Wendy Barrie (Kay).

The Dead Zone. 1983. 103m. color. Director: David Cronenberg. Writer: Jeffrey Boam; based on the novel by Stephen King. Cast: Christopher Walken (Johnny Smith); Brooke Adams (Sarah Bracknell); Tom Skerrit (Sheriff Bannerman); Herbert Lom (Dr. Sam Welzak).

Death Before Dishonor. 1987. 95m. color. Director: Lawrence Kubik. Writers: Kubik, John Catliff. Cast: Fred Dryer (Sgt. Jack Burns); Joey Gian (Ramirez); Sasha Mitchell (Ruggieri); Peter Parros (James).

Death Wish. 1973. 93m. color. Director: Michael Winner. Writer: Wendell Mayes; based on the novel by Brian Garfield. Cast: Charles Bronson (Paul Kersey); Hope Lange (Joanna Kersey); Vincent Gardenia (Frank Ochoa); Stuart Margolin (Aimes Jainchill); Steven Keats (Jack Toby).

The Deer Hunter. 1978. 183m. color. Director: Michael Cimino. Writer: Deric Washburn; based on a story by Cimino, Washburn, Louis Garfinkel, Quinn Redeker. Cast: Robert De Niro (Michael); John Cazale (Stan); John Savage (Steven); Christopher Walken (Nick); Meryl Streep (Linda).

The Defiant Ones. 1958. 97m. bw. Director: Stanley Kramer. Writers: Nathan Douglas, Harold Jacob Smith. Cast: Tony Curtis (John "Joker" Jackson); Sidney Poitier (Noah Cullen); Theodore Bikel (Sheriff Max Muller); Charles McGraw (Capt. Frank Gibbons).

Desperately Seeking Susan. 1985. 103m. color. Director: Susan Seidelman. Writer: Leora Barish. Cast: Rosanna Arquette (Roberta); Madonna (Susan); Aidan Quinn (Dez); Mark Blum (Gary); Robert Joy (Jim).

The Devil And Daniel Webster. 1941. 107m. bw. Director: William Dieterle. Writer: Dan Totheroh; based on a story by Stephen Benet. Cast: Edward Arnold (Daniel Webster); Walter Huston (Mr. Scratch); Jane Darwell (Ma Stone); Simone Simon (Belle).

Die Hard. 1988. 132m. color. Director: John McTiernan. Writers: Jeb Stuart, Steven deSouza. Cast: Bruce Willis (John McClane); Alan Rickman (Hans Gruber); Bonnie Bedelia (Holly McClane); Reginald Veljohnson (Sgt. Al Powell).

Dirty Dancing. 1987. 97m. color. Director: Emile Ardolino. Writer: Eleanor Bergstein. Cast: Jennifer Grey (Frances "Baby" Houseman);Patrick Swayze (Johnny Castle); Jerry Orbach (Dr. Jake Houseman); Cynthia Rhodes (Penny Johnson).

Dirty Harry. 1971. 102m. color. Director: Don Siegel. Writers: Harry Julian Fink, Rita M. Fink, Dean Riesner. Unpublished story by Fink & Fink. Cast: Clint Eastwood (Harry Callahan); Harry Guardino (Bressler); Reni Santoni (Chico); John Vernon (Mayor).

D. O. A. 1988. 100m. color. Director: Rocky Norton, Annabel Jankee. Story by Mr. Pague, Russell Rouse, Clarence Greene. Cast: Dennis Quaid (Dexter Cornell); Meg Ryan (Sydney

Fuller); Charlotte Rampling (Mrs. Fitzwaring); Daniel Stern (Hal Fetibsham).

Dr. Strangelove. 1964. 102m. bw. Director: Stanley Kubrick. Writers: Kubrick, Terry Southern, Peter George; based on a novel Red Alert by Peter George. Cast: Peter Sellers (Group Capt. Lionel Mandrake/President Merkin Muffley/Dr. Strangelove); George C. Scott (Gen. "Buck" Turgidson); Peter Bull (Ambassador de Sadesky); Sterling Hayden (Gen. Jack D. Ripper).

Double Indemnity. 1944. 106m. bw. Director: Billy Wilder. Writers: Wilder, Raymond Chandler; based on a short story by James M. Cain in the book *Three of a Kind.* Cast: Fred MacMurray (Walter Neff); Barbara Stanwyck (Phyllis Dietrichson); Edward G. Robinson (Barton Keyes); Tom Powers (Mr. Dietrichson).

Down And Out In Beverly Hills. 1986. 97m. color. Director: Paul Mazursky. Writers: Mazursky, Leon Capetanos; based on the play "Boudu saved from Drowning" by Rene Fauchois. Cast: Nick Nolte (Jerry Baskin); Richard Dreyfuss (David Whiteman); Bette Midler (Barbara Whiteman); Little Richard (Orvis Goodright).

Do The Right Thing. 1989. 120m. Director: Spike Lee. Writer: Spike Lee. Cast: Spike Lee (Mookie); Danny Aiello (Sal); Ossie Davis (Mr. Mayor).

Dressed To Kill. 1980. 105m. color. Director: Brian DePalma. Writer: DePalma. Cast: Michael Caine (Dr. Robert Elliott); Angie Dickinson (Kate Miller); Nancy Allen (Liz Blake); Keith Gordon (Peter Miller).

Drums Along The Mohawk. 1939. 103m. color. Director: John Ford. Writers: Lamar Trotti, Sonya Levien; based on the novel by Walter Edmonds. Cast: Claudette Colbert (Lana 'Magdalana' Martin); Henry Fonda (Gil Martin); Edna May Oliver (Mrs. Sarah McKlennar); Eddie Collins (Christian Reall).

E. T. 1982. 115m. color. Director: Steven Spielberg. Writer: Melissa Mathison. Cast: Dee Wallace (Mary); Henry Thomas (Elliott); Peter Coyote (Keys); Robert McNaughton (Michael).

Earth Vs. The Flying Saucers. 1956. 82m. bw. Director: Fred Sears. Writers: George Worthing Yates, Raymond Marcus. Cast: Hugh Marlowe (Dr. Russell Marvin); Joan Taylor (Carol

Marvin); Donald Curtis (Major Huglin); Morris Ankrum (Gen. Hanley).

Easy Rider. 1969. 94m. color. Director: Dennis Hopper. Writers: Peter Fonda, Hopper, Terry Southern. Cast: Peter Fonda (Wyatt); Dennis Hopper (Billy); Jack Nicholson (George Hanson).

Easy Street. 1916. 22n. bw. (silent) Director: Charles Chaplin. Writer: Charles Chaplin. Cast: Charles Chaplin, Edna Purviance, Albert Austin, Eric Campbell.

Eddie And The Cruisers. 1983. 92m. color. Director: Martin Davidson. Writers: Davidson, Arlene Davidson. Cast: Tom Berenger (Frank); Michael Pare (Eddie); Joe Pantoliano (Doc); Matthew Laurance (Sal).

18 Again. 1988. 100m. color. Director: Paul Flaherty. Writers: Josh Goldstein, Jonathan Prince. Cast: George Burns (Jack Watson); Charlie Schlatter (David Watson); Tony Roberts (Arnold); Anita Morris (Madelyn).

Empire Of The Sun. 1988. 152m. color. Director: Steven Spielberg. Writers: Tom Stoppard, Menno Meyjs; based on the novel by J.C. Ballard. Cast: Christian Bale (Jim Graham); John Malkovich (Pasie); Miranda Richardson (Mrs. Victor); Nigel Havers (Dr. Rawlins).

Escape From New York. 1981. 99m. color. Director: John Carpenter. Writers: Carpenter, Nick Castle. Cast: Kurt Russell (Snake Plissken); Lee Van Cleef (Bob Hauk); Ernest Borgnine (Cabby); Donald Pleasence (The President).

Executive Action. 1973. 91m. color. Director: David Miller. Writer: Dalton Trumbo; based on a story by Donald Freed, Mark Lane. Cast: Burt Lancaster (Farrington); Robert Ryan (Foster); Will Geer (Ferguson); Gilbert Green (Paulitz).

Executive Suite. 1954. 104m. bw. Director: Robert Wise. Writer: Ernest Lehman; based on the novel by Cameron Hawley. Cast: Fredric March (Loren Shaw); William Holden (McDonald Walling); June Allyson (Mary Walling); Barbara Stanwyck (Julia Tredway); Walter Pidgeon (Frederick Alderson); Shelley Winters (Eva Bardeman); Paul Douglas (Josiah Dudley).

The Exorcist. 1973. 121m. color. Director: William Friedkin. Writer: William P. Blatty; based on Blatty's novel.

Cast: Ellen Burstyn (Mrs. MacNeil); Max Von Sydow (Fr. Merrin); Jason Miller (Fr. Karras); Linda Blair (Regan).

A Face In The Crowd. 1957. 125m. bw. Director: Elia Kazan. Writer: Budd Schulberg; based on his short story "The Arkansas Traveler." Cast: Andy Griffith (Lonesome Rhodes); Lee Remick (Betty Lou Fleckum); Walter Matthau (Mel Miller); Patricia Neal (Marcia Jeffries).

Fail Safe. 1964. 111m. bw. Director: Sidney Lumet. Writer: Walter Bernstein; based on the novel by Eugene Burdick, Harvey Wheeler. Cast: Henry Fonda (The President); Walter Matthau (Groeteschele); Dan O'Herlihy (Gen. Black); Frank Overton (Gen. Bogan).

Fame. 1980. 134m. color. Director: Alan Parker. Writer: Christopher Gore. Cast: Irene Cara (Coco); Lee Curreri (Bruno); Laura Dean (Lisa); Paul McCrane (Montgomery); Barry Miller (Ralph).

A Farewell To Arms. 1957. 152m. color. Director: Charles Vidor. Writer: Ben Hecht. Based on the novel by Ernest Hemingway. Cast: Jennifer Jones (Catherine Barkely); Rock Hudson (Frederick Henry); Vittorio De Sica (Alessandro Rinaldi); Alberto Sordi (Fr. Galli).

Field Of Dreams. 1989. 107m. color. Director: Phil Alden Robinson. Writer: Robinson; based on a book Shoeless Joe by W.P. Kinsella. Cast: Kevin Costner (Ray Kinsella); Amy Madigan (Annie Kinsella); Ray Liotta (Shoeless Joe Jackson).

The Fighting 69th. 1940. 90m. bw. Director: William Keighley. Writers: Norman Raine, Fred Niblo, Jr., Dean Franklin. Cast: James Cagney (Jerry Plunkett); Pat O'Brien (Fr. Duffy); George Brent (Wild Bill Donovan); Jeffrey Lynn (Joyce Kilmer).

The Fighting Sullivans. 1944. 111m. bw. Director: Lloyd Bacon. Writer: Mary McCall, Jr.; based on a true story by Jules Schermer, Edward Doherty. Cast: Anne Baxter (Katherine Mary); Thomas Mitchell (Mr. Sullivan); Selena Royle (Mrs. Sullivan); Edward Ryan (Al).

Firefox. 1982. 137m. color. Director: Clint Eastwood. Writers: Alex Lasker, Wendell Wellman; based on a novel by Craig Thomas. Cast: Clint Eastwood (Mitchell Gant); Freddie Jones (Kenneth Aubrey); David Huffman (Buckholz); Warren Clarke (Pavel Upenskoy).

First Blood. 1982. 97m. color. Director: Ted Kotcheff. Writers: Michael Kozoll, William Sackheim, Q. Moonblood; based on the novel by David Morrell. Cast: Sylvester Stallone (Rambo); Richard Crenna (Trautman); Brian Dennehy (Teasle); David Caruso (Mitch).

Foolish Wives. 1921. 85m. bw. (silent) Director: Erich von Stroheim. Writer: Stroheim. Cast: Erich von Stroheim (Count Sergius Karamzin); Mae Busch (Princess Vera Petschnikoff); Maude George (Princess Olga Petschnikoff).

Footlight Parade. 1933. 102m. bw. Directors: Lloyd Bacon, William Keighley, Busby Berkeley. Writers: Manuel Seff, James Seymour. Cast: James Cagney (Chester Kent); Joan Blondell (Nan Prescott); Ruby Keeler (Bea Thorn); Dick Powell (Scotty Blair).

Forbidden Fruit. 1921. Director: Cecil B. DeMille. Writer: Jeanie MacPherson. Cast: Agnes Ayres (Modern Cinderella); Clarence Burton (Her husband); Kathryn Williams (Fairy Godmother); Forrest Stanley (The Prince).

The Formula. 1980. 117m. color. Director: John G. Avildsen. Writer: Steven Shagan; based on the novel by Steven Shagan. Cast: George C. Scott (Barney Caine); Marlon Brandon (Adam Steiffel); Marthe Keller (Lisa); John Gielgud (Dr. Esau).

42nd Street. 1933. 98m. bw. Director: Lloyd Bacon. Writers: James Seymour, Rian James; based on the novel by Bradford Ropes. Cast: Warner Baxter (Julian Marsh); Bebe Daniels (Dorothy Brock); George Brent (Pat Denning); Una Merkel (Lorraine Fleming).

Four Friends. 1981. 114m. color. Director: Arthur Penn. Writer: Steve Tesich. Cast: Craig Wasson (Danilo Prozor); Jodi Thelen (Georgia Miles); Michael Huddleston (David Levine); Jim Metzler (Tom Donaldson).

The Four Seasons. 1981. 107m. color. Director: Alan Alda. Writer: Alda. Cast: Alan Alda (Jack Burroughs); Carol Burnett (Kate Burroughs); Len Cariou (Nick Callan); Sandy Dennis (Anne Callan).

Frantic. 1988. 110m. color. Director: Roman Polanski. Screenplay by Polanski and Gerald Brach. Cast: Harrison Ford (Dr. Richard Walker); Betty Buckley (Sonda); Emmanuelle Seigner (Waif).

Friday The 13th. 1980. 95m. color. Director: Sean Cunningham. Writer: Victor Miller. Cast: Betsy Palmer (Mrs. Voorhees); Adrienne King (Alice); Jeannine Taylor (Marcie); Robbi Morgan (Annie).

The Front. 1976. 95m. color. Director: Martin Ritt. Writer: Walter Bernstein. Cast: Woody Allen (Howard Prince); Zero Mostel (Hecky Brown); Herschel Bernardi (Phil Sussman); Michael Murphy (Alfred Miller).

Full Metal Jacket. 1988. 120m. color. Director: Stanley Kubrick. Writers: Kubrick, Michael Herr, Gustav Husford; based on the novel The Short Timers by Gustav Hasford. Cast: Matthew Modine (Pvt. Joker); Adam Baldwin (Animal Mother); (Vincent D'Orofrio (Lawrence Pyle); Lee Ermey (Gunnery Sgt. Hartman).

G-Men. 1935. 85m. bw. Director: William Keighley. Writer: Seton I. Miller; based on the novel Public Enemy No. 1 by Gregory Rogers. Cast: James Cagney (James "Brick" Davis); Ann Dvorak (Jean Morgan); Margaret Lindsay (Kay McCord); Robert Armstrong (Jeff McCord).

Gabriel Over The White House. 1933. 87m. Director: Gregory LaCava. Writers: Carey Wilson, Bertram Bloch; based on the novel Rinehard by T.F. Tweed. Cast: Walter Huston (Hon. Judson Hammond); Karen Morley (Pendota Molloy); Franchot Tone (Hartley Beekman); C. Henry Gordon (Nick Diamond).

Gandhi. 1982. 188m. color. Director: Richard Attenborough. Writer: John Briley. Cast: Ben Kingsley (Mahatma Gandhi); Candice Bergen (Margaret Bourke-White); Edward Fox (Gen. Dyer); John Mills (The Viceroy).

Gentleman's Agreement. 1947. 118m. bw. Director: Elia Kazan. Writer: Moss Hart; based on the novel by Laura Hobson. Cast: Gregory Peck (Phil Green); Dorothy McGuire (Kathy); John Garfield (Dave); Celeste Holm (Anne).

Getting Straight. 1970. 126m. color. Director: Richard Rush. Writer: Robert Kaufman; based on the novel by Ken Kolb. Cast: Elliott Gould (Harry Bailey); Candice Bergen (Jan); Robert F. Lyons (Nick); Jeff Corey (Dr. Wilhunt).

Giant. 1956. 201m. color. Director: George Stevens. Writers: Fred Guiol, Ivan Moffat; based on the novel by Edna Ferber. Cast: Rock Hudson (Bick Benedict); Elizabeth Taylor

(Leslie   Benedict);   James   Dean   (Jett   Rink);
Mercedes McCambridge (Luz Benedict).

The Godfather. 1972. 175m. color. Director: Francis
Coppola. Writers: Francis Coppola, Mario Puzo; based on the
novel by Puzo. Cast: Marlon Brando (Don Vito Corleone); Al
Pacino (Michael Corleone); Robert Duvall (Tom Hagen); James
Caan (Sonny Corleone); Richard Castellano (Clemenza).

The Godfather, Part II. 1974. 200m. color. Director: Francis
Coppola. Writers: Francis Coppola, Mario Puzo. Cast: Al Pacino
(Michael Corleone); Robert DeNiro (Vito Corleone); Diane Keaton
(Kay Corleone); Robert Duvall (Tom Hagen).

Going My Way. 1944. 130m. bw. Director: Leo McCarey.
Writers: Frank Butler, Frank Cavett, Leo McCarey; based on a
story by Leo McCarey. Cast: Bing Crosby (Fr. Chuck O'Malley);
Barry Fitzgerald (Fr. Fitzgibbon); Rise Stevens (Genevieve
Linden); Frank McHugh (Fr. Timothy O'Dowd).

Gold Diggers Of 1933. 1933. 94m. bw. Director: Mervyn
LeRoy. Writers: Erwin Gelsey, James Seymour, David Boehm,
Ben Markson. Cast: Warren William (J. L. Bradford); Joan
Blondell (Carol); Aline MacMahon (Trixie Lorraine); Ruby Keeler
(Polly Parker); Dick Powell (Brad Roberts/Robert Treat
Bradford).

Gone With The Wind. 1939. 220m. color. Director: Victor
Fleming. Writer: Sidney Howard; based on the novel by Margaret
Mitchell. Cast: Clark Gable (Rhett Butler); Vivien Leigh (Scarlett
O'Hara); Olivia de Havilland (Melanie Hamilton); Leslie Howard
(Ashley Wilkes); Thomas Mitchell (Gerald O'Hara).

Good Morning Vietnam. 1987. 119m. color. Director: Barry
Levinson. Writer: Mitch Markowitz. Cast: Robin Williams
(Adrian Cronaver); Forest Whitaker (Edward Garlick); Tung
Thanh Tran (Tuan Trinh); Chintara Sukapatana (Trinh).

The Good Mother. 1988. 113m. color. Director: Leonard
Nimoy. Writer: Michael Bortman; based on the novel by Sue
Miller. Cast: Diane Keaton (Anna); Liam Neeson (Leo); Jason
Robards (Muth); Ralph Bellamy (Grandfather); Teresa Wright
(Grandmother).

The Graduate. 1967. 105m. color. Director: Mike Nichols.
Writers: Calder Willingham, Buck Henry; based on the novel by
Charles Webb. Cast: Dustin Hoffman (Ben Braddock); Anne

Bancroft (Mrs. Robinson); Katharine Ross (Elaine Robinson); Murray Hamilton (Mr. Robinson).

The Grapes Of Wrath. 1940. 129m. bw. Director: John Ford. Writer: Nunnally Johnson; based on the novel by John Steinbeck. Cast: Henry Fonda (Tom Joad); Jane Darwell (Ma Joad); John Carradine (Casey); Charley Grapewin (Grandpa Joad).

The Great Dictator. 1940. 127m. bw. Director: Charles Chaplin. Writer: Charles Chaplin. Cast: Charles Chaplin (Hynkel); Paulette Goddard (Hannah); Jack Oakie (Napaloni); Reginald Gardiner (Schultz).

The Great McGinty. 1940. 81m. bw. Director: Preston Sturges. Writer: Preston Sturges. Cast: Brian Donlevy (Dan McGinty); Akim Tamiroff (The Boss); Muriel Angelus (Catherine McGinty); Louis Jean Heydt (Thompson).

The Great Train Robbery. 1903. 10m. bw. (silent) Director: Edwin S. Porter. Writer: Edwin S. Porter. Cast: Marie Murray, Bronco Billy Anderson, George Barnes.

The Green Berets. 1968. 141m. color. Directors: John Wayne, Ray Kellogg. Writer: James Lee Barrett; based on the novel by Robin Moore. Cast: John Wayne (Col. Mike Kirby); David Janssen (George Beckworth); Jim Hutton (Sgt. Petersen); Aldo Ray (Sgt. Muldoon).

Guess Who's Coming To Dinner. 1967. 108m. color. Director: Stanley Kramer. Writer: William Rose. Cast: Spencer Tracy (Matt Drayton); Katharine Hepburn (Christina Drayton); Katharine Houghton (Joey Drayton); Sidney Poitier (John Prentice).

Gunga Din. 1939. 117m. bw. Director: George Stevens. Writers: Joel Sayre, Fred Guiol, Ben Hecht, Charles MacArthur; based on a story by Ben Hecht, Charles MacArthur, Wm. Faulkner, suggested by the poem by Rudyard Kipling. Cast: Cary Grant (Sgt. Cutter); Victor McLaglen (Sgt. MacChesney); Douglas Fairbanks, Jr. (Sgt. Ballantine); Sam Jaffe (Gunga Din).

Hairspray. 1988. 89m. color. Director: John Waters. Writer: John Waters. Cast: Ricki Lake (Tracy Turnblad); Shawn Thompson (Corny Collins); Franklin von Tussle (Sonny Bono); Edna and Arvin (Divine).

Halloween. 1978. 93m. color. Director: John Carpenter. Writers: John Carpenter, Debra Hill. Cast: Donald Pleasance (Loomis); Jamie Lee Curtis (Laurie); Nancy Loomis (Annie); P.J. Soles (Lynda).

Hamburger Hill. 1988. 110m. color. Director: John Irvin. Writer: Jim Corabatsos. Cast: Anthony Barrile (Languilliu); Michael Patrick (Boatman Motown); Don Cheadle (Washburn); Michael Dolan (Murphy).

Hannah And Her Sisters. 1986. 104m. color. Director: Woody Allen. Writer: Woody Allen. Cast: Woody Allen (Mickey); Michael Caine (Elliot); Mia Farrow (Hannah); Carrie Fisher (April); Barbara Hershey (Lee).

Heartbreak Ridge. 1986. 128m. color. Director: Clint Eastwood. Writer: James Carabatsos. Cast: Clint Eastwood (Tom Highway); Marsha Mason (Aggie); Major Powers (Everett McGill); Sgt. Webster (Moses Gunn).

Hearts Of The World. 1918. 80m. bw. (silent) Director: David Griffith. Writer: David Griffith. Cast: Lillian Gish, Dorothy Gish, Robert Harron, Josephine Crowell.

Hell's Angels. 1930. 135m. bw. (some scenes in color) Directors: Howard Hughes, Marshall Neilan, Luther Reed. Writers: Howard Estabrook, Harry Behn, Joseph March; based on a story by Neilan March. Cast: Ben Lyon (Monte Rutledge); James Hall (Roy Rutledge); Jean Harlow (Helen); John Darrow (Karl Arnstedt).

Heroes For Sale. 1933. 73m. bw. Director: William Wellman. Writers: Robert Lord, Wilson Mizner. Cast: Richard Barthelmess (Tom); Aline MacMahon (Mary); Loretta Young (Ruth); Berton Churchill (Mr. Winston).

The Hidden. 1986. 96m. color. Director: Jack Sholder. Writer: Bob Hunt. Cast: Michael Nouri (Tom Beck); Kyle MaLachlan (Lloyd Gallagher); Ed O'Ross (Cliff Willis); Clu Gulager (Ed Flynn).

High Noon. 1952. 85m. bw. Director: Fred Zinnemann. Writer: Carl Foreman; based on the story "The Tin Star" by John Cunningham. Cast: Gary Cooper (Will Kane); Grace Kelly (Amy Kane); Thomas Mitchell (Jonas Henderson); Lloyd Bridges (Harvey Pell).

Hitler's Children. 1942. 80m. bw. Director: Edward Dmytryk. Writer: Emmet Lavery; based on the book *Education for Death* by Gregor Ziemer. Cast: Tim Holt (Karl Bruner); Bonita Granville (Anna Muller); Otto Kruger (Col. Henkel); Kent Smith (Prof. Nichols).

Home Of The Brave. 1949. 88m. bw. Director: Mark Robson. Writer: Carl Foreman; based on a play by Arthur Laurents. Cast: Frank Lovejoy (Mingo); Lloyd Bridges (Finch); Douglas Dick (Maj. Robinson); Steve Brodie (T.J.).

I Am A Fugitive From A Chain Gang. 1932. 93m. bw. Director: Mervyn LeRoy. Writers: Sheridan Gibney, Brown Holmes, Howard J. Green; based on an autobiography *I am a Fugitive from a Georgia Chain Gang* by Robert Burns. Cast: Paul Muni (James Allen); Glenda Farrell (Maria Woods); Helen Vinson (Helen); Preston Foster (Pete).

I Married A Communist. 1950. bw. (originally named Woman on Pier 13, 1949.) Director: Robert Stevenson. Writers: Charles Grayson, Robert Hardy Andrews; based on a story by George W. George, George F. Slavin. Cast: Laraine Day (Nan Collins); Robert Ryan (Brad Collins); John Agar (Don Lowry); Thomas Gomez (Vanning).

I Was A Communist For The FBI. 1951. 83m. bw. Director: Gordon Douglas. Writers: Crane Wilbur, Matt Cvetic; based on a *Saturday Evening Post* article "I Posed as a Communist for the FBI" by Matt Cvetic. Cast: Frank Lovejoy (Matt Cvetic); Dorothy Hart (Eve Merrick); Phil Carey (Mason); James Millican (Jim Blandon).

Imitation Of Life. 1959. 125m. color. Director: Douglas Sirk. Writers: Eleanore Griffin, Allan Scott; based on the novel by Fannie Hurst. Cast: Lana Turner (Lora Meredith); Juanita Moore (Annie Johnson); John Gavin (Steve Archer); Susan Kohner (Sarah Jane, age 18).

The Immigrant. 1917. 20m. bw. (silent) Director: Charles Chaplin. Writer: Charles Chaplin. Cast: Charles Chaplin, Edna Purviance, Albert Austin, Henry Bergman, Eric Campbell.

In The Heat Of The Night. 1967. 109m. color. Director: Norman Jewison. Writer: Sterling Silliphant; based on the novel by John Ball. Cast: Sidney Poitier (Virgil Tibbs); Rod Steiger (Bill Gilespie); Warren Oates (Sam Wood); Quentin Dean (Delores Purdy).

Innerspace. 1987. 120m. color. Director: Joe Dante. Writers: Jeffrey Boam, Chip Proser; based on a story by Chip Proser. Cast: Dennis Quaid (Lt. Tuck Pendelton); Martin Short (Jack Putter); Meg Ryan (Lydia Maxwell); Kevin McCarthy (Victor Scrimshaw).

Intolerance. 1916. 115m. bw. (silent) Director: D.W. Griffith. Writer: D.W. Griffith. Cast: Mae Marsh (The dear one); Lillian Gish (The woman who rocks the cradle); Constance Talmadge (Marguerite deValois); Robert Harron (The boy).

Intruder In The Dust. 1949. 87m. bw. Director: Clarence Brown. Writer: Ben Maddow; based on the novel by William Faulkner. Cast: Juano Hernandez (Lucas Beauchamp); Elizabeth Patterson (Miss Habersham); David Brian (John Gavin Stevens); Claude Jarmon, Jr. (Chick Mallison).

Invaders From Mars. 1953. 73m. color. Director: William Cameron Menzies. Writers: Richard Blake, John Battle, Menzies; based on a story by John Battle. Cast: Helena Carter (Dr. Patricia Blake); Arthur Franz (Dr. Stuart Kelston); Leif Erickson (George MacLean); Hillary Brooke (Mary MacLean).

Invasion Of The Body Snatchers. 1956. 80m. bw. Director: Don Siegel. Writer: Daniel Mainwaring; based on a novel *The Body Snatchers* by Jack Finney. Cast: Kevin McCarthy (Miles Bennel); Dana Wynter (Becky Driscoll); Larry Gatges (Dr. Dan Kauffmann); King Donovan (Jack).

Invasion USA. 1952. 73m. bw. Director: Alfred E. Green. Writer: Robert Smith; based on a story by Robert Smith, Franz Spencer. Cast: Dan O'Herlihy (Mr. Ohman); Gerald Mohr (Vince); Peggie Castle (Carla).

The Iron Curtain. 1948. 87m. bw. Director: William Wellman. Writer: Milton Krims; based on the memoirs of Igor Gouzenko. Cast: Dana Andrews (Igor Gouzenko); Gene Tierney (Anna Gouzenko); Berry Kroeger (Grubb); Edna Best (Mrs. Foster).

Iron Eagle. 1986. 116m. color. Director: Sidney J. Furie. Writers: Kevin Elders, Sidney J. Furie. Cast: Louis Gossett, Jr. (Chappy); Jason Gedrick (Doug); David Suchet (Minister of Defense); Tim Thomerson (Ted).

The Iron Triangle. 1989. 91m. color. Director: Eric Weston. Writers: Eric Weston, John Bushelman, Larry Hilbrand. Cast:

Beau Bridges (Capt. Keene); Liem Whatley (Hu); Haing Ngor (Capt. Tuong).

It. 1927. 72m. bw. (silent) Director: Clarence Badger. Writers: Hope Loring, Louis D. Lighton. Cast: Clara Bow, Antonio Moreno, William Austin, Jacqueline Gadson, Gary Cooper, Elinor Glyn.

It Happened One Night. 1934. 105m. bw. Director: Frank Capra. Writer: Robert Riskin; based on a story "Night Bus" by Samuel Hopkins Adams. Cast: Clark Gable (Peter Warne); Claudette Colbert (Ellie Andrews); Walter Connolly (Alexander Andrews); Roscoe Karns (Oscar Shapeley).

It's A Wonderful Life. 1946. 129m. bw. Director: Frank Capra. Writers: Frances Goodrich, Albert Hackett, Frank Capra; based on a story "The Greatest Gift" by Philip Van Doren Stern. Cast: James Stewart (George Bailey); Henry Travers (Clarence); Donna Reed (Mary Hatch); Lionel Barrymore (Mr. Potter); Thomas Mitchell (Uncle Billy).

Jaws. 1975. 124m. color. Director: Steven Spielberg. Writers: Peter Benchley, Carl Gottlieb; based on the novel by Peter Benchley. Cast: Robert Shaw (Quint); Roy Scheider (Police Chief Martin Brody); Richard Dreyfuss (Matt Hooper); Lorraine Gary (Ellen Brody).

Joe. 1970. 107m. color. Director: John G. Avildsen. Writer: Norman Wexler. Cast: Peter Boyle (Joe Curran); Dennis Patrick (Bill Compton); Audrey Caire (Joan Compton); Susan Sarandon (Melissa Compton).

Julia. 1977. 116m. color. Director: Fred Zinnemann. Writer: Alvin Sargent; based on a story in the book *Pentimento* by Lillian Hellman. Cast: Jane Fonda (Lillian Hellman); Vanessa Redgrave (Julia); Jason Robards, Jr. (Dashiel Hammett); Maximilian Schell (Johann).

The Kaiser, Beast Of Berlin. 1918. 7 reels. bw. (silent) Director: Rupert Julian. Writer: Elliott Clawson. Cast: Rupert Julian (The Kaiser); Allan Sears (Capt. von Wohlbold); Nigel de Brulier (Capt. von Neigel); Jay Smith (Field Marshal von Hindenburg); Mark Fenton (Adm. von Tirpitz).

The Kaiser's Finish. 1918. 8 reels. bw. (silent) Director: John Joseph Harvey, Clifford P. Saum. Cast: Earl Schenck, Vic DeLinsky, Claire Whitney, Jean Sunderland, Percy Standing.

The Killing Fields. 1984. 139m. color. Director: Roland Joffe. Writer: Bruce Robinson; based on "Death and Life of Dith Pran" by Sydney Schanberg. Cast: Sam Waterston (Sydney Schanberg); Dr. Haing S. Ngor (Dith Pran); John Malkovich (Al Rockoff).

Kleptomaniac. 1904. Director: Edwin S. Porter.

Kramer Vs. Kramer. 1979. 105m. color. Director: Robert Benton. Writer: Robert Benton; based on the novel by Avery Corman. Cast: Dustin Hoffman (Ted Kramer); Justin Henry (Billy Kramer); Meryl Streep (Joanna Kramer); Jane Alexander (Margaret Phelps).

The Last Emperor. 1987. 160m. color. Director: Bernardo Bertolucci. Writers: Mark Peploe, Bernardo Bertolucci, Enzo Ungari. Cast: John Lone (Aisin-Gioro Pu Yi); Joan Chen (Wan Juhg); Peter O'Toole (Reginald Johnston); Ying Ruocheng (The Governor).

The Last Hurrah. 1958. 121m. bw. Director: John Ford. Writer: Frank Nugent; based on the novel by Edwin O'Connor. Cast: Spencer Tracy (Frank Skeffington); Jeffrey Hunter (Adam Caulfield); Diane Foster (Maeve); Pat O'Brien (John Gorman).

Less Than Zero. 1987. 96m. color. Director: Marek Kanieuska. Writer: Harley Peyton; based on the novel by Bret Easton Ellis. Cast: Andrew McCarthy (Clay Easton); Jami Gertz (Blair); Robert Downey, Jr. (Jullian Wells); James Spader (Rip).

Lethal Weapon. 1987. 110m. color. Director: Richard Donner. Writer: Shane Black. Cast: Mel Gibson (Martin Riggs); Danny Glover (Roger Murtaugh); Gary Busey (Joshua); Mitchell Ryan (The General).

Lilac Time. 1928. 90m. bw. (silent/with sound effects) Director: George Fitzmaurice. Writer: Carey Wilson. Cast: Colleen Moore, Gary Cooper, Eugenie Besserer, Burr McIntosh, Arthur Lake.

The Little American. 1917. Cast: Mary Pickford.

Little Big Man. 1970. 147m. color. Director: Arthur Penn. Writer: Calder Willingham; based on the novel by Thomas Berger. Cast: Dustin Hoffman (Jack Crabb); Martin Balsam (Allardyce Merriweather); Faye Dunaway (Mrs. Pendrake); Chief Dan George (Old Lodge Skins).

Little Caesar. 1931. 80m. color. Director: Mervyn LeRoy. Writers: Francis Faragoh, Robert N. Lee, Darryl Zanuck; based on the novel by W.R. Burnett. Cast: Edward G. Robinson (Cesare Bandello/Rico-Little Caesar); Douglas Fairbanks, Jr. (Joe Massara); Glenda Farrell (Olga Strasoff); William Collier, Jr. (Tony Passa).

Little Shop Of Horrors. 1986. 88m. color. Director: Frank Oz. Writer: Howard Ashman, based on his play. Cast: Rick Moranis (Seymour Ivelborn); Ellen Greene (Audrey); Vincent Gardenia (Mr. Mushnik); Steve Martin (Orin Scrivello).

Looking For Mr. Goodbar. 1977. 135m. color. Director: Richard Brooks. Writer: Richard Brooks; based on the novel by Judith Rosner. Cast: Diane Keaton (Theresa Dunn); Tuesday Weld (Katherine Dunn); William Atherton (James Morrissey); Richard Kiley (Mr. Dunn).

Lost In America. 1985. 91m. color. Director: Albert Brooks. Writers: Albert Brooks, Monica Johnson. Cast: Albert Brooks (David Howard); Julie Hagerty (Linda Howard).

Making Mr. Right. 1987. 100m. color. Director: Susan Seidelman. Writers: Frank and Floyd Byars. Cast: John Malkovich (Jeff Peters/Ulysses); Ann Magnuson (Frankie Stone); Glenn Headly (Trish); Ben Masters (Steve Marcus).

The Manchurian Candidate. 1962. 126m. bw. Director: John Frankenheimer. Writer: George Axelrod, Frankenheimer, based on the novel by Richard Condon. Cast: Frank Sinatra (Bennett Marco); Laurence Harvey (Raymond Shaw); Janet Leigh (Rosie); James Gregory (Sen. John Iselin).

Mannequin. 1937. 92m. bw. Director: Frank Borzage. Writer: Lawrence Hazard; based on a story "Marry for Money" by Katharine Brush. Cast: Joan Crawford (Jessie Cassidy); Spencer Tracy (John L. Hennessey); Alan Curtis (Eddie Miller); Ralph Morgan (Briggs).

Matewan. 1987. 132m. color. Director: John Sayles. Cast: Chris Cooper (Joe); Will Oldham (Danny); Mary McDonnell (Elema); James Earl Jones (Few Clothes).

McCabe and Mrs. Miller. 1971. 120m. Director: Robert Altman. Writers: Robert Altman, Brian Mackay; based on the novel *McCabe* by Edmund Naughton. Cast: Warren Beatty (John McCabe); Julie Christie (Constance Miller); Rene Auberjonois (Sheehan); Shelley Duvall (Ida Coyle).

Meet John Doe. 1941. 135m. bw. Director: Frank Capra. Writer: Robert Riskin; based on a story "The Life and Death of John Doe" by Robert Presnell, Richard Connell. Cast: Gary Cooper (John Doe/Long John Willoughby); Barbara Stanwyck (Ann Mitchell); Edward Arnold (D.B. Norton); Walter Brennan (Colonel).

The Milagro Beanfield War. 1988. 118m. color. Director: Robert Redford. Writers: David Ward, John Nichols; based on the novel by John Nichols. Cast: Chick Vennara (Joe Mondragon); Christopher Walken (Kyril Montana); John Heard (Charlie Bloom); Sonia Braga (Ruby Archuleta).

Missing. 1982. 122m. color. Director: Constantine Costa-Gavras. Writers: Costa-Gavras, Donald Stewart; based on *The Execution of Charles Horman* by Thomas Hauser. Cast: Jack Lemmon (Ed Horman); Sissy Spacek (Beth Horman); Melanie Mayron (Terry Simon); John Shea (Charles Horman).

Missing In Action. 1984. 101m. Director: Joseph Zito. Cast: Chuck Norris (James Braddock); General Tran (James Hong); M. Emmet Walsh.

Missing In Action, 2: The Beginning. 1985. 96m. Director: Lance Hool. Cast: Chuck Norris (James Braddock); Soon-Teck Oh (Colonel Yin).

Mission To Moscow. 1943. 123m. bw. Director: Michael Curtiz. Writer: Howard Koch; based on a book Joseph E. Davies. Cast: Walter Huston (Ambassador Joseph E. Davies); Ann Harding (Mrs. Davies); Oscar Homolka (Maxim Litvinov); George Tobias (Freddie).

Mississippi Burning. 1989. 127m. color. Director: Alan Parker. Writer: Chris Gerolaw. Cast: Gene Hackman (Anderson); William Defoe (Ward); Frances McDormand (Mrs. Pell); Brad Doury (Deputy Pell).

Mr. Deeds Goes To Town. 1936. 115m. bw. Director: Frank Capra. Writer: Robert Riskin; based on a story "Opera Hat" by Clarence Budington Kelland. Cast: Gary Cooper (Longfellow Deeds); Jean Arthur (Babe Bennett); Raymond Walburn (Walter); Lionel Stander (Cornelius Cobb).

Mr. Smith Goes To Washington. 1939. 130m. bw. Director: Frank Capra. Writer: Sidney Buchman; based on a book *The Gentleman from Montana* by Lewis R. Foster. Cast: James Stewart

(Jefferson Smith); Claude Rains (Sen. Joseph Paine); Jean Arthur (Saunders); Thomas Mitchell (Diz Moore).

Mrs. Miniver. 1942. 134m. bw. Director: William Wyler. Writers: Arthur Wimperis, George Froeschel, James Hilton, Claudine West; based on the novel by Jan Struther. Cast: Greer Garson (Mrs. Kay Miniver); Walter Pidgeon (Clem Miniver); Teresa Wright (Carol Beldon); Richard Ney (Vin Miniver).

The Money Pit. 1986. 91m. color. Director: Richard Benjamin. Writer: David Giler. Cast: Tom Hanks (Walter Fielding); Shelley Long (Anna Crowley); Alexander Godunov (Max Beissart); Maureen Stapleton (Estelle).

The Mortal Storm. 1940. 100m. bw. Director: Frank Borzage. Writers: Claudine West, George Froeschel, Anderson Ellis; based on the novel by Phyllis Bottome. Cast: Margaret Sullavan (Freya Roth); Robert Young (Fritz Marlberg); James Stewart (Martin Brietner); Frank Morgan (Prof. Roth).

Musketeers Of Pig Alley. 1912. Director: D.W. Griffith. Cast: Lillian Gish, Harry Carey.

My Favorite Year. 1982. 92m. color. Director: Richard Benjamin. Writers: Norman Steinberg, Dennis Palumbo; based on a story by Dennis Palumbo. Cast: Peter O'Toole (Alan Swann); Mark Linn-Baker (Benjy Stone); Jessica Harper (K.C. Downing); Joseph Bologna (King Kaiser).

My Man Godfrey. 1936. 94m. bw. Director: Gregory LaCava. Writers: Morrie Ryskind, Eric Hatch, Gregory LaCava; based on a story "1101 Park Avenue" by Eric Hatch. Cast: Carole Lombard (Irene Bullock); William Powell (Godfrey Parke); Alice Brady (Angelica Bullock); Mischa Auer (Carlo).

My Son John. 1952. 122m. bw. Director: Leo McCarey. Writers: Myles Connolly, Leo McCarey, John Mahin; based on a story by Leo McCarey. Cast: Helen Hayes (Lucille Jefferson); Robert Walker (John Jefferson); Dean Jagger (Dan Jefferson); Van Heflin (Stedman).

Nashville. 1975. 159m. color. Director: Robert Altman. Writer: Joan Tewkesbury. Cast: Geraldine Chaplin (Opal); David Arkin (Norman); Barbara Baxley (Lady Pearl); Ned Beatty (Delbert Reese).

The Nation's Peril. 1915. 5 reels. bw. (silent) Director: George W. Terwilliger. Writer: Harry Chandlee. Cast: Ormi

Hawley (Ruth Lyons); William H. Turner (Adm. Lyons); Earl Metcalf (Lt. Sawyer); Eleanor Barry (Mrs. Sawyer).

Network. 1976. 120m. color. Director: Sidney Lumet. Writer: Paddy Chayefsky. Cast: Peter Finch (Howard Beale); William Holden (Max Schumacher); Faye Dunaway (Diana Christensen); Robert Duvall (Frank Hackett).

Never Say Never Again. 1983. 137m. color. Director: Irvin Kershner. Writer: Lorenzo Semple, Jr.; based on a story by Kevin McClory, Jack Whittingham, Ian Fleming. Cast: Sean Connery (James Bond); Klaus Marie Brandauer (Largo); Max von Sydow (Blofeld); Barbara Carrera (Fatima Blush).

1969. 1988. 95m. color. Director: Ernest Thompson. Cast: Robert Downey, Jr. (Ralph); Kiefer Sutherland (Scott); Bruce Dern (Cliff); Mariette Hartley (Jessie).

1984. 1955. 91m. bw. Director: Michael Anderson. Writer: William P. Templeton, Ralph Bettinson; based on the novel by George Orwell. Cast: Michael Redgrave (Gen. O'Connor); Edmond O'Brien (Winston Smith); Jan Sterling (Julia); David Kossoff (Charrington).

1984. 1984. 115m. Director: Michael Bradford. Cast: John Hurt (Winston Smith); Richard Burton (O'Brien); Suzanna Hamilton (Julia).

Ninotchka. 1939. 110m. bw. Director: Ernst Lubitsch. Writers: Charles Brackett, Billy Wilder, Walter Reisch; based on a story by Melchior Lengyel. Cast: Greta Garbo (Lena Yakushova "Nin"); Melvyn Douglas (Count Leon Dolga); Sig Rumann (Michael Ironoff); Alexander Granach (Kopalski).

No Way Out. 1987. 114m. color. Director: Roger Donaldson. Cast: Kevin Costner (Tom Farrell); Gene Hackman (David Brice); Sean Young (Susan Atwell).

Norma Rae. 1979. 110m. color. Director: Martin Ritt. Writers: Irving Ravetch, Harriet Frank, Jr. Cast: Sally Field (Norma Rae); Beau Bridges (Sonny); Ron Leibman (Reuben); Pat Hingle (Vernon).

The North Star. 1943. 105m. bw. Director: Lewis Milestone. Writer: Lillian Hellman; based on a story by Lillian Hellman. Cast: Anne Baxter (Marina); Farley Granger (Damian); Jane Withers (Claudia); Eric Roberts (Grisha).

Objective Burma! 1945. 142m. bw. Director: Raoul Walsh. Writers: Randall McDougall, Lester Cole, Alvah Bessie; based on a story by Alvah Bessie. Cast: Errol Flynn (Maj. Nelson); James Brown (Sgt. Treacy); William Prince (Lt. Jacobs); George Tobias (Gabby Gordon).

An Officer And A Gentleman. 1982. 126m. color. Director: Taylor Hackford. Writer: Douglas Day Stewart. Cast: Richard Gere (Zack Mayo); Debra Winger (Paula Pokrifki); Louis Gossett (Sgt. Emil Foley); David Keith (Sid Worley).

The Omen. 1976. 111m. color. Director: Richard Donner. Writer: David Seltzer. Cast: Gregory Peck (Robert Thorn); Lee Remick (Katherine Thorn); David Warner (Jennings); Billie Whitelaw (Mrs. Baylock).

On Golden Pond. 1981. 109m. color. Director: Mark Rydell. Writer: Ernest Thompson; based on his play. Cast: Henry Fonda (Norman Thayer, Jr.); Katharine Hepburn (Ethel Thayer); Jane Fonda (Chelsea Thayer Wayne); Doug McKeon (Billy Ray).

On The Beach. 1959. 133m. bw. Director: Stanley Kramer. Writers: John Paxton, James Lee Barrett; based on the novel by Nevil Shute. Cast: Gregory Peck (Dwight Towers); Ava Gardner (Moira Davidson); Fred Astaire (Julian Osborn); Anthony Perkins (Peter Holmes).

On The Waterfront. 1954. 108m. bw. Director: Elia Kazan. Writer: Budd Schulberg. Story suggested by articles by Malcolm Johnson. Cast: Marlon Brando (Terry Malloy); Eva Marie Saint (Edie Doyle); Lee J. Cobb (Johnny Friendly); Rod Steiger (Charley Malloy).

One Flew Over The Cuckoo's Nest. 1975. 129m. color. Director: Milos Forman. Writers: Laurence Hauben, Bo Goldman; based on the novel by Ken Kesey and a play by Dale Wasserman. Cast: Jack Nicholson (Randle McMurphy); Louise Fletcher (Nurse Mildred Ratched); William Redfield (Harding); Will Sampson (Chief Bromden).

One, Two, Three. 1961. 115m. bw. Director: Billy Wilder. Writers: Billy Wilder, I.A.L. Diamond; based on a play "Egy, Ketto, Harom" by Ferenc Molnar. Cast: James Cagney (C.R. MacNamara); Horst Buchholz (Otto Ludwig Piffl); Arlene Francis (Phyllis MacNamara); Pamela Tiffin (Scarlett Hazeltine).

Ordinary People. 1980. 124m. color. Director: Robert Redford. Writer: Alvin Sargent; based on the novel by Judith Guest. Cast: Donald Sutherland (Calvin), Mary Tyler Moore (Beth); Timothy Hutton (Conrad); Judd Hirsch (Berger).

Orphans Of The Storm. 1922. 124m. bw. (silent) Director: D.W. Griffith. Writer: D.W. Griffith. Cast: Lillian Gish (Henriette Girard); Dorothy Gish (Louise); Joseph Schildkraut (Chevalier de Vaudrey); Lucille LaVern (Mother Frochard).

Our Dancing Daughters. 1928. 86m. bw. (silent) Director: Harry Beaumont. Writer: Josephine Lovitt. Cast: Joan Crawford (Diana Medford); Johnny Mack Brown (Ben Blaine); Dorothy Sebastian (Beatrice); Anita Page (Ann).

Our Daily Bread. 1934. 74m. bw. Director: King Vidor. Writers: Elizabeth Hill, King Vidor, Joseph Mankiewicz. Cast: Karen Morley (Mary Sims); Tom Keene (John Sims); John Qualen (Chris); Barbara Pepper (Sally).

Out Of The Past. 1947. 97m. bw. Director: Jacques Tourneur. Writer: Geoffrey Homes; based on the novel *Build My Gallows High* by Geoffrey Homes. Cast: Robert Mitchum (Jeff Bailey); Jane Greer (Kathie Moffett); Kirk Douglas (Whit Sterling); Rhonda Fleming (Meta Carson).

The Parallax View. 1974. 102m. color. Director: Alan J. Pakula. Writers: David Giler, Lorenzo Semple, Jr.; based on the novel by Loren Singer. Cast: Warren Beatty (Joseph Frady); Paula Prentiss (Lee Carter); William Daniels (Austin Tucker); Hume Cronyn (Editor Edgar Rintels).

Patterns. 1956. 83m. bw. Director: Fielder Cook. Writer: Rod Serling;based on his TV play. Cast: Van Heflin (Fred Staples); Everett Sloane (Walter Ramsey); Ed Begley (William Briggs); Beatrice Straight (Nancy Staples).

Patton. 1970. 170m. color. Director: Franklin Schaffner. Writers: Francis Coppola, Edmund North; based on the book *Patton: Ordeal and Triumph* by Ladislas Farago and *A Soldier's Story* by Gen. Omar Bradley. Cast: George C. Scott (Gen. George Patton, Jr.); Karl Malden (Gen. Omar Bradley); Michael Bates (Field Marshall Sir Bernard Law Montgomery); Stephen Young (Capt. Chester Hansen).

Peggy Sue Got Married. 1986. 105m. color. Director: Francis Coppola. Cast: Kathleen Turner (Peggy Sue); Nicholas

Cage (Charlie Bodell); Barry Miller (Richard Norvik); Catherine Hicks (Carol Heath).

The Phantom President. 1932. 80m. bw. Director: Norman Taurog. Writers: Walter DeLeon, Harlan Thompson; based on the novel by George F. Worts. Cast: George M. Cohan (T.K. Blair/Doc Peter Varney); Claudette Colbert (Felicia Hammond); Jimmy Durante (Curly Cooney); George Barbier (Jim Ronkton).

The Philadelphia Story. 1940. 112m. bw. Director: George Cukor. Writer: Donald Ogden Stewart; based on a play by Philip Barry. Cast: Katharine Hepburn (Tracy Lord); Cary Grant (C.K. Dexter Haven); James Stewart (Macauley Connor); Ruth Hussey (Elizabeth Imbrie).

Pillow Talk. 1959. 105m. color. Director: Michael Gordon. Writers: Stanley Shapiro, Maurice Richlin; based on a story by Russell Rouse, Clarence Greene. Cast: Doris Day (Jan Morrow); Rock Hudson (Brad Allen); Tony Randall (Jonathan Forbes); Thelma Ritter (Alma).

Pinky. 1949. 102m. bw. Director: Elia Kazan. Writers: Philip Dunne, Dudley Nichols; based on the novel *Quality* by Cid R. Sumner. Cast: Jeanne Crain (Pinky/Patricia Johnson); Ethel Barrymore (Miss Em); Ethel Waters (Granny Johnson); William Lundigan (Dr. Thomas Adams).

Platoon. 1986. 120m. Director: Oliver Stone. Cast: Charlie Sheen (Chris Taylor); Tom Berenger (Barnes); William Dafoe (Elias).

Power. 1986. 111m. color. Director: Sidney Lumet. Cast: Richard Gere; Julie Christie; Gene Hackman; Kate Capshaw.

The President's Analyst. 1967. 103m. color. Director: Theodore J. Flicker. Writer: Theodore J. Flicker. Cast: James Coburn (Dr. Sidney Schaefer); Godfrey Cambridge (Don Masters); Severn Darden (Kropotkin); Joan Delaney (Nan Butler).

Pride Of The Marines. 1945. 119m. bw. Director: Delmer Daves. Writers: Albert Maltz, Marvin Borowsky; based on a story by Roger Butterfield. Cast: John Garfield (Al Schmid); Eleanor Parker (Ruth Hartley); Dane Clark (Lee Diamond); John Ridgely (Jim Merchant).

The Private Lives Of Elizabeth And Essex. 1939. 106m. color. Director: Michael Curtiz. Writers: Norman Reilly Raine, Aeneas MacKenzie; based on a play "Elizabeth the Queen" by Maxwell

Anderson. Cast: Bette Davis (Queen Elizabeth); Errol Flynn (Robert Devereaux); Olivia de Havilland (Lady Penelope Gray); Donald Crisp (Francis Bacon).

The Public Enemy. 1931. 83m. bw. Director: William Wellman. Writers: Kubec Glasmon, John Bright; based on a story "Beer and Blood" by John Bright. Cast: James Cagney (Tom Powers); Edward Woods (Matt Doyle); Jean Harlow (Gwen Allen); Joan Blondell (Mamie).

The Purple Rose Of Cairo. 1985. 82m. Director: Woody Allen. Cast: Karen Akers (Kitty Haynes); Mia Farrow (Cecilia); Jeff Daniels (Tom Baxter/Gil Shepherd); Danny Aiello (Monk)

Raiders Of The Lost Ark. 1981. 115m. color. Director: Steven Spielberg. Writer: Lawrence Kasdan; based on a story by George Lucas, Philip Kaufman. Cast: Harrison Ford (Indiana Jones); Karen Allen (Marion Ravenswood); Ronald Lacey (Toht); Paul Freeman (Bellog).

Rambo: First Blood II. 1985. 93m. color. Director: George P. Cosmatos. Writer: Kevin Jarre. Cast: Sylvester Stallone (Rambo); Richard Crenna (Trautman); Charles Napier (Murdock); Steven Berkoff (Podoveky).

Rear Window. 1954. 112m. color. Director: Alfred Hitchcock. Writer: John Michael Hayes; based on the novel by Cornell Woolrich. Cast: James Stewart (L.B. Jeffries); Grace Kelly (Lisa Fremont); Raymond Burr (Lars Thorwald); Judith Evelyn (Miss Lonely Hearts).

Rebel Without A Cause. 1955. 111m. color. Director: Nicholas Ray. Writer: Stewart Stern; based on a story "The Blind Run" by Dr. Robert Lindner. Cast: James Dean (Jim); Natalie Wood (Judy); Jim Backus (Jim's Father); Sal Mineo (Plato).

The Red Danube. 1949. 119m. bw. Director: George Sidney. Writers: Gina Kaus, Arthur Wimperis; based on the novel *Vespers in Vienna* by B. Marshall. Ethel Barrymore (Mother Superior); Walter Pidgeon (Col. Michael Nicobar); Janet Leigh (Maria Buhlen); Peter Lawford (Maj. John McPhimister).

Red Dawn. 1984. 114m. color. Director: John Milius. Writer: Kevin Reynolds. Cast: Powers Boothe, Ron O'Neal, Patrick Swayze (Jed); C. Thomas Howell.

The Red Menace. 1949. 81m. bw. Director: R.G. Springsteen. Writers: Albert DeMond, Gerald Geraghty; based on a story by Albert DeMond. Cast: Robert Rockwell (Bill Jones); Hanne Axman (Nina Petrovka); Sheperd Menken (Henry Solomon); Barbara Fuller (Mollie O'Flaherty).

Reds. 1981. 200m. color. Director: Warren Beatty. Writers: Warren Beatty, Trevor Griffiths. Cast: Warren Beatty (John Reed); Diane Keaton (Louise Bryant); Edward Herrman (Max Eastman); Jerzy Kosinski (Grigory Zinoview).

Return Of The Secaucus Seven. 1980. 110m. color. Director: John Sayles. Writer: John Sayles. Cast: Mark Arnott (Jeff); Gordon Clapp (Chip); Maggie Cousineau (Frances); Brian Johnston (Norman Gaddis).

Rio Bravo. 1959. 141m. color. Director: Howard Hawks. Writers: Jules Furthman, Leigh Brackett; based on a story by Barbara Hawks McCampbell. Cast: John Wayne (John Chance); Dean Martin (Dude); Ricky Nelson (Colorado Ryan); Angie Dickinson (Feathers).

Risky Business. 1983. 98m. color. Director: Paul Brickman. Writer: Paul Brickman. Cast: Tom Cruise (Joel); Rebecca DeMornay (Lana); Joe Pantoliano (Guido); Richard Masur (Rutherford).

The River. 1984. 122m. color. Director: Mark Rydell. Writers: Robert Dillon, Julian Barry. Cast: Mel Gibson (Tom Garvey); Sissy Spacek (Mae Garvey); Scott Glenn (Joe Wade).

River's Edge. 1987. 99m. color. Director: Tim Hunter. Writer: Neal Jimenez. Cast: Crispin Glover (Layne); Keanu Reeves (Matt); Ione Skye Leitch (Clarissa); Daniel Roebuck (Samson "John" Jollette).

The Road Warrior. 1982. 94m. color. Director: George Miller. Writers: Terry Hayes, George Miller, Brian Hannat. Cast: Mel Gibson (Max); Bruce Spence (Gyro Captain); Vernon Wells (Wez); Emil Minty (Feral Kid).

The Roaring Twenties. 1939. 104m. bw. Director: Raoul Walsh. Writers: Jerry Wald, Richard Macaulay, Robert Rossen; based on a story by Mark Hellinger. Cast: James Cagney (Eddie Bartlett); Humphrey Bogart (George Hally); Priscilla Lane (Jean Sherman); Jeffrey Lynn (Lloyd Hart).

Robocop. 1987. 103m. color. Director: Paul Verhowen. Writers: Edward Neumeier, Michael Miner. Cast: Peter Weller

(Alex J. Murphy/RoboCop); Nancy Allen (Anne Lewis); Ronny Cox (Richard "Dick" Jones); Kurtwood Smith (Clarence J. Boddicker).

Rocky. 1976. 119m. color. Director: John G. Avildsen. Writer: Sylvester Stallone. Cast: Sylvester Stallone (Rocky Balboa); Burgess Meredith (Mickey); Talia Shire (Adrian); Burt Young (Paulie).

Rocky IV. 1985. color. Director: Sylvester Stallone. Writer: Sylvester Stallone. Cast: Sylvester Stallone (Rocky Balboa); Ralph Lundgren (Ivan Drago); Talia Shire (Adrian); Care Weathers (Apollo Creed).

Rollover. 1981. 118m. color. Director: Alan J. Pakula. Writer: David Shaber; based on a story by Shaber, Howard Kohn, David Weir. Cast: Jane Fonda (Lee Winters); Kris Kristofferson (Hub Smith); Hume Cronyn (Maxwell Emery); Josef Sommer (Roy Lefcourt).

Roxanne. 1987. 107m. color. Director: Fred Schepisi. Writer: Steve Martin; based on the play "Cyrano de Bergerac" by Edmond Rostand. Cast: Steve Martin (Charlie "CD" Bales); Daryl Hannah (Roxanne Kowalski); Rick Rossovich (Chris McDonell); Shelley Duvall (Dixie).

The Running Man. 1987. 100m. color. Director: Paul Michael Glaser. Cast: Arnold Schwarznegger (Ben Richards); Richard Dawson (Damon Killian); Maria Conchita Alonso (Amber Mendez).

Running On Empty. 1988. 116m. color. Director: Sidney Lumet. Writer: Naomi Foner. Cast: Christine Lahti (Annie Pope); River Phoenix (Danny Pope); Judd Hirsch (Arthur Pope).

Safety Last. 1923. 70m. bw. (silent) Directors: Sam Taylor, Fred Newmeyer. Writers: Harold Lloyd, Sam Taylor, Tim Whelan, Hal Roach. Cast: Harold Lloyd (the boy); Mildred Davis (the girl); Noah Young (the law).

Salvador. 1986. 125m. color. Director: Oliver Stone. Writers: Oliver Stone, Richard Boyle. Cast: James Woods (Richard Boyle); James Belushi (Dr. Rock); Michael Murphey (Ambassador Kelly); John Savage (John Cassady).

Santa Fe Trail. 1940. 110m. bw. Director: Michael Curtiz. Writer: Robert Buckner. Cast: Errol Flynn (Jeb Stuart); Olivia de Havilland (Kit Carson Halliday); Raymond Massey (John Brown); Ronald Reagan (George Armstrong Custer).

Saturday Night Fever. 1977. 119m. color. Director: John Badham. Writer: Norman Wexler; based on a story by Nik Cohn. Cast: John Travolta (Tony Manero); Karen Lynn Gorney (Stephanie); Barry Miller (Bobby); Joseph Call (Joey).

Scarface. 1932. 99m. bw. Director: Howard Hawks. Writers: Ben Hecht, Seton Miller, John Lee Mahin, W.R. Burnett, Fred Pasley; based on the novel by Armitage Trail. Cast: Paul Muni (Tony Camonte); Ann Dvorak (Cesca Camonte); George Raft (Guido Rinaldo); Boris Karloff (Gaffney).

The Sea Hawk. 1940. 126m. bw. Director: Michael Curtiz. Writers: Seton Miller, Howard Koch. Cast: Errol Flynn (Capt. Geoffrey Thorpe); Flora Robson (Queen Elizabeth); Brenda Marshall (Donna Maria Alvarez de Cordoba); Henry Daniell (Lord Wolfingham).

The Searchers. 1956. 119m. color. Director: John Ford. Writer: Frank Nugent; based on the novel by Alan LeMay. Cast: John Wayne (Ethan Edwards); Jeffrey Hunter (Martin Pawley); Natalie Wood (Debbie Edwards); Vera Miles (Laurie Jorgensen).

The Secret Of My Success. 1987. 109m. Director: Herbert Ross; story by Mr. Carothers. Cast: Michael J. Fox (Brantley Foster); Helen Slater (Christy Willis); Richard Jordan (Howard Prescott); Margaret Whitton (Vera Prescott).

The Seduction Of Joe Tynan. 1979. 107m. color. Director: Jerry Schatzberg. Writer: Alan Alda. Cast: Alan Alda (Joe Tynan); Barbara Harris (Ellie); Meryl Streep (Karen Traynor); Melvyn Douglas (Sen. Birney).

Sergeant York. 1941. 134m. bw. Director: Howard Hawks. Writers: Abem Finkel, Harry Chandler, Howard Koch, John Huston; based on *War Diary of Sgt. York, Sgt. York and His People* by Sam Cowan and *Sgt. York-Last of the Long Hunters* by Tom Skeyhill. Cast: Gary Cooper (Alvin York); Joan Leslie (Gracie Williams); Walter Brennan (Pastor Rosier Pile); George Tobias (Michael Ross).

Seven Days In May. 1964. 120m. bw. Director: John Frankenheimer. Writer: Rod Serling; based on the novel by Fletcher Knebel and Charles Bailey II. Cast: Kirk Douglas (Col. Martin Casey); Burt Lancaster (Gen. James M. Scott); Fredric March (Pres. Jordan Lyman); Ava Gardner (Eleanor Holbrook).

Shampoo. 1975. 109m. color. Director: Hal Ashby. Writers: Robert Towne, Warren Beatty. Cast: Warren Beatty

(George Roundy); Julie Christie (Jackie Shawn); Lee Grant (Felicia Carr); Goldie Hawn (Jill).

The Shootist. 1976. 100m. color. Director: Don Siegel. Writers: Miles Swarthout, Scott Hale; based on the novel by Glendon Swarthout. Cast: John Wayne (John Bernard Books); Lauren Bacall (Bond Rogers); James Stewart (Dr. Hostetler); Ron Howard (Gillom Rogers).

Shoulder Arms. 1918. 24m. bw. (silent) Director: Charles Chaplin. Writer: Charles Chaplin. Cast: Charles Chaplin, Edna Purviance, Sydney Chaplin.

Silkwood. 1983. 131m. color. Director: Mike Nichols. Writer: Nora Ephron, Alice Arlen. Cast: Meryl Streep (Karen Silkwood); Kurt Russell (Drew Stephens); Cher (Dolly Pelliker); Craig T. Nelson (Winston).

Since You Went Away. 1944. 172m. bw. Director: John Cromwell. Writer: David O. Selznick; based on the novel *Together* by Margaret Buell Wilder. Cast: Claudette Colbert (Anne Hilton); Jennifer Jones (Jane); Shirley Temple (Bridget "Brig" Hilton); Joseph Cotten (Lt. Anthony Willett).

Soldier Blue. 1970. 112m. color. Director: Ralph Nelson. Writer: John Gay; based on the novel *Arrow in the Sun* by Theodore Olsen. Cast: Candice Bergen (Cresta Marybelle Lee); Peter Strauss (Pvt. Honus Gant); Donald Pleasance (Isaac Q. Cumber); Bob Carraway (Lt. John McNair).

Something Wild. 1986. 113m. color. Director: Jonathan Demme. Cast: Jeff Daniels; Melanie Griffith; Ray Liotta.

Song Of Russia. 1943. 107m. bw. Director: Gregory Ratoff. Writer: Paul Jarrico, Richard Collins. Cast: Robert Taylor (John Meredith); Susan Peters (Nadya Stepanova); John Hodiak (Boris); Robert Benchley (Hank Higgins).

Sparrows. 1926. 9 reels. bw. Director: William Beaudine. Writer: C. Gardner Sullivan; based on a story by Winifred Dunn. Cast: Mary Pickford (Mama Mollie); Gustav von Seyffertitz (Grimes); Roy Stewart (Richard Wayne); Mary Louise Miller (Doris Wayne).

Stand By Me. 1986. 87m. color. Director: Rob Reiner. Writers: Raynold Gideen, Bruce Evans; based on the Stephen King novella, *The Body.* Cast: Wil Wheaton (Gordie Lachance);

River Phoenix (Chris Chambers); Corey Feldman (Teddy Duchamp); Jerry O'Connell (Vern Tassio).

Star Wars. 1977. 121m. color. Director: George Lucas. Writer: George Lucas. Cast: Mark Hamill (Luke Skywalker); Harrison Ford (Han Solo); Carrie Fisher (Princess Leia Organa); Peter Cushing (Grand Moff Tarkin).

State Of The Union. 1948. 124m. bw. Director: Frank Capra. Writers: Anthony Veiller, Myles Connolly; based on a play by Howard Lindsay, Russel Crouse. Cast: Spencer Tracy (Grant Matthews); Katharine Hepburn (Mary Matthews); Van Johnson (Spike McManus); Angela Lansbury (Kay Thorndyke).

The Story Of G. I. Joe. 1945. 109m. bw. Director: William Wellman. Writer: Leopold Atlas, Guy Endore, Philip Stevenson; based on a story by Ernie Pyle. Cast: Burgess Meredith (Ernie Pyle); Robert Mitchum (Lt. Walker); Freddie Steele (Sgt. Warnicki); Wally Cassell (Pvt. Dondaro).

Straw Dogs. 1971. 118m. color. Director: Sam Peckinpah. Writers: David Zelag Goodman, Peckinpah; based on the novel *The Siege of Trencher's Farm* by Gordon M. Williams. Cast: Dustin Hoffman (David Sumner); Susan George (Amy Sumner); Peter Vaughan (Tom Hedden); T. P. McKenna (Maj. Scott).

The Strawberry Statement. 1970. 103m. color. Director: Stuart Hagmann. Writer: Israel Horovitz; based on the novel by James Simon Kumen. Cast: Bruce Davison (Simon); Kim Darby (Linda); Bud Cort (Elliot); Murray MacLeod (George).

Superman. 1978. 143m. color. Director: Richard Donner. Writers: Mario Puzo, David Newman, Leslie Newman, Robert Benton. Cast: Marlon Brando (Jor-El); Gene Hackman (Lex Luthor); Christopher Reeve (Superman/Clark Kent); Margot Kidder (Lois Lane).

Taxi Driver. 1976. 112m. color. Director: Martin Scorsese. Writer: Paul Schrader. Cast: Robert DeNiro (Travis Bickle); Cybill Shepherd (Betsy); Jodie Foster (Iris Steensman); Peter Boyle (Wizard).

Tell Them Willie Boy Is Here. 1969. 97m. color. Director: Abraham Polonsky. Writer: Abraham Polonsky; based on the novel *Willie Boy . . . A Desert Manhunt* by Harry Lawton. Cast: Robert Redford (Christopher Cooper); Katharine Ross (Lola); Robert Blake (Willie Boy); Susan Clark (Liz Arnold).

Terms Of Endearment. 1983. 130m. color. Director: James L. Brooks. Writer: James L. Brooks; based on the novel by Larry McMurtry. Cast: Debra Winger (Emma Horton); Shirley MacLain (Aurora Greenway); Jack Nicholson (Garrett Breedlove); Danny DeVito (Vernon Dahlart).

Testament. 1983. 90m. color. Director: Lynne Littman. Writer: John Young; based on the novel *The Last Testament* by Carol Amen. Cast: Jane Alexander (Carol Wetherly); William Devane (Tom Wetherly); Ross Harris (Brad Wetherly); Roxana Zal (Mary Liz Wetherly).

Them! 1954. 93m. bw. Director: Gordon Douglas. Writers: Ted Sherdeman, Russell Hughes; based on a story by George Worthing Yates. Cast: James Whitmore (Sgt. Ben Peterson); Edmund Gwenn (Dr. Harold Medford); Joan Weldon (Dr. Patricia Medford); James Arness (Robert Graham).

The Thief Of Bagdad. 1924. 12 reels. Director: Raoul Walsh. Writer: Lotta Woods; based on a story by Elton Thomas. Cast: Douglas Fairbanks (Thief of Bagdad); Snitz Edwards (His Evil Associate); Charles Belcher (The Holy Man); Julanne Johnston (The Princess).

The Thing. 1951. 87m. bw. Director: Christian Nyby. Writer: Charles Lederer; based on the novel *Who Goes There* by John Wood Campbell. Cast: Kenneth Tobey (Capt. Pat Hendry); James Arness (The Thing); Margaret Sheridan (Nikki Nicholson); Robert Cornthwaite (Dr. Arthur Carrington).

This Island Earth. 1955. 87m. Directors: Joseph Newman, Jack Arnold. Writers: Franklin Coen, Edward O'Callaghan; based on the novel by Raymond F. Jones. Cast: Jeff Morrow (Exeter); Faith Domergue (Dr. Ruth Adams); Rex Reason (Cal Meacham); Russell Johnson (Steve Carlson).

This Is The Army. 1943. 120m. color. Director: Michael Curtiz. Writers: Casey Robinson, Claude Binyon; based on a play by Irving Berlin. Cast: Irving Berlin (himself); George Murphy (Jerry Jones); Joan Leslie (Eileen Dibble); George Tobias (Maxie Staloff).

This Modern Age. 1931. 76m. Director: Nicholas Grinde. Writers: Sylvia Thalberg, Frank Butler, John Meehan; based on the story *Girls Together* by Mildred Cram. Cast: Joan Crawford (Valentine Winters); Pauline Frederick (Diane Winters); Neil Hamilton (Bob Blake); Monroe Owsley (Tony).

Three Days Of The Condor. 1975. 117m. color. Director: Sydney Pollack. Writers: Lorenzo Semple, Jr., David Rayfiel; based on the novel by James Grady. Cast: Robert Redford (Joe Turner); Faye Dunaway (Kathy Hale); Cliff Robertson (Higgins); Max von Sydow (Joubert).

Tin Men. 1987. 112m. color. Director: Barry Levinson. Writer: Barry Levinson.   Cast: Richard Dreyfuss (Bill "BB" Babowsky); Danny DeVito (Ernest Tilley); Barbara Hershey (Nora Tilley).

To Be Or Not To Be. 1942. 99m. bw. Director: Ernst Lubitsch.   Writer: Edwin Justus Mayer; based on a story by Lubitsch, Melchior Lengyel. Cast: Carole Lombard (Maria Tura); Jack Benny (Joseph Tura); Robert Stack (Lt. Stanislav Sobinski); Felix Bressart (Greenberg).

To Kill A Mockingbird. 1962. Director: Robert Mulligan. Writer: Horton Foote; based on the novel by Harper Lee. Cast: Gregory Peck (Atticus Finch); Mary Badham (Jean Louise Finch); Phillip Alford (Jem Finch); John Megna (Dill Harris).

Tootsie. 1982. 116m. color. Director: Sydney Pollack. Writers: Larry Gelbart, Murray Schisgal; based on a story by Don McGuire,   Gelbart.   Cast: Dustin   Hoffman   (Michael Dorsey/Dorothy Michaels); Jessica Lange (Julie); Teri Garr (Sandy); Dabney Coleman (Ron).

Top Gun. 1986. 109m. color. Director: Tony Scott. Writers: Jim Cash, Jack Epps, Jr. Cast: Tom Cruise (Maverick); Kelly McGillis (Charlie); Val Kilmer (Iceman); Tom Skerrit (Viper).

Top Hat. 1935. 101m. bw. Director: Mark Sandrich. Writers: Dwight Taylor, Allan Scott; based on the musical "The Gay Divorcee" by Dwight Taylor, Cole Porter. Cast: Fred Astaire (Jerry Travers); Ginger Rogers (Dale Tremont); Edward Everett Horton (Horace Hardwick); Helen Broderick (Madge).

Tough Guys. 1986. 100m. color. Director: Jeff Kanew. Writers: James Orr, Jim Cruickshank.   Cast: Burt Lancaster (Harry Doyle); Kirk Douglas (Archie Long); Charles Durning (Yablonski); Alexis Smith (Belle).

Trading Places. 1983. 106m. color. Director: John Landis. Writers: Timothy Harris, Herschel Weingrod. Cast: Dan Aykroyd (Louis Winthorpe III); Eddie Murphy (Billy Ray Valentine); Ralph Bellamy (Randolph Duke); Don Ameche (Mortimer Duke).

The Tramp. 1915. Director: Charles Chaplin.

Tucker. 1988. 110m. color. Director: Francis Ford Coppola. Writers: Arnold Schulman, David Seidler. Cast: Jeff Bridges (Preston Tucker); Joan Allen (Vera); Martin Landau (Abe); Frederic Forrest (Eddie).

Twilight's Last Gleaming. 1977. 146m. color. Director: Robert Aldrich. Writers: Ronald Cohen, Edward Huebsch; based on the novel *Viper Three* by Walter Wager. Cast: Burt Lancaster (Lawrence Dell); Richard Widmark (Martin Mackenzie); Charles Durning (Pres. Stevens); Melvyn Douglas (Zachariah Guthrie).

2001: A Space Odyssey. 1968. 160m. color. Director: Stanley Kubrick. Writers: Kubrick, Arthur Clarke; based on a short story "The Sentinel" by Arthur Clarke. Cast: Keir Dullea (David Bowman); Gary Lockwood (Frank Poole); William Sylvester (Dr. Heywood Floyd); Daniel Richter (Moonwatcher).

Uncommon Valor. 1983. 105m. color. Director: Ted Kotcheff. Writer: Joe Gayton. Cast: Gene Hackman (Col. Rhodes); Robert Stack (MacGregor); Fred Ward (Wilkes); Reb Brown (Blaster).

Under Fire. 1983. 127m. color. Director: Roger Spottiswoode. Writers: Ron Shelton, Clayton Frohman; based on a story by Clayton Frohman. Cast: Nick Nolte (Russell Price); Ed Harris (Oates); Gene Hackman (Alex Grazier); Joanna Cassidy (Claire).

Wake Island. 1942. 78m. bw. Director: John Farrow. Writers: W.R. Burnett, Frank Butler. Cast: Brian Donlevy (Maj. Caton); MacDonald Carey (Lt. Cameron); Robert Preston (Joe Doyle); William Bendix (Smacksie Randall).

A Walk In The Sun. 1945. 117m. bw. Director: Lewis Milestone. Writer: Robert Rossen; based on a story by Harry Brown. Cast: Dana Andrews (Sgt. Tyne); Richard Conte (Rivera); John Ireland (Windy); George Tyne (Friedman).

Walking Tall. 1973. 125m. color. Director: Phil Karlson. Writer: Mort Briskin. Cast: Joe Don Baker (Buford Pusser); Elizabeth Hartman (Pauline Pusser); Gene Evans (Sheriff Al Thurman); Noah Beery, Jr. (Grandpa Carl Pusser).

Wall Street. 1987. 125m. color. Director: Oliver Stone. Writers: Oliver Stone, Stanley Weiser. Cast: Charlie Sheen (Bud

Fox); Michael Douglas (Gordon Gekko); Daryl Hannah (Darien Taylor); Martin Sheen (Carl Fox).

The War Of The Worlds. 1953. 85m. color. Director: Byron Haskin. Writer: Barre Lyndon; based on the novel by H.G. Wells. Cast: Gene Barry (Dr. Clayton Forrester); Ann Robinson (Sylvia Van Buren); Les Tremayne (Gen. Mann); Lewis Martin (Pastor Matthew Collins).

Wargames. 1983. 113m. color. Director: John Badham. Writers: Lawrence Lasker, Walter Parkes. Cast: Matthew Broderick (David); Dabney Coleman (McKittrich); John Wood (Falken); Ally Sheedy (Jennifer).

Washington Merry-Go-Round. 1932. 78m. bw. Director: James Cruze. Writer: Jo Swerling; based on a story by Maxwell Anderson. Cast: Lee Tracy (Button Gwinnett Brown); Constance Cummings (Alice Wylie); Alan Dinehart (Norton); Walter Connolly (Sen. Wylie).

Watch On The Rhine. 1943. 114m. bw. Director: Herman Shumlin. Writers: Dashiell Hammett, Lillian Hellman; based on a play by Lillian Hellman. Cast: Bette Davis (Sara Muller); Paul Lukas (Kurt Muller); Geraldine Fitzgerald (Marthe de Brancovis); Lucile Watson (Fanny Farrelly).

Way Down East. 1920. 13 reels. bw. Director: D.W. Griffith. Writer: Antony Paul Kelly; based on a play by Lottie Blair Parker, Joseph R. Grismer. Cast: Lillian Gish (Anna More); Richard Barthelmess (David Bartlett); Lowell Sherman (Lennox Sanderson); Mary Hay (Kate Brewster); Emily Fitzroy (Maria Poole).

West Side Story. 1961. 153m. color. Directors: Robert Wise, Jerome Robbins. Writer: Ernest Lehman; based on a stage play by Arthur Laurents. Cast: Natalie Wood (Maria); Richard Beymer (Tony); Russ Tamblyn (Riff); Rita Moreno (Anita).

White Nights. 1985. 135m. Director: Taylor Hackford. Cast: Mikhail Baryshnikov (Nikolai Rodchenko); Gregory Hines (Raymond Greenwood).

Why Change Your Wife? 1920. Director: Cecil B. DeMille. Writer: William DeMille. Cast: Thomas Meighan, Gloria Swanson, Bebe Daniels, Theodore Kosloff.

Wild Boys Of The Road. 1933. 77m. bw. Director: William Wellman. Writer: Earl Baldwin; based on a story "Desperate

Youth" by Daniel Ahearn. Cast: Frankie Darro (Eddie Smith); Dorothy Coonan (Sally); Edwin Phillips (Tommy); Rochelle Hudson (Grace).

Wild Horse Rustlers. 1943. bw. Director: Sam Newfield. Writer: Steve Braxton. Cast: Bob Livingston (Tom Cameron); Al St. John (Fuzzy Q. Jones); Lane Chandler (Smoky/Hans Beckman).

Wild In The Streets. 1968. 96m. color. Director: Barry Shear. Writer: Robert Thom; based on a story "The Day it all Happened, Baby" by Robert Thom. Cast: Shelley Winters (Mrs. Flatow); Christopher Jones (Max Flatow/Max Frost); Diane Varsi (Sally LeRoy); Ed Begley (Sen. Allbright).

The Wild One. 1953. 79m. bw. Director: Laslo Benedek. Writer: John Paxton; based on a story by Frank Rooney. Cast: Marlon Brando (Johnny); Mary Murphy (Kathie); Robert Keith (Harry Bleeker); Lee Marvin (Chino).

Wilson. 1944. 154m. color. Director: Henry King. Writer: Lamar Trotti. Cast: Alexander Knox (Woodrow Wilson); Charles Coburn (Prof. Henry Holmes); Geraldine Fitzgerald (Edith Wilson); Thomas Mitchell (Joseph Tumulty).

Wings. 1927. 13 reels. bw. (silent) Director: William Wellman. Writers: Hope Loring, Louis D. Lighton; based on a story by John Monk Saunders. Cast: Clara Bow (Mary Preston); Charles "Buddy" Rogers (Jack Powell); Richard Allen (David Armstrong); Jobyna Ralston (Sylvia Lewis).

The Winning Of Barbara Worth. 1926. 9 reels. bw. Director: Henry King. Writer: Frances Marion; based on a story by Harold Bell Wright. Cast: Ronald Colman (Willard Holmes); Vilma Bauky (Barbara Worth); Charles Lane (Jefferson Worth); Paul McAllister (The Seer).

Without A Clue. 1988. 108m. color. Director: Thom Eberhardt. Writers: Gary Murphy, Larry Strauther; based on character created by Arthur C. Doyle. Cast: Michael Caine (Sherlock Holmes); Ben Kingsley (Watson); Jeffrey Jones (Inspector Lestrade).

Yankee Doodle Dandy. 1942. 126m. bw. Director: Hugh MacMullan. Writers: Robert Buckner, Edmund Joseph; based on a story by Buckner. Cast: James Cagney (George M. Cohan); Joan Leslie (Mary); Walter Huston (Jerry Cohan); Richard Whorf (Sam Harris).

You Only Live Once. 1937. 86m. bw. Director: Fritz Lang. Writers: Gene Towne, Graham Baker; based on a story by Gene Towne. Cast: Sylvia Sidney (Joan Graham); Henry Fonda (Eddie Taylor); Barton McLane (Stephen Whitney); Jean Dixon (Bonnie Graham).

Young Mr. Lincoln. 1939. 100m. bw. Director: John Ford. Writer: Lamar Trotti. Cast: Henry Fonda (Abraham Lincoln); Alice Brady (Abigail Clay); Marjorie Weaver (Mary Todd); Arleen Whelan (Hannah Clay).

Zabriskie Point. 1970. 112m. color. Director: Michelangelo Antonioni. Writers: Antonioni, Fred Gardner, Sam Shepard, Tonino Guerra, Clare Peploe; based on a story by Antonioni. Cast: Mark Frechette (Mark); Daria Halprin (Daria); Rod Taylor (Lee Allen); Paul Fix (Cafe Owner).

Subject Index